Love's Last Madness

Sant Darshan Singh
1921–1989

Love's Last Madness

Poems on a Spiritual Path

Darshan Singh

Revised Edition

Translation and Commentary by
Barry Lerner and Harbans Singh Bedi

Editing by Jeff Lydon

Epigraph
BOOKS
Rhinebeck, New York

Revised edition published 2018
Library of Congress Control Number: 2018958979

ISBN 978-1-948796-38-5 (softcover)
ISBN 978-1-948796-39-2 (e-book)

First edition © 2001 by Barry Lerner and Harbans Singh Bedi,
published 2001 by Hohm Press

Library of Congress Cataloging-in-Publication Data for first edition:

Darshan Singh, 1921–1989
Love's last madness: poems on a spiritual path / by Darshan Singh, translated with commentary by Barry Lerner and Harbans Singh Bedi
p.cm.
Includes bibliographical references.
ISBN 1-890772-14-3 (softcover)
1. Ghazals, Urdu—Translations into English. 2. Ghazals, Urdu—History and criticism
I. Lerner, Barry, 1953– II. Bedi, Harbans Singh, 1922– III. Title.
PK2211.E3 D3 2001
891.4'39171—dc21 20011039420

Translations of the verses contained in this book were neither reviewed nor endorsed by the author, Sant Darshan Singh, or by Sant Rajinder Singh, his heir and successor.

Photo of Sant Darshan Singh, p. iii, courtesy of David Edmonston

Book design, typesetting, and cover design: Sue Balcer • www.justyourtype.biz
Cover photo: Bruce Rolff/Shutterstock.com

EPIGRAPH BOOKS
Rhinebeck, NY
www.epigraphps.com

In Loving Remembrance of

Sant Darshan Singh

میں اکیلا تو نہیں، ذوقِ جنوں ہے ہم سفر
ظلمتِ شب کے بھنور سے لاؤں گا نورِ سحر
درشن

I do not walk alone—love's mad zeal is my companion;
Out of the vortex of night's gloom I'll distill the light of dawn.
Darshan

मैं अकेला तो नहीं, ज़ौक़-ए-जुनूँ है हम-सफ़र
ज़ुल्मत-ए-शब के भंवर से लाऊँगा नूर-ए-सहर
'दर्शन'

Contents

Preface to the Revised Edition

The great spiritual master Sant Darshan Singh is arguably among the most profound voices in twentieth-century Urdu poetry. But beyond this, he deserves a prominent place in the gallery of the world's inspired mystic poets. As such, he is a fount of knowledge for anyone seeking insight into the path of love for God and the life of the spirit. For the benefit of those who could not read his poetry in the original, he brought out three small collections of his verses in English translation. While Sant Darshan wrote most of his poetry in Urdu, he did compose four lyric poems, or *ġhazals*,[1] in Persian. I was greatly honored when, in March 1985, during a short visit I made to Kirpal Ashram in Delhi, Sant Darshan asked me to translate these Persian ghazals. It was equally surprising to me that, later, after he had told me how much he liked my translations, he gave no instructions as to what he wanted done with them. Seemingly the whole undertaking had led to nothing.

Time passed and, in the first week of July 1988, Sant Darshan made his final visit to the Sawan Kirpal Meditation Center in Bowling Green, Virginia. On the afternoon before he left, I had the opportunity to have a private conversation with the Master (for so we called him), during which he asked me how I was doing with my Persian and Arabic. At this, my face fell. Abashed, I told him that because of my job teaching English, I had spent hardly any time on them. We then turned to other matters. I saw the Master again very late that night when he walked into the Center's large meditation hall to bid farewell to the many people that had gathered there. Slowly, gracefully walking up the center aisle, his eyes lovingly sweeping the eyes in each row, the Master looked at my wife and me on the aisle and passed on by. After continuing for several yards, he suddenly turned around and walked back over to me. Gazing intently into my eyes, he said, "I want you to keep up with your Arabic and Persian. And I'd like you to translate some of my poetry." Hearing this, I was flabbergasted. Although I was thrilled to be asked to translate more of this great man's poetry, I had never before translated from Urdu, only from Persian and Hindi. Folding my hands in the

Indian gesture of respect, I replied, "I'll do my best, Master." Then he turned and continued walking up the aisle.

In spite of the Master's request, I did nothing—the task was simply too intimidating. Even so, in April 1989, during a phone call to him in Delhi, I mentioned his request that I translate some of his poetry and told him I'd like to translate from *Matā'-e Nūr* (Treasure House of Light—his latest collection of poems published some months previously in Delhi) but didn't have the book. The Master graciously replied that when he came to Washington, DC, at the end of June, he would give the book to me personally. Sadly, that was not meant to be, as Sant Darshan Singh left this world some six weeks later on May 30. It was only after this heartbreaking event that I felt impelled to attempt a translation of some of his verses from his first published collection of poems, *Talāsh-e Nūr*, for a memorial service in Washington. Emboldened by that effort and having obtained a copy of *Matā'-e Nūr*, I soon began work on translating from that book, which is primarily a collection of the ghazals that he considered to be his best. Nearly five years later, the second draft of the translation was complete. Now the purpose of my seemingly purposeless Persian translations, done nine years earlier, made sense.

For months, I was in a quandary over whom to ask to check my work, as I knew no experts in Urdu literature living in the Washington area. Thus, my unexpected discovery that Mr. Harbans Singh Bedi, an acquaintance from Delhi whom Sant Darshan Singh himself consulted when editing *Matā'-e Nūr*, had moved to a house only a fifteen-minute walk from mine seemed like a miracle. Bedi Sahib and I spent the next six years working together on the book, revising it several times over, and he proved to be the most sensitive reader and skilled translator of Urdu poetry I could have hoped to find. His new translations of many verses, stylistic improvements to others, and contributions to the commentary and introduction immeasurably improved the quality of the book. What began as a solo project evolved into a truly collaborative effort that has brought both of us joy and a friendship we cherish.

This revised edition of *Love's Last Madness*, published seventeen years after the original, was itself the fruit of another five years of labor. The book contains all of the poems from *Matā'-e Nūr* not previously translated by Sant Darshan Singh in his books *The Cry of the Soul, A Tear and a Star*, and *Love at Every Step*, as well as some miscellaneous verses from three of his other poetry collections. It also incorporates corrections and additions to the commentary, notes, and bibliography of the first edition; a more exact transliteration system; and refinements in the translations of most of the verses. Despite the many improvements we have made, however, I am all too conscious of the shortcomings in the translations and commentary, for which I take sole responsibility, as it was I who made the final decisions as to what appears in the book. Were I to revise the translations a thousand times over, I could still never adequately express the beauty of the original verses or capture the totality of their meaning. When the task is impossible, the results can only be humbling.

Many people over the years have had a hand in bringing this project to completion. I was lucky to have wonderful Persian, Hindi, and Urdu teachers during the course of my studies at the University of Chicago and the American Institute of Indian Studies in New Delhi, and I am grateful to all of them for everything they taught me—especially to Professors Heshmat Moayyad, Norman Zide, Colin Masica, Kali Charan Bahl, and C.M. Naim of the University of Chicago—as well as to Professor Sanaa Azmi of Georgetown University, who taught me Arabic.

In addition, I must recognize the special contributions of two old friends: Professor Mumtaz Ahmad spent many hours patiently answering my translation questions in the early stages of the project, and novelist David Newcomb painstakingly reviewed the original manuscript and made invaluable improvements to the introduction and the poetry of a number of translated verses. Harichand Chadda, Professor Vinod Sena, P.S. Nagpal, S.P. Sahni, and Professor Chander Shekhar were also very generous with their time and comments when I conferred with them in Delhi in 1990 and 1996 and in subsequent correspondence.

For suggestions, inspiration, and help, even in small ways, with either the first or the revised edition, I offer my thanks to Dharam Arora, Kimti Lal Arora, Shilpa Arora, Anju Chopra, Carolyn Coe, Sheila Rogers DeMare, Ron Filewich, Frances M. Frommelt, Matthew Girard, Jack Griffin, Richard Handel, Khwaja Shamsul Hasan, Dr. Hormoz Hekmat,

Matt Hinrichs, Sonia Hossain, Yusuf Jaafar, Davinder Khanna, Dr. Abdul Wasi Latifi, Professor John Michael, Professor Sulayman S. Nyang, Steve Pollack, Steve Polyanchek, Professor Frances Pritchett, Eliot Jay Rosen, Regina Sara Ryan, Amar Nath Sharma, Professor Shaligram Shukla, Dr. Moazzam Siddiqi, Dr. Darshan Singh, Gaurav Singh, Martha Smith, Arran Stephens, Sarah Weyand, and John Wolf, as well as to my parents and family.

I am also very thankful to my friend Elżbieta Stafford, a librarian at Georgetown University, and to I.R. Malik in Delhi for their assistance in procuring books that we needed; to Sue McCallum for searching extensively for material in Sant Darshan Singh's recorded talks; to David Edmonston for all the efforts he made to provide his beautiful photograph of Sant Darshan Singh for the book's frontispiece; to David Kliger for his work on the transliteration table and advice on creating images of Urdu and Hindi text; to Leslie J. Girard, Bill Goble, Jon Samel, Daniela Schiano Di Cola, and John Stafford for their computer help; and to my sister, Marcy Samel, for the time she spent proofreading the revised manuscript and the recommendations she made to improve the book.

There are no words to express my gratitude to my brother, Jeff Lydon, for the tremendous amount of time he spent editing the revised edition of the book. His insightful suggestions for improving the accuracy and poetic quality of the translations and coherence of the commentary entries, along with his unfailing moral support, were truly indispensable.

Harbans Bedi and I regard this project as a blessing from our spiritual guides—Hazur Baba Sawan Singh; Sant Kirpal Singh; Sant Darshan Singh; and Sant Darshan Singh's spiritual successor, Sant Rajinder Singh. Without their help and loving influence, this book would not have been started, completed, or published.

Finally, there is my dear wife, Annie, whose help and support have been incredible. Her love and sacrifices are hidden on every page.

جو کچھ کہا تو تِرا حُسن ہو گیا محدود[2]

Any effort to define would but limit your beauty.

जो कुछ कहा तो तिरा हुस्न हो गया महदूद

Barry Lerner
September 14, 2018
Arlington, Virginia

Transliteration System for Urdu, Hindi, Persian, and Arabic

~ Consonants ~

Script (Urdu Alphabetical Order)	Urdu / Hindi	Persian	Arabic
ब / ب	b	b	b
भ / بھ	bh	–	–
प / پ	p	p	–
फ / پھ	ph	–	–
त / ت	t	t	t
थ / تھ	t’h	–	–
ट / ٹ	ṭ	–	–
ठ / ٹھ	ṭ’h	–	–
स / ث	ṡ	ṡ	th
ज / ج	j	j	j
झ / جھ	jh	–	–
च / چ	ch	ch	–
छ / چھ	chh	–	–
ह / ح	ḥ	ḥ	ḥ
ख़ / خ	ḳh	ḳh	ḳh
द / د	d	d	d
ध / دھ	dh	–	–
ड / ڈ	ḍ	–	–
ढ / ڈھ	ḍh	–	–
ज़ / ذ	ż	ż	<u>th</u>
र / ر	r	r	r
ड़ / ڑ	ṛ	–	–
ढ़ / ڑھ	ṛh	–	–

ज़ / ز	z	z	z
ज़ / ژ	zh	zh	–
स / س	s	s	s
श / ش	sh / śh	sh	sh
ष / ش	– / s̲h̲	–	–
स / ص	ṣ	ṣ	ṣ
ज़ / ض	ẓ	ẓ	d̲h̲
त / ط	ṯ	ṯ	ṯ
ज़ / ظ	ẕ	ẕ	T̲h̲
– / ع	‘	‘	‘
ग़ / غ	ġh	ġh	ġh
फ़ / ف	f	f	f
क़ / ق	q	q	q
क / ک	k	k	k
ख / کھ	kh	–	–
ग / گ	g	g	–
घ / گھ	gh	–	–
ल / ل	l	l	l
म / م	m	m	m
न / ن	n	n	n
ण / ن	– / ṇ	–	–
व / و	v or w; ẉ in خوا or خوی	v or w; ẉ in خوا or خوی	w
ह / ہ	h	h	h
य / ي	y	y	y
– / ء	– / ’	’	’

~ Vowels ~

Script (Urdu Alphabetical Order)	Urdu / Hindi	Persian	Arabic
आ / آ	ā	ā	ā
अ / اَ	a	a	a
उ / اُ	u	o	u
ऊ / اُو	ū	ū	ū
इ / اِ	i or ě	e	i
ई / اِی	ī	ī	ī
ए / اے	e	اَی / ei	اَی / ai
ऐ / اَے	ai	–	–
ओ / او	o	ow	–
औ / اَو	au	–	au
अह / اَہ or اَح medial position	ěh or ěḥ, usually when stressed	–	–
ए / اضافت	e	e	–
◌ं, ◌ँ / ں	ṅ	–	–
– / ىٰ	á	á	á
– / ٰ	â	â	â
– / اً	n̲	n̲	n̲

Introduction

Sant Darshan Singh (1921–1989)

The author of these poems was a remarkable human being, a modern-day Renaissance man. Had he been only a poet, Darśhan Siṅgh's achievements—five acclaimed volumes of poetry, four Urdu academy awards, and a reputation as the finest Urdu mystic poet of his times—would have been enough to earn him accolades and a place in Indian literary history.[3] (Hereinafter, we will refer to Darshan Singh either by his nom de plume, "Darshan," or by his spiritual title, *saṅt* (saint, God-realized spiritual master) as is most appropriate for the context.) Darshan, however, did not devote himself to one discipline alone. In an age of specialization, his mastery extended beyond the world of poetry to encompass his roles as civil servant, family man, and community servant as well. But it was yet another pursuit—achieving mastery as a mystic—that was closest to his heart. Simultaneous with his other endeavors, totally hidden from the eyes of the world, Darshan devoted himself to realizing God and bringing his individual will into harmony with that of the Divine. To accomplish this, he followed an ancient spiritual path known as Sant Mat, whose cornerstone was meditation guided by a preceptor who had himself realized the Almighty. Darshan's father, Kirpāl Siṅgh, was passionately devoted to such a spiritual master—Hazūr Bābā Sāwan Siṅgh of Beas in Punjab—and was so advanced in meditation that Sawan Singh ultimately chose him to carry on his spiritual mission. Thus, Darshan was steeped in this spiritual tradition right from his childhood. As he himself wrote, "I grew up in the lap of mysticism."[4]

> I was born into a family with a charged spiritual atmosphere. From the time I opened my eyes, I enjoyed a bliss and peace which many do not experience all their lives. My father, Sant Kirpal Singh Ji, was highly evolved, and four years before my birth he began seeing in his meditations Hazur Baba Sawan Singh Ji, who was to become his Master and mine. Thus, I grew up in a home which was charged with mystic ecstasy. I was three years old when my father met Hazur

> Baba Sawan Singh Ji and received initiation. I remember how my parents would be sitting in meditation in the morning. I would sit by their side and try to imitate them.[5]

Growing up in this loving ambience and inspired by his father's example, Darshan began cultivating the art of meditation. All the while, he was guided lovingly by Baba Sawan Singh to develop a consuming passion for attaining mystical union with the Creator.

Despite his routine of strict spiritual discipline, Darshan, unlike an ascetic or a monk, was engaged in the affairs of the world. Following a principle he later called "positive mysticism," he embraced the responsibilities of daily life, becoming a devoted husband, loving father, and conscientious employee. As he carried out his worldly duties, however, he kept his attention focused on God and continued meditating regularly. The divine revelations he received in meditation served as the lodestar that guided his every activity. The world, like meditation, thus became a sphere in which he could express his love for the Divine. Love, for him, meant serving others, beginning, as he would say, with one's family and expanding outward to include one's community, one's nation, and ultimately the world.[6]

To earn his living, he entered into public service with the government of India. Over the course of his thirty-seven-year career, he held diverse posts, rising to the high post of deputy secretary in the Department of Supplies and Disposal.[7] He proved himself to be an officer of integrity and unblemished honesty. By his own personal account, he was offered, on more than one occasion, exorbitant amounts of money as bribes and never took a penny.[8] His door was always open to his subordinates to help them with their personal problems, and he would work late to make up for the time he had spent with them.[9] As he wrote in his autobiography,

> during my career I held positions in which I was responsible for the administration of thousands of people. Many people came crying to me that injustices had been done to them. I would try to alleviate their miseries and help them out of their difficulties to the extent possible. When people have problems and are not getting love and affection at home or understanding from their officers, naturally they are prone

to misbehave at times. But if you guide them with love, and give them the necessary facilities to improve, then they do begin working efficiently. . . . I have yet to come across anyone who is not amenable to love.

Generally, when tea was served in our offices, the first one to receive it was the boss. But I had trained my staff to do the opposite. I would have them serve everyone else first, and serve me last. So whoever came in my office during tea time, whether a sweeper or a fellow officer, would get a cup of tea, and they would be the first to be served.

Peons, sweepers, and the lowest paid workers usually had no access to the senior officers. But I allowed all of them to come to me and discuss their problems. As a result, I would generally stay after work for about an hour or more extra to make up for the time I spent helping people with their dilemmas. Every day before leaving the office I had the satisfaction of helping between fifteen and twenty of those low-paid people who could turn to no one else.[10]

Such was his compassion that, upon his retirement in 1979, many members of his staff, from officers to peons, wept, for no other superior officer had treated them with such love.[11]

This attitude of respect for all and a desire to serve others was one that Kirpal Singh had instilled in Darshan from the time he was a small boy. From the age of five Darshan involved himself in tasks around the ashram (spiritual colony), such as minding the shoes of visitors, working in the *laṅgar* (free kitchen), or operating Hazur Baba Sawan Singh's hand-driven fan.[12] Kirpal Singh would often visit ailing and needy disciples in hospitals or at their homes to boost their spirits or give them money for medicine or expenses, and young Darshan would frequently accompany him.[13] Further, after Baba Sawan Singh had entrusted Kirpal Singh with the guidance and initiation of spiritual seekers in April 1948, and the family moved to Delhi, Darshan continued working for his father's mission in both the literary and administrative spheres, often making the long ride across town to give service at the ashram in the middle of the night.[14] On August 19, 1974, when Sant Kirpal Singh transferred to Darshan his spiritual power and his work as a spiritual master, Darshan took on the burdensome responsibilities of putting thousands of spiritual seekers on the inner, mystic path and guiding them through worldly and spiritual travails.[15] Just as meditation once had done, now personal interviews, correspondence, and preparation for public talks kept him up all night when he returned home from the office. When he retired from government service, these ever-growing obligations replaced his office duties. Sant Darshan considered this spiritual work to be another means of giving selfless service, and he never took money for it. He supported himself and his family solely through his government pension. Even in the ashram, where he lived in his later years, he rented at a very high rate the house in which he lived, for he considered that house to be the property of the *sangat* (spiritual community).[16]

To foster interreligious harmony and human integration, Sant Darshan organized or presided over several international conferences, including the Sixth World Fellowship of Religions Conference (1981), the Asian Conference of Religion and Peace (1981), and the inaugural and concluding sessions of the Fifteenth International Human Unity Conference (1988).[17] Moreover, when anti-Sikh riots ravaged Delhi from October 31 to November 5, 1984, Sant Darshan was instrumental in protecting local Sikh families and keeping peace in his neighborhood. The Master sent food, water, and tea to Sikh families who had holed up in their houses out of fear, told them to make sure their outside lights were turned on, and had the ashram replace any burned-out light bulbs. He then called the people of the neighborhood together for a meeting and urged them to remain peaceful. He also announced that the ashram's langar would remain open twenty-four hours a day. Thus, the ashram became a shelter in which anyone could take refuge. Finally, the Master organized neighborhood patrols jointly composed of the local police and the ashram *sevādārs* (volunteer workers).[18] As a result, Vijay Nagar (in the north of Delhi) was one of the neighborhoods in the city to report no violence.[19]

So great was Sant Darshan Singh's penchant to give to others that, in the last few years of his life, after a major heart attack had destroyed a substantial part of his heart's pumping capacity, he refused to go to the hospital and, in no time, resumed his normal, exhausting day-and-night schedule of selfless service.[20] Yet, never did he complain of his pain, and nothing could dampen his infectious sense of humor. Compassionate to the core, he could not bear to see anyone suffer. Thus, when his personal physician advised him to rest, he replied, "If humanity is in unrest, how can I rest?"[21] When he astonished his doctors with a perfect, "stress-free" performance on a treadmill test, Sant Darshan told them, "You have developed gadgets to test the functioning of this fist-sized heart of flesh; do you have any gadgets to measure the functioning of the mystic heart of love?"[22] He had sympathy for all and did not spare himself in serving others.

Just as Baba Sawan Singh had served as Darshan's mentor on the spiritual path, Darshan also looked to him for guidance in his worldly profession. As a young man, Darshan had ambition to become an engineer or doctor. Baba Sawan Singh, however, saw a different future for him and advised him to pursue Persian and English literature, as well as history, at prestigious Government College, Lahore.[23] This prescription seems to have launched Darshan on his career as a poet, for it was not long before his artistic urges surfaced and he began writing poetry. Instructed in his craft by the renowned poets Sūfī Ġhulām Muṣṯafá Tabassum and Ḥaẕrat Shamīm Karhānī, and inspired by his own father and Baba Sawan Singh, Darshan immersed himself in the world of mystical poetry.[24] When Baba Sawan Singh assigned the task of writing the monumental spiritual treatise *Gurmat Siddhānt* (The Principles of the Path of the Masters) to Kirpal Singh, Kirpal Singh in turn delegated the collection of mystical quotations from Persian literature to Darshan.[25] This proved to be an invaluable education because the rich legacy of mystical themes in Persian carried over into Urdu poetry. In time, Darshan became known as one of the most important mystical poets in the Urdu language. He wrote hundreds of poems, which were published in five collections over a thirty-year period: *Talāsh-e Nūr* (Quest for Light) (1965), *Manzil-e Nūr* (Abode of Light) (1969), *Matā'-e Nūr* (Treasure House of Light) (1988), and posthumously, *Jādah-e Nūr* (Pathway of Light) (1992) and *Mauj-e Nūr* (Wave of Light) (1996). Frequently, he read his poetry on All India Radio and, later, on the national government's Doordarshan television channel.[26] His accomplishment was such that when award-winning Urdu poet Jāṅ Niṡār Aḵhtar published his two-volume anthology *Hindostān Hamārā* (Our India), covering Urdu poetry of the previous four hundred years, he included in the book's section on India's spiritual leaders more verses of Darshan's than of any other poet.[27] Darshan is also among the poets most represented in *Naġhmah-e Rūḥ: Ṣūfiānah Ġhazaloṅ kā Intiḳhāb* (The Melody of the Soul: A Selection of Sufi Ghazals), an anthology of spiritual Urdu poetry by another award-winning Urdu writer and literary critic, Inderjīt Lāl, who dedicated his book to Sant Darshan.[28] Additionally, Darshan had the distinction of winning four Urdu academy awards for his poetry.[29]

Mystical poetry is not a new phenomenon in Urdu literature. The mystical tradition has been an integral part of Urdu poetry since its origin in the sixteenth century, enriched by contributions from a dozen or so poets of note who were either practicing Sufis (most notably Ḳhẉājah Mīr Dard, 1721–1785) or who explored mystical themes in their verses.[30] In the context of this tradition, Darshan's poetry is remarkable for its distinctive and comprehensive treatment of mystical themes embracing all aspects of human life. His mystical approach can be conveniently examined under the categories of the practice of the mystical path, which influences every action of mundane existence; the master-disciple relationship (expressed through the conventional Urdu poetic symbols of the lover and the beloved); inner mystical experience and ecstasy; and religious or human unity as an outgrowth of mystical experience. Moving from one of these themes to the other as his inspiration carried him, Darshan, like Mir Dard, infused his verses with simple, lyrical fervor. This style appeals to the common person, striking a sympathetic chord of identification.

Profound talent notwithstanding, Darshan refused to take credit for his achievements.[31] Such humility was not an artifice adopted to impress the public but a state grounded in his awareness of a higher reality, the power of divinity creating all, inspiring all, moving all. His poetry and his spiritual illumination he would invariably call divine gifts. Similarly, later in life when Darshan took on the role of spiritual master, he attributed to his own spiritual teachers all credit for benefits his followers received—his spiritual masters were the givers; he was only the channel. It was perhaps this spirit of humility, born of love, that paradoxically was the greatest measure of the scale of his accomplishments.

Sant Mat—The Theory of the Mystic Path

The mystical path traveled by Darshan is called Sant Mat—the Path of the Masters—and a full appreciation of his poetry requires some understanding of this path. It should be clearly understood that the practices of Sant Mat are not the modern product of the evolution of spirituality, or a kind of reinterpretation of ancient tradition. Rather, we find very explicit references to these practices in the writings of great mystics of all religions.[32] Sant Mat postulates that the uncreated, eternal, blissful, and loving Divine Consciousness willed itself into expression from its absolute state, manifesting as a vibratory current of ethereal Light and Sound. As this current emanated from its source, it created the entire cosmos, bringing into existence a series of realms of successively diminishing consciousness and increasing materiality. The most rarefied of these regions is one of pure consciousness, while the grossest plane, the physical universe, is nearly devoid of consciousness.[33]

At the time of creation, "drops" of the manifested "Ocean of Divine Consciousness," or souls, "separated" from that ocean and became successively enveloped by the body-mind coverings required to function in the realms of increasing materiality. Each body-mind covering conditioned a soul's consciousness further until, reaching the physical region, the soul had completely forgotten its source and its essence, and had identified itself with its physical body and seemingly conscious mind. Thus the soul lost recognition of itself as a conscious entity.[34]

In this state of utter delusion, the soul imagines itself an actor separate from the Divine Mover, and restlessly seeks, by pursuing the things of the material world, the happiness it knew at its source. Ever desiring and acting, it creates karmas, the seeds of future reactions, which further condition the soul's consciousness and destiny, and which must be borne in one life after another.[35] At some point, however, the emobdied soul's consciousness has evolved sufficiently for it to recognize not only the futility of material goals but also its own helpless condition, and it sincerely cries out to the Divine for release from the cycle of births and deaths. The Almighty then brings it into contact with a fully evolved, enlightened soul—one whose consciousness is already attuned with the Divine and who has become a channel for it.[36] Such a soul is variously called a *sant*, *satguru* (master of truth), or *murshid-e kāmil* (perfect master).[37]

Central to Sant Mat is the tenet that the master takes on the responsibility for awakening spiritual seekers to their true nature as souls and showing them the way to escape from the cycle of transmigration.[38] He accomplishes this by teaching them Surat Shabd Yoga, a practice of withdrawing one's attention (*surat*) from the outer world through a process of inward concentration, or meditation, and uniting it (*yoga*) with the ever-reverberating current of Divine Light and Sound (*Shabd*) within. According to Sant Mat, the attention is the outer expression of the soul, and once the attention is concentrated in meditation and fully absorbed in this enrapturing current, the soul, guided and protected by the ethereal form of its enlightened teacher, is able to soar on this Radiant and Audible Life Stream back to its divine source.[39] As it proceeds on its inner journey, the soul transcends each successive region, divesting itself of its material coverings and expanding its consciousness. On reaching the fourth region (the third region beyond the physical), it escapes the realms of illusion and realizes its true identity as soul, divine in essence; on reaching the fifth region (the fourth region beyond the physical), known as Sach Khaṅḍ or Muqām-e Ḥaq, it enters the realm of pure spirit and begins merging back in its divine source, the infinite, all-conscious Ocean of Love.[40] Gradually it is reabsorbed into its absolute, unmanifested state in the eighth or "Wonder Region" of Anāmī Deśh.[41] Having brought about this divine union, the enlightened guide's responsibility is fulfilled, for the soul's long exile is finally over. Now imbued with love for God, the soul perpetually radiates this love, no matter in which region it is working; transformed into a selfless servant of creation, it has become a conscious co-worker of the divine plan.

The Mystic Path through Darshan's Poetry

Mysticism is popularly perceived as an abstruse mystery, far removed from normal life. Sant Darshan Singh, however, in keeping with the tradition of Sant Mat, believed that mystical insight develops in the thick of life. One need not retreat from life's routine challenges to be granted a vision of an inner reality and revelations of the Divine. Mysticism, for Sant Darshan, was rooted in what he considered the driving force of life—love. Hence, it was love that he made the foundation of both his mystic credo and poetic thought. He observed that, at all stages of life, humans crave affection and acceptance from others. Provision of this "nourishment" leads to happiness, while its denial creates misery.[42] However, by virtue of their material nature, all objects of love in this world ultimately perish, and to count on lasting fulfillment by loving them is to be lost in delusion.[43] To find love that lasts forever requires directing one's attention to God, the source of eternal love,[44] which, as Darshan expressed in the following two verses, is the creative power or energy that moves and upholds all of creation:

Love accomplishes everything in this world of possibilities . . .[(42:9)*]

Love is the beginning and the end of both worlds.[45]

(**Numbers in parentheses following a verse indicate poem and verse number for the poems of Darshan translated in this book.*)

To commune with this divine power of love, seekers of God must confront the negative forces within themselves and delve to the very core of their being.[46] Darshan writes,

Only one who dives far below the turbulent vortex
Emerges from the sea with that rarest pearl in hand.[(10:1)]

For Sant Darshan, this quest to find love in the depths of the self is the essence of mysticism and proves to be the fulfillment of human life and the purpose for which God created the cosmos.

Achieving complete realization of self unveils visions of God;
Blind to your being, how can you know the Lord?[(1:4)]

When human beings are the aim of God, how tragic they ask: where lies our aim?
God is hidden in the human heart, but all search: where is God?[(1:1)]

As God is the source of love and the soul is born out of the Divine, the soul is, in essence, love.[47] But the soul has been cut off from its divine source and is a wandering exile seeking the way back home, far beyond this world.[48]

Where I set out from is a mystery, my existence a journey from the womb of time,
Somewhere inconceivable my origin, my ultimate abode not of this world.[(59:6)]

The night of exile engulfs my heart—not a light in sight;
My only desire—to see the dawn in my homeland.[20:3]

Many, of course, attempt to find a way back to God through religion. While Sant Darshan Singh had great respect for the teachings of the world's religions, he nonetheless considered formal religious practices to be preliminary, exoteric steps to developing purity of heart and devotion—steps incapable of providing the transcendental, esoteric revelations that in his view are the core of the spiritual life.[49]

Why do you seek in the temple? What will you find in the Ka'ba?
Open your inner eye, look in the temple of your heart.[6:2]

Let them try to imprison Him in temple, mosque and church!
The seeing eye finds the Beloved's presence in every mote.[3:7]

The visionary eye ranges beyond the Ka'ba and Sinai—
God is not veiled from those with the eye to see.[54:1]

How easy to be enamored of the lights in temple and mosque—
What the heart needs is the moth's passion for fire.[45:2]

According to the teachings of Sant Mat, this passion for God-realization stirs the compassion of the Almighty, who leads the seeker to someone "who has himself rescued his soul from the illusion of the world and united it with its creator."[50] While such a liberated being may seem an ordinary human, his appearance belies the fact that he has become a "conscious co-worker of the divine plan" and has access to the most exalted of spiritual realms.[51]

Look not on me as a beggar in the tavern—
The range of my flight is to the highest heaven.[68:4]

Darshan even suggests that a God-realized soul takes on the role of spiritual guide over the course of a number of births to relieve the suffering of those seeking deliverance from the world.

I have come, as before, from the threshold of the Friend,
Summoned once again by the cries of the times.(35:6)

For Sant Darshan, the inner path to the Divine is accessible through "dying while living," or rising above body-consciousness through the process of meditation.[52] When a spiritual master in the tradition of Sant Mat initiates a seeker into its spiritual practices, he links the aspirant's soul with the Shabd, or *Nām*—the current of Divine Light and Sound that brought creation into being and sustains it still.[53] Darshan refers to "dying while living" and the creative power of the Shabd in this striking verse:

Reveal the secret of "Die before death!" my divine confidant,
Then make the mystery of " 'Be!' and it was," now veiled,
an open book.(69:4)

Before a seeker is able to make any appreciable headway on the inner path, however, a period of preparation is required. A desire to discover the reality of life behind the world of appearance, though necessary, is not sufficient. Sant Darshan made it clear that to gain proficiency in meditation entails earnest, regular practice and, simultaneously, cultivation of high moral principles.[54] By doing so, one is able to gradually outgrow sensual cravings and rise above worldly attachments.[55] In the following verse, Darshan warns of the necessity of escaping sensual cravings:

How hard to forgo desire after intimate pleasure!
Better pass over this vale of thorns like a zephyr.(40:1)

While travelers on the mystic path do not reject life in the world, they must face an endless array of trials and temptations, the overcoming of which both proves and strengthens their love for the Divine. In Darshan's poetry, an ideal lover treads the path undauntedly, with persistence and determination.

My footsteps never faltered, though the path of love at times
Wound through jungle, wound through desert, wound around my
neck like a rope.(76:2)

In reality, however, it is a spiritual guide's profound love for his disciples that gives them the ability to persevere on the path and transforms them into true lovers of God. Sant Darshan was fond of quoting the Persian Sufi saying "Love first emanates from the beloved's heart."[56] The spiritual guide's love is so compelling that the disciple falls irresistibly in love with him.[57] It is the spiritual master who initiates the game of love and excites responsive love from the disciple.

What a thrill when beauty herself compels us to look!
Were she not waiting restlessly, how would she capture our eyes?(78:8)

(In our translation, we have characterized the beloved sometimes in feminine and sometimes in masculine terms. For a discussion of the beloved's gender, see "Gender in the Ghazal" section, below.)

Once the disciple begins to gaze upon the spiritual master with love, the process of transformation is immeasurably quickened, for it is then that the disciple can catch what Sant Darshan calls the master's "lyrical glances." Through these "glances of grace," the master's spiritual energy radiates to his disciples, helping to purify their characters and free their souls from the bondage of pleasure, pain, and desire.[58]

To whomever but one glance of your grace is sent
Lives estranged from this world, and to the next, indifferent.(34:1)

In his verses, Darshan made frequent use of the millennium-old Sufi images of wine and *sāqī*, or "cupbearer," as mystical symbols. When we examine the context in which these symbols are used, we find the cupbearer represents the spiritual master, and wine is equivalent to the luminous and intoxicating spiritual energy the master radiates through his glance of grace.

Of what use to me are the goblet and carafe
When bubbling wine is pouring forth from my beloved's eyes!(84:2)

How to convey the wonder that reigns in the court of the friend!
Dancing is the beloved's light, cup and carafe are ecstatic!(3:1)

As mentioned earlier, Sant Darshan stressed the importance of freeing oneself of desires and cultivating detachment from the world. In the following verses, he takes up these themes, this time using the symbols of wine and goblet:

To sink this world and the next in a glass of wine—
What can perform this feat but the saqi's eyes![(54:6)]

O cupbearer, pour self-absorbed Darshan a cup of your wine—
The vintage that frees the heart from all sense of me and mine.[(53:4)]

Central to both Sant Mat and the poetry of Darshan is the paradoxical tenet that love is the goal of the mystic journey and the means of attaining that goal. For Darshan, however, love can be called "love" only when it has become *junūṅ*—that is, it has reached such a feverish intensity that it burns up everything except remembrance of the beloved and a "mad" passion to reach his abode.[59] In his verses Darshan frequently refers to this state of *junūṅ*.

I do not walk alone—love's mad zeal is my companion;
Out of the vortex of night's gloom I'll distill the light of dawn.[(80:1)]

Such madness proves to be both a blessing and an ordeal, for seekers who have fallen in love with their master find relief from their yearning only on achieving mystical union with him. Sant Darshan wrote of how, paradoxically, the path leads to the highest bliss and to the anguish of separation and tears.[60] Those in this condition spend their nights in meditation in hopes of meeting the elusive beloved.

My nights of anguish will not see my eyes defiled by sleep—
I would never shame my resolve to keep awake.[(23:1)]

The state of sublime madness is beyond the ken of intellect, which is confined to the material planes of consciousness and incapable of discerning the Divine. Incessantly active in rationalizing and judging experience, the intellect blocks transcendence of body-consciousness and surrender of the ego to the divine will, which is the sine qua non of love.[61]

Only by stilling the intellect and becoming mad with love can one become receptive to divine revelations and find the way to the divine goal.

The idol temple of intellect is a house of darkness,
Void of any corner illumined by madness.[(15:3)]

No one would find the goal beyond reach, O Darshan,
If they had my love-madness to subdue the mind.[(7:5)]

Interestingly, such madness protects the lover from the pain of life in the world and provides intuitive perception of the meaning of life.[62]

With full consciousness of sorrow, who can bear to be alive?
How can reason grasp my secret of self-oblivion?[(42:2)]

Losing awareness of self, I awoke to the secret of life—
A boon of self-oblivion, not the fruit of discernment.[(57:7)]

In a related context, Darshan shows that this state of self-oblivion is brought on by gazing into the master's eyes, and that by doing so, we receive the same intoxicating "wine" that flows from his "lyrical glances."[63]

Who knows what state I was in when our eyes met!
All awareness of my existence was gone.[(78:1)]

When the cupbearer cast a glance,
Such rapture in my soul it bred
That blissfully drunk I watched entranced
As the tavern reeled around my head![(81:4)]

The beloved's glance sent my heart into rapture—
A bliss I'd failed to find in the cup of wine.[(46:4)]

Such glances uplift seekers into a state in which they are madly in love with the beloved.

From all eternity the saqi's glance has worked a wonder—
Lulling intellect to sleep, awakening love's madness.[(14:5)]

If not the bewitching glance from a God-realized man,
What transforms rational life into love's madness?[39:2]

Moreover, these glances send the soul soaring in spiritual flight and provide a source of effulgent, mystic visions that reveal the secrets of the universe.[64]

The wine of truth the saqi keeps concealed in his eyes;
Whatever is poured in a cup just deceives thirst.[6:4]

Wonder of wonders! What grace flows within the saqi's tavern!
The secrets of both worlds are revealed in his cup.[6:1]

The master's glances are, for the disciple, the key to salvation of the soul.

What could grant me the gift of life everlasting?
A life-infusing glance is what I want.[67:3]

Thus far, we have only alluded to the mystical visions and divine revelations that the seeker experiences in meditation. However, Darshan did write verses that directly depicted such experiences. From a close look at some of these verses in conjunction with statements from his spiritual discourses, we can roughly approximate the progression of experiences a seeker undergoes on entering transcendental regions beyond the scope of sensory perception.

Central to Sant Darshan's teachings is the premise that one who relies on the physical eyes rather than the inner, spiritual eye to discern reality is asleep to the truth and lives in delusion.[65]

When I awaken, I'll see reality for what it is—
My existence now is but a bewildering dream.[4:4]

Does the evidence of the eyes bear true witness?
The eyes can see you only to the limits of seeing.[18:10]

It is through the inner eye that one can perceive the Divine Light.[66]

What can I say of the grace he showers as I gaze within!
Darshan, the moment I close my eyes, the beloved's light begins.(3:9)

Sant Darshan writes that the darkness seekers confront when they focus their attention at the third or single eye ultimately breaks into points of light.[67] With more concentrated attention, they begin hearing the inner sound current at its lowest levels.[68] As their concentration improves, their experiences of the inner Light and Sound develop: the sound grows more enchanting, and the points of light are replaced by a starry sky, an inner moon, and eventually an inner sun.[69] In the following verse, Darshan warns against getting lost in the beauty of these elementary stages, urging seekers to cross them to reach higher planes of perception:

For you that moon and sun are enchanting snares—
Beware lest your gaze be caught and you rise no higher!(78:2)

As their longing for their spiritual master grows and their inner concentration deepens, the disciples begin to get their first glimpses of the ethereal form of their spiritual guide.

When, with tearful eyes, I looked up into the night of sorrow,
I saw you smiling down on me from amidst the stars.(18:2)

Their yearning to meet their inner guide in fullness now inflamed to a desperate pitch, the disciples' concentration at the eye focus becomes unwavering, allowing them to rise completely above body-consciousness and come face to face with their enrapturing, radiant divine beloved.[70]

When she removed her veil, all were dazzled
By the vision of Sinai's lightning in their midst.(71:2)

Whose radiant visions are these appearing within me!
Even the darkest night is relieved of darkness.(46:6)

O Darshan, I was preordained to see his radiant visions—
A thousand thanks my world is not in darkness.(54:11)

At this point, the disciples begin hearing the Inner Music pealing forth with an "indescribable beauty and magnetic power [that] pulls [them] up irresistibly."[71] According to Sant Darshan, "one who has once heard the magic of the divine Symphony within is lost forever in its wonder."[72]

Who is aware of this wonder—without instruments
A symphony resounds in the music hall of the heart![(6:5)]

Sitting alone in silence, I often have to wonder—
Is there a musician playing in this blissful space of my heart?[(6:7)]

Minstrel, make music—sans strings or reed—in the presence of supreme beauty!
Every beat of your heart is an enrapturing melody.[(69:5)]

This Music produces "an intoxication which places the lovers in perpetual communion with the Beloved."[73] Thereafter, anywhere they travel in the physical world or the inner spiritual regions, they find their resplendent beloved before them.

Wherever I go on earth I see his beauty,
In heaven after heaven I gaze on my beloved.[(3:3)]

No corner of his court is void of his resplendent light;
Every atom celebrates with radiance from the beloved's face.[(3:2)]

It is at this stage that the detachment the disciples began cultivating while novices on the path reaches its fruition. The world ceases to have any hold on them, for its joys have become insipid in the face of the bliss they experience in the inner spiritual regions.[74]

Saqi, whoever comes by even a tinge of awakening
We see sitting in your assembly, oblivious to this world.[(9:6)]

I am forever grateful—you've blessed me with paradise!
A thought of you transports me to a world of enchanting beauty.[(11:6)]

Thus, as the disciples, through the aid of the mystic adept, traverse the higher planes of spiritual consciousness, they eventually penetrate the veil of ego and realize their pristine identity as divine souls.[75] When they reach this stage, the master absorbs their souls into his Shabd form,[76] a process called *fanā' fī'shhaikḥ* by the Sufis. Their momentum accelerated by their ever-intensifying desire for divine union, such souls then move onward, transcending the realms of time and space, to the plane of pure consciousness and the court of the Lord, and then beyond toward their final goal.

My restless heart led me as far as the empyrean,
And then a torrent of yearning swept me beyond.[(10:2)]

Ultimately, the soul experiences what the Sufis have called *fanā' fī'llâh*,[77] absorption into the nameless, formless Ocean of All Consciousness, the divine source from whence the soul emanated. One in such a state has lost all sense of individual existence. As Darshan ironically puts it,

Meet enraptured Darshan—he'll reveal the secrets of consciousness,
Though now he's in a place where he's unconscious of himself.[(57:9)]

O Darshan, I am lost in remembrance of my friend—
Exulting in my self-oblivion![(68:5)]

With the long and torturous quest at an end, the disciple now knows the bliss of endless love and the ecstasy of what the Sufis term *waḥdat al-wujūd*—the unity of existence. In this state, the disciple experiences God everywhere, and sees within him- or herself the entire creation—the macrocosm in the microcosm.

In every atom I beheld your scintillating beauty
In a world where intellect stands bewildered.[(18:4)]

When I looked with the eye of love, it stood revealed—
Within each sand grain spreads a boundless desert.[(62:10)]

Having become the embodiment of love, the disciple no longer seeks to fulfill individualistic desires, but lives to bestow love on all, making personal sacrifices in the service of others to share in their suffering.

Friends, by morning you'll find my ashes here too—
My heart burns in the same fire of grief as the moth.(6:3)

Sparing no thought for themselves, indifferent to their own pain,
Consumed are your mad lovers by the suffering on the earth.(55:2)

Listen, ascetic, though this is my heart, it has no concern for itself—
Filled with the world's sorrows, what room is left for its own?(32:3)

Mysticism is inextricably intertwined with the soul's primal urge to experience a consummate love, and it is this urge that Darshan makes the focus of his poetry. Suffering intensely its separation from the Creator, the soul, as Darshan depicts it, embarks on a journey leading back to its source in the most sublime spiritual realms. Here the soul reunites with its divine Beloved and is immersed in the everlasting bliss of divine love, a love that the soul then shares with the entire creation.

The Roots of Urdu Poetry

Darshan wrote most of his poetry in Urdu, a language that evolved from the Śaurasenī (or Western) Apabhraṃśa-based dialect spoken in Delhi around the thirteenth and fourteenth centuries.[78] Later called Khaṛī Bolī, this early form of Urdu was a composite of the dialects of Hariyanvi, Kauravi (the country dialects north of Delhi), Punjabi, and Rajasthani (Mewati).[79] The name "Urdu" was not used for the language of Delhi for about half a millennium. Persian literary sources from the late twelfth and early thirteenth centuries refer to the language of Delhi as Hindvī, Hindī, Hinduī, or Dehlavī.[80] Amīr Ḳhusrow (1253–1325), the most distinguished Persian poet of the early Delhi Sultanate period, mentioned in the introduction to his third *dīvān* (formal collection of poems) in 1294 that he had composed Hindvi verses for the enjoyment of his friends, though, with Persian being the court and literary language, he apparently did not consider these verses serious enough to be recorded in a divan.[81] It was not until the last quarter of the eighteenth century that the word "Urdu," truncated from the Mughal-era Persian phrase *zabān-e urdū-e mu'allá-e shāhjahānābād*—the language of the exalted royal city-court of Shahjahanabad (now known as "the walled city of Delhi")—was used by the poet Shaiḳh Ġhulām Hamdānī Muṣ'ḥafī to describe the poetry in Hindvi that had begun to prevail in Delhi early in the century and supplant Persian as the language of poetry.[82]

The conquest of Delhi by the Turkish invader Muḥammad Ġhorī (1149–1206) from Afghanistan in 1193, which led to the consolidation of Muslim rule over northern India, profoundly affected the language of Delhi over the next six and a half centuries. This occurred primarily through the agency of the Persian used as the language of administration by the Muslim rulers up through the end of the Muġhal Empire,[83] as well as through the mingling of the local populations with the Persian-speaking ruling class, which came to depend on Khari Boli for social intercourse and commerce with the locals.[84]

From the mid-sixteenth to mid-seventeenth centuries, with the transfer of the Mughal imperial capital to Agra, Hindvi saw further linguistic development through the influence of Braj Bhā<u>sh</u>ā.[85] Yet, marginalized by Persian—the language of the royal court—and by Braj Bhasha and Awadhī—the languages of the regional courts and *saguṇa bhaktī* and Sufi poets—Hindvi (with the exception of the poetry of Kabīr (1398–1518)), did not become a vehicle for literary expression in the North until the seventeenth century.[86]

Hindvi did, however, spread from Delhi to western, central, and southern India, empowered by "the dynamics of the interflow between capital and region, the privilege of the north as the center of power."[87] The spread of Hindvi was further promoted through military and civil service reassignments to Gujarat under Sul<u>t</u>ān 'Alā'u'ddīn Ḳhaljī (1297); Sul<u>t</u>ān Muḥammad bin Tuġhluq's enforced transfer of the population of Delhi to Daulatabad in the Deccan region of the South (1327); the flight of people from the sacking of Delhi by the Turco-Mongol conqueror Tīmūr (1398); traveling merchants; and Sufis who were encouraged by their *pīrs* (spiritual preceptors) to establish their own centers in distant regions.[88] Consequently, because of these Sufis, Hindvi came to flourish as a literary language in Gujarat (where it became known as Gujrī) and then in the Deccan (where it became known as Dakhinī).[89]

The extraordinarily rapid rise of Hindvi as a language of poetry in Delhi in the early eighteenth century, where it was also called Reḳhtah, and later in Lucknow in the latter half of that century, was enabled by the "slow maturing" of Dakhini in the courts of Bijapur and Golkunda during the fifteenth and sixteenth centuries and the patronage of these kingdoms' rulers.[90] However, the Mughal emperor Auraṅgzeb's conquest of the independent Muslim kingdoms in the South in 1686–87 upended this system of patronage,[91] and the influx of soldiers, officials, and others from Delhi that followed influenced Dakhini and ultimately led to the transformation of Urdu poetry.[92]

The poet who led this poetic revolution was the great Valī Aurangābādī (1665–1708), who "blended the Deccani and Gujarati idioms with the polite and more sophisticated language of the north, and following the traditions of standard Persian literature, . . . transferred to Urdu poetry ideas and images with which readers of Persian poetry were familiar."[93] Vali's visit to Delhi in 1700 and the appearance of his divan in Delhi in 1720 inspired many poets there to adopt his style and "showed in no uncertain measure how complex, sophisticated, abstracted, metaphoric poetry was possible in a language other than Persian or Indo-Persian," a language that we can identify as early Urdu but which was known in Delhi as Hindi or Rekhta in those times.[94]

This development ushered in the classical period of Urdu poetry when, at the hands of such poets as satirist Mirzā Saudā (1717–1780), Sufi Mīr Dard (1719–1785), narrative romanticist Mīr Ḥasan (1736/7–1787), and anguished love lyrist Mīr Taqī Mīr (1723–1810) (considered along with Mirzā Asadu'llâh Ḳhān Ġhālib by many as the greatest of Urdu poets), Urdu flourished and achieved the same refined literary status that Persian previously had.[95] Later, Ghalib (1796–1869), through the complexity of his thought and images evoking a poignant and ironic dolor, raised Urdu poetry to profound artistic heights and inspired all Urdu poets who came after him, including such exalted twentieth-century greats as Muḥammad Iqbāl (1873–1938) and Faiẓ Aḥmed Faiẓ (1911–1984).[96] Darshan, whom the late Dr. Unwān Chishtī, noted Urdu poet and chairman of the Department of Urdu at Jamia Milya University in New Delhi, called "the leading mystic poet in the Urdu language in our times,"[97] affirmed the value of Iqbal and Faiz's styles and the importance of the grand mainstream Urdu poetic tradition, writing that "our literary heritage has behind it centuries of effort, and we must not allow it to be lost. . . . We have only to look at the poetry of Dr. Mohammad Iqbal or Faiz Ahmed Faiz to see that a poet can express with perfect ease and directness the most complex and subtle insights without abandoning existing modes. I myself have not found it difficult to render my sentiments and thoughts in verse while accepting the bounds of poetic tradition."[98]

Accordingly, in our efforts in the commentary and notes to explain particular verses of Darshan's, we have often quoted relevant verses of other Urdu and Persian poets to place Darshan's verses in the context of the ghazal tradition.

The Ghazal—Form

The most popular of all literary forms in Urdu is the ghazal, and it is this poetic form in which Darshan primarily composed. The word ghazal is derived from Arabic. Etymologically it means to talk and act in an amorous and enticing manner with women.[99] Essentially, the ghazal is a lyric meant to celebrate love, but its structure may strike one unacquainted with it as unusual, if not bewildering. The best of lyrics with which one may be familiar depict the lover celebrating his sweetheart's beauty and soliciting her love. Moreover, these lyrics have a thematic unity. The reader of a ghazal, however, soon discovers that, more often than not, its verses are unrelated to each other, leaping from concept to concept, even giving expressions to thoughts that are at variance with what has appeared earlier in the poem. Readers may be struck by the fact that the unity to which they are accustomed—a poem having a beginning, middle and end—is absent. The ghazal does not start out with a thought, develop it to a climax, and then round it out with an epigrammatic statement. It is the tradition of the ghazal for the verses to be fragmentary, each one an intensely concentrated, self-contained expression of a particular mood or thought. One reason why each verse is distinct from the others is the rigid rhyme scheme, which is germane to this particular genre and which, along with the meter, holds the poem together. The internal rhyme and word endings of each couplet must correspond to each other. Thus, it is extremely difficult to explore and develop a single theme throughout the poem. We offer two examples, one from the compositions of Ghalib, the other from those of Darshan, which bring out the constraint placed on the poet by the rhyme scheme. The repeating internal rhyme (*qāfiyah*) is in bold type; the word(s) repeated as a refrain (*radīf*) following the internal rhyme are italicized. The first verse of the ghazal contains the rhyme and refrain in both lines, while subsequent verses employ the rhyme and refrain in the second line only. First, we present the simpler rhyme scheme of Ghalib's:

yĕh nah t'hī hamārī qismat kĕh viṣāl-e y**ār** *hotā*
agar aur jīte rĕhte yĕhī intiẕ**ār** *hotā*

tĕre va'de par jīye ham to yĕh jān jhūṭ jānā
kĕh ḳhẉushī se mar nah jāte agar i'tib**ār** *hotā*

ko'ī mere dil se pūchhe tĕre tīr-e nīm-kash ko
yĕh ḳhalish kahāṅ se hotī jo jigar ke p**ār** *hotā*[100]

Here is a more complicated scheme of Darshan's:

bāteṅ ḳhẉud apne dil se k**īye** *jā rahā hūṅ maiṅ*
tanhā'ī ko fareb d**īye** *jā rahā hūṅ maiṅ*

ab un kā ġham bhī vajh-e tasallī nahīṅ rahā
yĕh ġham bhī apne sāt'h l**īye** *jā rahā hūṅ maiṅ*

jis rah-guzar se guzrā hai un kā ḳhyāl bhī
us rah-guzar pĕ sajde k**īye** *jā rahā hūṅ maiṅ*[101]

The ghazal's roots in oral tradition also contribute to its fragmentary content. The poetic attitudes of the Persian ghazal tradition, from which much of the spirit and tone of Urdu poetry derive, were social, characterizing the poet as "reciting in a 'circle', or 'gathering', or 'assembly', or breaking away from it only in a fit of literary frenzy. Behind this fiction lay the reception-room or hall of royal court or feudal mansion, where men of letters competed for the patron's favour and rewards; a rivalry of which today's *mushā'ira* [poetic symposium] is an imitation."[102] The atmosphere of these gatherings was extremely competitive, the poets reciting or singing their verses in the presence of the patron, other poets, and an audience of literary connoisseurs, with an eye to winning appreciation and critical acclaim. In order to make an impressive showing, hold the audience's attention, and win superiority over the other poets, a poet had to compose verses containing a great variety of thoughts and deliver them in a dramatically compelling manner. Musha'iras are still very popular today, and the atmosphere is one of intimate interaction between poets and their listeners. After reciting one line or an entire verse, the poet pauses for the reaction of the audience, who express their appreciation by shouting, "Wāh, wāh!" (Bravo, well done!), repeating the line or verse themselves, and calling for the poet to recite it again. Often they are able to guess a rhyme word or phrase before it comes, and join in like a chorus.[103] Normally, while two or three of the verses are of very high poetic merit, original in expression and profound in sensibility, the other verses are meant to add to the length of the poem, ease emotional tension, provide comic relief, or display technical skill and artistic talent.[104] Hence, the poem as a whole reads with an uneven and disconnected quality, displaying diversity of both mood and poetic intensity. Now, with the passage of time, the vogue is to write ghazals that achieve a consistency of mood or explore the diverse aspects of one thought. Poets now view sentiments from various angles, often concluding a poem with an aphorism. Many of Darshan's ghazals uphold this new development.

In the ghazal's final verse, poets characteristically include their *taḳhalluṣ*, or nom de plume. The sentiment attributed to the takhallus may be expressed in the first, second, or third person, as convenient. The takhallus is often used to heighten irony as the poets reflect on their condition or situation.

The Ghazal—Themes

The ghazal most likely originated around the beginning of the eighth century in Arabia. In time it became the chief form of love poetry in Islamic culture, taking hold of the minds of poets in Iran, Turkey, Afghanistan, and India. Just as it imported its verse form, meter, and diction from the Persian ghazal tradition, the Urdu ghazal incorporated the Persian ghazal's stock of imagery, which can be varied and recomposed inexhaustibly.[105] Despite the continued influence of Islamic culture on the Urdu ghazal's themes and images, the ghazal's content is neither essentially religious nor even solely concerned with love. On the contrary, giving free rein to their thoughts, poets make observations on the human condition, expressing their joys, sorrows, and despondency that fate is so cruel and life so fleeting. They may give voice to feelings of patriotism or protest the tyranny of the governing classes. Frequently they expose the hypocrisy of the religious authorities or ridicule the conventional practitioner of religion, who misses the true essence of spirituality and is content with ritualistic observances as a matter of religious duty. However, as has been previously mentioned, it is primarily their feelings of love and their urge to find peace through communion with the Divine that poets express in the ghazal.

That the poet "assumed frequently a tone of repining, lamenting a hard lot in a bad world, the demeanor of a martyr, despised and rejected by men and mistress" was due, through the nineteenth century, to the capricious nature of feudal patronage, which often left him beset by misfortune and publicly disgraced.[106] "Composing under the eye of an autocratic patron and of an inflexible religion[, the poet] could not give vent to his gloomier feelings in any open manner, or seem to be finding fault with the order of things as by God and the Sultan established.[107] . . . Against the omnipotence of Church and State there could be no rebellion; but veiled protest was allowable, under the form of praise of the individual prepared to defy convention, which as a harmless safety-valve became itself a tolerated part of the convention."[108]

At musha'iras hosted by the patron, who might himself recite some of his own verses under his own nom de plume,

> the patron was not supposed to be present in his own person: art requires some, if only fictitious, equality among its devotees.[109] . . . It was, then, the 'Saqi' who was supposed to preside, and be the center of attraction: the wine-pourer, elevated into a mysteriously fascinating woman with whom all present were supposed to be hopelessly in love—an idealized, rarified version of the educated courtesan whose reception-room was the nearest that Muslim India could come to a European salon. It was under colour of bewailing the hard-heartedness of this demigoddess that the poet could most easily give voice to his grievances against life at large. A true poet would be expressing something deeper than his own private disappointments.[110]

The grievance most readily aired and the dominant theme explored in Urdu poetry is that of unfulfilled love. The poet's love life amounts to little more than frustration over waiting and longing for the beloved. The beloved is almost invariably inaccessible, and the poet's consciousness of her unapproachability only intensifies his feeling of yearning. At the same time, the beloved is regarded as having attributes more sublime than those of a mere mortal and, in comparison, the poet feels himself to be unequal and unworthy of her. (One finds close similarities of this idealization of the beloved in the tradition of courtly love in the West.) The lack of response on her part is taken by him to be willful torment. The lover is generally a tortured soul, and he is led to depict the beloved as not only the cause of his torment but also the perpetrator of cruelty. He is further tormented by the thought that, compared with himself, his rival in love is more successful in gaining her favor. The scenario generally takes on the dynamic of an eternal triangle, with the beloved standing on a high pedestal, the sincere and faithful lover receiving only ill-treatment, and the rival, because of his wiles, succeeding where the sincere lover fails. In the light of his unwavering devotion, the beloved's habitual rejection is, to the lover, utterly inexplicable.

Critics of Urdu literature have attributed this convention of frustrated love to the Indian social context,[111] as well as to the influence of ‘Uthrī love poetry in seventh- and eighth-century Arabia.[112] Certainly, the theme of unrequited love finds ample expression in the Persian ghazal tradition. In any event, this convention takes on a special significance in Darshan's poetry, where the lover's torments are symbolic of those a lover of God suffers at the hands of the divine beloved (the spiritual master). Thus, the confrontation with God is another aspect of the lover's quarrel, when the lovers find their love ignored by the divine beloved, who adopts every device to compel their love and then irrationally, cruelly rebuffs them. The theme of human and divine love is so integral to the ghazal that the same verse can be frequently read as carrying a double meaning, expressive of either sensual desire or longing for God. Thus, the pain in an Urdu love poem may be interpreted at two levels: the suffering the lover undergoes over the estranged, unresponsive sweetheart, and the anguish devotees suffer in their love of God. As Victor Kiernan notes,

> a divine Beloved could melt imperceptibly into an earthly one, an ideal feminine, an unattainable mistress who was also the wine-pourer at the never-ending feast, as uncertain, coy, and hard to please as Fortune, dispenser of life's never-ending deceptions.[113] . . . Ambiguity belonged to the essence of this

> style, in its visionary landscape things melted into one another like dreams, and everything had a diversity of meanings, or rather, any precisely definable 'meaning' was lost in a diffused glow. A poet might really have mystic moods, or might really be in love—with a woman, or, as in Greece or Rome, with a man; but for his poetry, for his hearers, that was not the real point, any more than for us when we listen to a piece of music whose composer may have felt religious, or been in love.[114]

Yet why should this love remain unfulfilled, with the lover doomed to suffering and frustration? The lover's despair is inevitable because the object of love is, by definition, unapproachable. In a mystical sense, the lover is the exiled soul yearning for its true home in the Oversoul. Since this love is not satisfied, the yearning only grows in intensity. The lover, however, ultimately comes to cherish this yearning as the highest expression of love, and the yearning thus becomes a kind of fulfillment:[115] it is the fire of longing that is life itself; it is the hope for union that can be put into words.

Because of the frequent intermingling of profane and celestial love in the ghazal, it is often difficult to sift the mystical from the earthly, as verses may be read at both levels. Verses that overtly speak of the beloved's beauty, the enjoyment of wine, and the distracted lover can have a veiled meaning and give a subterranean insight into the mystical experience: the beloved may be the divine beloved; the wine, the divine power that induces spiritual ecstasy; and the lover's madness, a state beyond the domain of emotion and intellect in which the lover intuitively perceives reality. Though it cannot be claimed that this symbolism persists throughout a ghazal, its use became quite the convention among Urdu poets, even though the majority were not practicing mystics. Considering his upbringing and training as a mystic suffused with the values of spirituality, however, Darshan's mind is imbued with love of the Divine. Hence, the inaccessible beloved for Darshan usually refers to his spiritual master or to the Almighty and, therefore, not to the ostensible human beloved of the image.

The Lyric Voice of Darshan's Poetry

In a ghazal, poets are generally heard speaking in the first person, projecting their personal experience of love, their own pangs and longings, the jealousies suffered at the hands of a rival, and the calculated cruelty of the beloved. This is the archetypal form of the ghazal, which has been preserved right up to modern times. Even personalized experiences take on the form of the stereotype because the themes explored are uniformly the same; the nature of love and the effects it has are almost indistinguishable from one poet to the next. The better poets are able to find a more refined expression and seek a profounder meaning. Even if a person studies the poet's life very closely, it is difficult to discern which expressions of love have actually arisen from some true incident. Many of the classical Urdu poets wrote so copiously, very often to meet the demands of a musha'ira or to please their patrons, that it defies reason to believe that their works are replete with biographical details. In contrast, the modern Urdu poets who have taken part in a political struggle or embraced an ideology have deviated from the traditional practice and given very fine utterance to their personal beliefs and ideals. For example, the poetry of Iqbal or Faiz is philosophical and idealistic in content, though it does not reject vivid expression of the poet's love for another human being. Nevertheless, Urdu scholar Frances Pritchett warns that "it is always hazardous to take a work of art, simply because it is written in the first person, as an accurate account of its author's life. The narrator may be an invented persona, or the author may have reshaped the events of his own life for any of a number of (artistic or other) reasons."[116]

When it comes to Darshan's mystical poetry, however, the poet makes it very clear that it is not based on flights of imagination, as it may have been with other Urdu poets who expressed mystical ideas that had been made fashionable by the writings of well-known Sufis. As he states in his discourse "Love at Every Step," "Mysticism deals with reality. It is not the child of imagination. My poetry springs from my personal experiences. Behind every word there is some incident, some event, which made a deep impression on me."[117] In his autobiography, he expands on the theme of his poetic inspiration: "My poetry is not born out of imagination. Each verse has to do with meaningful incidents in my life. It is personal experience. . . . I have lived every verse I have written. Actually, I can not say my poetry has been written, for it is not a matter of writing; it is a matter of intuition. It is a matter of revelation. It comes of its own accord."[118] Sant Darshan provides further insight into the reservoir of his poetic inspiration in his essay "My Concept of Poetry":

> The poet's spirit is quickened by his environment and by his experiences. His heart is the repository of life's joys and sorrows, its successes and failures. When the creative moment arrives, external influences and personal experiences are woven together inextricably, and his verse comes forth as revelation. His poetry then conveys to us a crystallization of what is most intense and heartfelt in his life.
>
> My own poetry is an unfettered expression of such moments of inspiration. In fact, I compose only when I am in a state of poetic exaltation. I do not believe in sitting down to write poetry through an act of will.[119]

Because Sant Darshan is unequivocal that his verses are revelations based on real events and personal experiences in his life, we have chosen, in conformity with his own practice while commenting on his own verses, to identify his poetry's lyric voice with the voice of the poet.

Gender in the Ghazal

As the ghazal is the poetry of love, it often presents the lover holding imaginary or face-to-face converse with the beloved, or his making statements about the beloved. The love object is by convention indeterminate, and may be a man or a woman, an ideology, or God. Darshan's poetry is essentially mystical in content; it speaks of his yearning for union with the divine beloved or complains of the suffering the beloved inflicts upon him by denying him access. The imagery of the Urdu ghazal is replete with descriptions of the beloved's feminine charms and beauty. Darshan belongs to the mainstream of ghazal writing, and his references to the beloved are in feminine terms, though the undercurrent of thought is mystical, and the implied beloved is usually his spiritual preceptor or God. However, adopting the male gender to refer to them in our translations would have been at odds with the feminine imagery conventionally used to describe the beloved and made the reading of the verses awkward. For this reason, we have followed Darshan's frequent practice of referring to the beloved as feminine unless a masculine reference to directly indicate the spiritual master or God would be more appropriate to the context.[120]

Problems Encountered in Translating and Annotating

Sensitive readers of Urdu conversant with the tradition of Urdu ghazal writing and having firsthand experience of life as lived in North India and Pakistan would not require, in many cases, much in the way of explanation of the verses collected here. To them the meaning would be clear in the context of the literary tradition with which they are familiar. In contrast, even readers of English literature familiar with the nuances of its love poetry may find themselves out of depth, or see inconsistencies, paradoxes, or inexplicable images that leave them perplexed. In other cases, simple and terse verses whose meaning may appear obvious in fact have an undercurrent of profound thought that may be missed without elucidation. Thus, to aid in understanding these elusive verses, we have provided explanations of their contexts or underlying meanings.

Annotating the poems has not been an easy task, for Urdu poetry is semantically fluid to an extreme. It is this fluidity that accounts for so much of its profundity, but at the same time poses such problems for the translator or scholar. In the case of Darshan's poetry, these problems are compounded, of course, by the poetry's mystical dimension, which is often veiled by the simple, literal meaning.

Over the years, as we studied the writings and attended the discourses of Sant Darshan Singh and his spiritual predecessors, and of his successor, Sant Rājinder Siṅgh, we have gained knowledge of their philosophy and world view. This knowledge we have naturally brought to bear on our translations and annotations. We believe our interpretations to be sound, but we do not claim to be the last word on the subject. Our purpose was to remain faithful to the original verses but still render them as poetically as possible. As every translator has admitted, this is nearly impossible to achieve: translating too literally creates lifeless, wooden verses and sometimes even distorts the poet's intended meaning; taking inordinate liberties in translating often leads to betraying a verse's original sense or tone. We hope to have struck enough of a balance that both truth and beauty are satisfied.

Mystical Symbols Frequently Employed in Darshan's Poetry

assembly

One frequently used symbol in Darshan's poetry is that of the *bazm*, or *mĕḥfil*, the beloved's assembly. In the milieu where Urdu developed, the setting for the assembly was originally a feudal court and, beginning in the eighteenth century and increasingly widespread in the nineteenth, an urban salon or brothel (*koṭhā*), a place where educated, refined, cultured courtesans (*ṯawā'if*) entertained men from elite circles with singing, dancing, and poetry, and where these men learned "the culture of tawa'if patronage, including courtly deportment and the sophisticated idiom of Urdu poetry."[121] The woman who was the center of attraction in this assembly was looked on as

> the queen of the mahfil, the candle (*shamma'*) among moths (*parvane*), and the proud target of their rivalry. She is the cupbearer (*saqi*) of the wine of ecstasy, but also the killer who wields the dagger (*khanjar*) of cruelty. Aesthetically and affectively, her listeners, the patrons, became her lovers, ardent, helpless, and silent. But her songs speak for them as well as to them. She is the voice not only of love (*'ishq*, *muhabbat*) but also of the lover (*'ashiq*), his suffering and his delights. An assembly of rivals is by definition a place of suffering, a contest of desire for a woman untrammeled by the constraints of patrilineal kinship ties.[122]

Frequently in Urdu poetry, the poet portrays himself as a sincere and faithful lover and his rivals as motivated merely by lust, and expresses his frustration when the beloved seems to favor his rivals over him.

In mystical symbolism, the assembly represents the *satsang* or *majlis-e ḥaq-jūyān*, the gathering of spiritual seekers presided over by an enlightened spiritual master. In this sense, too, the poet feels that the master withholds his favor and grace from him while bestowing it on others who are less deserving, and his torment over his perpetually unrequited love likewise finds expression in his poetry.

cupbearer
See "saqi" in this section, below.

darshan
The Hindi word *darshan*, which is Sant Darshan Singh's nom de plume, in a general sense means to behold a loved one and enjoy his or her elevating presence. According to the teachings of Sant Mat, however, true darshan is to receive the soul-uplifting glance of the spiritual master, or to lovingly absorb one's attention into the master's eyes so fully that one becomes completely and ecstatically lost in him, forgetting the world outside and one's individual existence.[123]

desert or wilderness
This image symbolizes the severe trials and tribulations lovers must face in their quest for the beloved. In addition, it can refer to the arid patches seekers often confront on the spiritual journey. In such a condition, their hearts are assailed by doubts and they feel bewildered and abandoned. Despite their hard struggle to make inner headway, they find themselves deprived of divine visions, and feel the love and grace they previously enjoyed have dried up.

eye or inner eye
In mysticism this is often referred to as the third or single eye. The spiritual journey begins when seekers concentrate their attention at this point between and behind the two eyebrows in meditation, withdrawing their attention from the external world and their physical bodies.

heart
Most often, Darshan uses this image to represent the seat of love, but it sometimes carries a mystical sense in which it signifies the inner world of the soul where divine revelations occur. Sant Darshan would often say that the heart of the mystic is at the third eye. (See 60:9 note.)

madness (*junūṅ*)
The word *junūṅ* means "madness, lunacy," and in the context of mystical literature is often translated as "the madness of love." *Junūṅ* suggests a state of rapture in the literal sense of possession by a spirit (*jinn*). The word calls to mind the Arabic story of Qais, who was so madly in love with his beloved Lailá that he took leave of his senses and was dubbed

"Majnūn," or "the mad one." *Junūṅ* is actually more than a frenzied state of mind, however. It suggests an overriding sublime obsession or ruling passion for one object, as well as an intuitive understanding that transcends reason. The intellect, whose powers are confined to the material planes of consciousness, incessantly attempts to rationalize and judge all experience in the service of the self-centered ego. As long as the intellect is engaged, it blocks clear inner vision and transcendence of body-consciousness in meditation and prevents complete self-surrender, which is the sine qua non of attaining love for God and God-realization. In the sphere of mysticism, *junūṅ* thus denotes the state of one who, having stilled and transcended the intellect, becomes absorbed in ecstatic love of God and gains a true perception of reality.

moth and candle

The moth and candle in Urdu and Persian poetry are symbols of the lover and beloved. Just as the moth is irresistibly drawn to the flame of the candle and burns to death in its fire, so a true lover of the spiritual master or God sacrifices his or her will in order to attain mystical union with the beloved.

saqi

In Persian and Urdu poetry, the saqi, or cupbearer, is responsible for pouring and serving wine in the tavern. Annemarie Schimmel, one of the greatest scholars of Islam and Sufism, writes of the innumerable Persian verses that depict "the [platonic] enchantment engendered by a fourteen-year-old boy of otherworldly beauty, a *saqi*, "cup bearer" (frequently referred to as a Christian youth or as a young Zoroastrian)."[124] In the Urdu milieu, a courtesan who entertained the clientele in her reception room with wine, poetry, song, and dance, and bestowed her favors on them, also came to be referred to as the saqi (see "assembly" in this section, above). In spiritual terms, the saqi represents the spiritual master, who serves the divine "wine" through his eyes and whose presence charms and inspires. (See "wine" in this section, below.)

tavern

The tavern is the place of congregation for lovers of God or seekers after spiritual truth. It is the abode of the mystical experience as opposed to the formal creed of temple, mosque, and church.

tavern master
This symbolizes the spiritual master, who lays bare the divine mysteries.

tresses
The beloved's long, curly locks represent the spiritual master's divine influence and grace, which encompass this world and the next.

veil
Since Urdu poetry carries the influences of Islamic culture, the beloved in the poems hides herself under a veil. Only when the veil is lifted can one get a glimpse of her ravishing beauty. The same holds true for the revelation of the divine beloved. According to Sant Mat, though God and the soul dwell in the same body, they are separated by a veil of illusion. The soul lives in separation from and ignorance of God and its own divine nature. This veil covering the inner eye is pierced or drawn aside by a combination of assiduous meditation and the grace of the spiritual master. (See "eye or inner eye" in this section, above.) On passing beyond the veil, the soul comes face to face with the radiant form of its spiritual master and begins traversing the inner planes on its spiritual journey back to its source.

wine
This image symbolizes the nectar of divine love, the divine current of spiritual Light and Sound that raises spiritual seekers above physical body-consciousness in meditation and intoxicates them with mystic insight and visions.

zephyr
When this gentle, refreshing breeze blows from the direction of the beloved's lane, carrying the beloved's fragrance, it reminds lovers of the beloved's scented tresses and fills the lovers with ecstasy. For them it is the beloved's message of love.

Selected Poetry:

Matā'-e Nūr[125]

Treasure House of Light

Translations of Urdu Ghazals

1

When human beings are the aim of God, how tragic they ask:
where lies our aim?
God is hidden in the human heart, yet all search:
where is God?[1:1*]

This is a clique of vain poseurs—speak not a word about love;
Everyone claims to be sincere, no one lacks devotion here!

All light is your reflection, all beauty mirrors your splendor.
Whose countenance has your radiance? Where is another like you?

Achieving complete realization of self unveils visions of God;
Blind to your being, how can you know the Lord?[1:4]

This valley—my heart—is desolate; alone, I'm engrossed in search—
Where are the pilgrims of love? Where is their caravan?

Tell those who trust in the captain to save our ship from
the raging seas:
Deliverance lies with the Lord, not in expertise.[1:6]

Let me stay bowed in worship here, never leave this sacred place;
Where else could broken Darshan find refuge but at your door?[†]

* For a discussion of numbered verses, refer to the Commentary.

† Note that both vowels in *D<u>a</u>rsh<u>a</u>n* are pronounced like the *u* in the English word *run*.

2

How did I ever think silence the language of love?
What I thought would not come to light was in plain sight.[2:1]

I hear my silence talked of in every lane—
"The suppression of a cry is itself a cry of pain."[2:2]

My beloved's regard was but a flash of light—
How innocently I'd found eternal bliss.[2:3]

In the end this too was claimed by the gardener, lightning and wind—
That handful of pitiful straws I called my nest.[2:4]

O Darshan, these eyes, which I'd fancied the voice of my love,
Even they couldn't convey the fathomless depths of my longing.

3

How to convey the wonder that reigns in the court of the friend!
Dancing is the beloved's light, cup and carafe are ecstatic!

No corner of his court is void of his resplendent light;
Every atom celebrates with radiance from the beloved's face.

Wherever I go on earth I see his beauty,
In heaven after heaven I gaze on my beloved.

O seeker bereft of radiant visions, look with the eyes of your heart!
How can you see the beloved's light with eyes of flesh and blood?

I took on humanity's sorrows, I gave my love to the world—
My entire life I've devoted to the work of my beloved.

Brushing past me, it stirred my heart and suddenly was gone—
Now even the morning breeze has learned to tease from my beloved!

Let them try to imprison Him in temple, mosque and church!
The seeing eye finds the Beloved's presence in every mote.

Seekers of your radiant visions are very close to your heart—
Eyes focused outside are infinitely far from the beloved's light.

What can I say of the grace he showers as I gaze within!
Darshan, the moment I close my eyes, the beloved's light begins.

4

The cup goes around—my life is in dance,
Rivaling the gyres of fortune, ceaseless in its whirling.

I see the saqi coming towards me with a cup spilling over with wine!
My entire being ignites like a lamp lighting up the night in spring.

All your talk of affliction's storms fails to frighten me—
No tempest is more turbulent than my life.

When I awaken, I'll see reality for what it is—
My existence now is but a bewildering dream.[4:4]

Go tell the darners at work in the night of waiting:
The cloak of my life has been torn since the dawn.[4:5]

Your life is a chandelier lighting beauty's sleeping chamber;
My life, a lamp guiding strangers on the road at night.[4:6]

How could I meet life face to face, O Darshan?
With every breath my life is fleeing from me.

5

Pass through this world of enchantment and charm with complete detachment—
Tomorrow will write your life in letters of gold.

Though we are gathered as before—same wine, same flagon, same goblet—
Without the saqi in our midst, the tavern is desolate.

Grief so overwhelming, to body and mind oblivious;
Who is the one whose absence drove each tippler completely mad?

What can the candle flame do now but tremble?
The moth has burned to ash in its own fiery love.

Restless from thirst in the tavern, should Darshan get your glance,
The flagon will overflow, the cup—ecstatic—begin to dance.

6

Wonder of wonders! What grace flows within the saqi's tavern!
The secrets of both worlds are revealed in his cup.[6:1]

Why do you seek in the temple? What will you find in the Ka'ba?
Open your inner eye, look in the temple of your heart.[6:2]

Friends, by morning you'll find my ashes here too—
My heart burns in the same fire of grief as the moth.[6:3]

The wine of truth the saqi keeps concealed in his eyes;
Whatever is poured in a cup just deceives thirst.

Who is aware of this wonder—without instruments
A symphony resounds in the music hall of the heart![6:5]

Saqi, is ignoring my desire your kind of mercy?
Endless, I hear, is the rapture from wine in your tavern.

Sitting alone in silence, I often have to wonder—
Is there a musician playing in this blissful space of my heart?[6:7]

Nowhere in life, O Darshan, could you ever hope to find
A joy to rival the bliss of the Master's tavern.

7

They cast the aura of renunciates, as humble as the dust,
But waiting at their doors I saw the sovereigns of the age.[7:1]

My heart smolders with that secret—could I but reveal it!
I await a kindred heart who I could trust to keep it.

I met him in Chishti's tavern as well—
The one I'd seen draining the cup of Nanak's love.[7:3]

My quest to probe the world's suffering turned into a nightmare—
At the core of every mote I saw a mountain.

No one would find the goal beyond reach, O Darshan,
If they had my love-madness to subdue the mind.[7:5]

8

Blossom season has come, yet who can explain—there must
be someone—
Why has the dust of autumn covered the mirror of spring?[8:1]

I, too, explored the path of seeking truth through intellect—
The wayfarers were sleepwalking, their guides wandering lost.[8:2]

How could I fear losing my way? Why dread the wilderness?
My longing for you will guide me, your remembrance be
my companion.

Even more sublime than beauty is the light of love—
Beauty lights her cloistered court; love is a lamp on the lonely road.[8:4]

Now, what's to become of my heart, lying here in ruins?
My eyes implore—she stays self-absorbed.

9

At dusk, at dawn I gaze upon Your beauty—
A dazzling spectacle of rising moon and sun.

The wayfarers have yet to discover your footprints—
They stand on the path to your threshold, absorbed in the stepstone.[9:2]

You showered us with glances of grace—still they were too few;
We with the eyes to see know the worth of your glance.[9:3]

Saqi, they've just arrived and taken their seats—
How is it that they've already gained intimacy?[9:4]

Those you inspire with the madness of prostration
See only your form before them, not your threshold.

Saqi, whoever comes by even a tinge of awakening
We see sitting in your assembly, oblivious to this world.

Those mad lovers consumed by passion to reach the goal
Are oblivious of other wayfarers—they see only the road.

O Master, such a strange state has come over your Darshan—
Anytime we see him his eyes are moist with tears.

10

Only one who dives far below the turbulent vortex
Emerges from the sea with that rarest pearl in hand.[10:1]

My restless heart led me as far as the empyrean,
And then a torrent of yearning swept me beyond.[10:2]

I'm stunned by what I see—the times convulsed by havoc;
My world of dreams has vanished with the past.

Faded, the memory of you sitting close—gone, the company of pain;
My heart abandoned me, taking all my friends away.

The art of drinking is dead, there's no respect for the wine—
The saqi has gone, and with him the tavern's decorum.[10:5]

In the book of my heart, we wrote our story of love—
The one chapter she tore up and tossed to the winds.[10:6]

There's no one else left in the raging sea of affliction—
The currents of time have swept away all my companions.

Why should the martyrs of love not live forever?
They left this world with all the essentials for life.[10:8]

Humankind has failed to illumine the earth with peace—
At least we've managed to land some men on the moon!

Even now I hear Mir's voice, crying out from his grave:
"Open your sleeping eyes! A flood is sweeping the city away!"[10:10]

O Darshan, the one prize left to you was your heart—
Even that priceless treasure a thief of hearts snatched away.

11

Without you I've fallen into a strange, listless state,
Removed from life's joys, indifferent to fate.

Myriad the hearts that beat in this world—
But which heart shares in humanity's pain?[11:2]

I'm dying for just one moment of peace;
This isn't life, but a dirge for life.

All things of this fleeting world betrayed me—
Only a perfect master proved my friend.

In this lustful company, how could love be true?
Here, there are cups in abundance—all quite empty of wine.

I am forever grateful—you've blessed me with paradise!
A thought of you transports me to a world of enchanting beauty.

They have a different heart, O friend—those lost in their own sorrows;
My heart grieves for the sorrows of the whole world.

The moon and sun—they gaze on me with reverence!
Who knows at whose feet I've bowed my head![11:8]

Friends, what can I say about her many-splendored hues?
Sometimes she's a flame of fire, at times a drop of dew.

When did this head of mine ever care for obeisance!
Who knows why it's finally bowed at your door!

Received from his graceful hand, a simple goblet of clay
Reveals no less, O Darshan, than the fabled cup of Jamshayd.[11:11]

12

Gone is the allure of love, faded from memory—
Now everyone weeps over worldly woes, beloved.

I took such pride, I placed such faith in it—
Now my heart's an assassin at my throat, beloved.

Where life's beauty stands revealed in every grain of sand,
Such is the world my eyes behold, beloved.

Could I but rest a moment in the thick shade of your tresses!
But who can find respite from the trials of the times, beloved?

What is it to me that others flock to temple and mosque!
The only holy place for me is wherever you are, beloved.

Grief gone to extremes was its own remedy;
No tear stains my eye, no complaint taints my lips, beloved.[12:6]

The present age has seen the human conscience torn to shreds,
So thorny the dilemmas of right and wrong, beloved.

Darshan, too, could have built a nest in the garden,
But the debt of thanks to the gardener he could not bear, beloved.[12:8]

13

I seek in the assembly a glance of love,
I seek a dawn for my night of desire.

Not aimless, my wandering in love's wilderness—
I am in search of the pathway to life.

Worship in temple and mosque brought no joy—
I now seek to bow before someone's door.[13:3]

Unwavering devotion, sharing in others' pain—
These are the essentials I must take on my journey.

Struck mad with love, we seek love everlasting—
We long for a dawn that will never pass.

Oh, for a place ruled by kindness and peace!
I seek nothing less than a city of love.

What I long to see are the flowers of spring—
Unlike those seeking lightning and fire.[13:7]

My quest for love's abode leaves my feet raw with blisters—
I seek the dawn for humanity's night of unfulfilled desire.

O Darshan, those dismayed by the darkness of the times
Watch raptly for the sun and moon at morning and at night![13:9]

14

Someone's austere nights bloomed with dawn's brilliant hues;
Borne by the weary morning breeze, spring arrived at last.[14:1]

The garden revels were not immune to anguish—
A rose flamed up like a candle, its bud's fire went out.

Idols decked in lavish splendor filled the idol house—
Your simple grace alone compelled my eyes.[14:3]

While my heart was weeping over the plight of the lamp,
Dawn marched right in with a mocking grin.[14:4]

From all eternity the saqi's glance has worked a wonder—
Lulling intellect to sleep, awakening love's madness.

Ineffable was the ecstasy that thrilled my thirsty gaze—
Opening her ravishing eyes, she gave me drink and drank me in!

Who was there to befriend him, roaming the lonely wilderness
But the long night of despair, which took him in its arms.

Autumn afflicts the earth, but she entered with such grace,
The blighted orchard of Darshan burst into blossom, surging
with spring!

15

My heart has not the slightest urge to indulge in wine,
But if she offered me a drink, how could I decline?

As for the dawn of the age of love—friends, what can I say?
I have yet to see a sign of that promised day.

The idol temple of intellect is a house of darkness,
Void of any corner illumined by madness.[15:3]

Too long the tavern of love has lain desolate;
Why question the saqi's absence—no tipplers ever visit.[15:4]

The garden is now a wasteland, the world that was is gone;
In vain you search for flowers where not even thorns survive.[15:5]

Don't ask about the dark, O Darshan, that enshrouds love's world—
Even on the gallows now we find no lamps are lit.[15:6]

16

Moonlight enchants, the garden enthralls; beside me she glows, resplendent—
Night fills with the exultation of a love-blessed woman.

O essence of modesty, what enchantment when alone with you!
With bashful eyes, you draw your skirt around you.[16:2]

Now the time is ripe for being robbed on the path of love;
O heart, don't try to flee—you are the bandit.[16:3]

How can I even begin to explain? How to make it make sense?
It is a sort of mysterious desire, a strange entanglement.[16:4]

The face of every friend is an endless array of masks;
My foes I recognize in any guise they try to pass.

All arrangements have been made to devastate the garden:
Blossoms invite the flower picker; my nest, the lightning bolts.[16:6]

Darshan, at every turn in the garden my feet are stopped in their tracks—
Is it some mischief done by the thorns or my coat hem's waywardness?[16:7]

17

I gained the wealth of the world, won prestige and renown,
I attained everything but failed to meet the compassionate Lord.[17:1]

It's as if I've seen these somewhere before—
The same signs I came upon in unknown valleys.[17:2]

Climbing over endless boulders strewn across the path,
I kept pressing onward toward the house of my beloved.

A thousand times fate has left me weeping
Since that day you met me with a loving smile.

Till the end of the world I will cherish the memory
Of those on life's journey who were kind to me.

How could one so blessed by fate
Seek another door when they've found yours?

It was no accident I broke my persecutors' hearts—
My heart had the mettle to bear endless pain.

The faithful in temple and mosque could provide no solution,
Embroiled as they were in debating "either, or."[17:8]

Darshan has spent his entire life in search—
Where can he find some moments of quiet and peace?

18

The worldly-wise I beheld distraught and dismayed;
Your lovers in their madness were cheerful in their trials.

When, with tearful eyes, I looked up into the night of sorrow,
I saw you smiling down on me from amidst the stars.[18:2]

The world—pain, life—pain, the beloved—pain, my heart—pain:
See how many thorns have caught my shirt and pierced my flesh!

In every atom I beheld your scintillating beauty
In a world where intellect stands bewildered.

With the rope of his wisdom, he captured the moon and sun—
In an age of madness, see what this true man has done![18:5]

I found all here are worshipers of the one manifested light—
Who can tell Muslim from Hindu in your assembly?

That mischievous, saucy breeze I kiss,
For I often see it mussing your tresses.

Possessed by love's madness, your lovers spurned both worlds;
Those who go by appearances took them for paupers.[18:8]

Where would they find the leisure to laugh at others?
Your mad lovers are too busy laughing at themselves!

Does the evidence of the eyes bear true witness?
The eyes can see you only to the limits of seeing.

I've seen souls in crystal palaces driven to distraction;
I've seen them shut away in prisons, where they were at peace.[18:11]

I'll never forget my despair in the night of longing
When I saw my own shadow abandon me.

My entire life I spent on the journey of love,
Watching my hopes at nightfall flee with the dawn.

19

Now the time is urgent to relieve suffering;
Alas, this age is ruled by callous indifference![19:1]

To millions he freely gives his heart—
Yet he claims he is chaste![19:2]

Scowl-furrowed brow, eyes flashing indignant—
Such are her ploys to entice my heart.

Someone's countenance kept intruding on my thoughts—
My heart strayed even as I prayed.[19:4]

At least just once she should soothe my pain!
If only just once to show respect!

Only the warrior who conquers the mind
Merits honor as "Vanquisher of Infidels."[19:6]

O Darshan, my whole being supplicates—
She is indifference incarnate.

20

Forgotten are the flowers—buried by the dust of our strivings;
Nothing remains of the garden but a faint memory.[20:1]

What are these shiny goals of our dreams! Wait for morning to come:
All our dreams amount to nothing but exhaustion.

The night of exile engulfs my heart—not a light in sight;
My only desire—to see the dawn in my homeland.[20:3]

Don't give up, my ardent eyes—keep on teasing her,
Though her only response till now is a ruffled brow.

Though autumn's dark night has fallen, I feel no despair—
I see a garden resplendent in full morning light.

To inspire my heart to break into song, O Darshan,
I need only feel the breeze off the Ganges and Jamna.[20:6]

21

Each hour I pass like a mourner; each breath—a sigh for dark times.
Is this really life, or am I just paying for some crime?

Day and night theirs is a journey of the part to the whole;
Some have called their destination "death."[21:2]

Others are racked by fear of life's misfortunes;
I meet the onslaughts of time with a cup of wine.

Love's state knows nothing of alteration;
My world never sees morning, and night never falls.

Is breathing in and out all there is to life?
Without understanding life's purpose, of what worth is life?

Alas, that the youth of today show signs of old age!
Should the morning sun be flickering like a lamp in the night?

O saqi, why should I ask you to quench my thirst?
Thirsting's reward, O Darshan, is pleasure in thirsting.

22

An exhilarant breeze is blowing, so pour till the cup of the ghazal spills over!
Once more the ghazal night enchants with the garden's fragrant call.

Come quickly, O beloved of spring, a ghazal gracing your lips—
Ghazal courtyards and rooftops are restless for your soft footsteps.[22:2]

How to describe the season's smile? It seems like a ghazal verse.
Black curls cascading onto her shoulders—a snare she's cast in the ghazal.

Her every graceful step inspires rays of dreams, flames of desire,
When that airy ghazal houri walks out in the starlight.[22:4]

This desolation as night fades out, these eyes wet with longing,
The anguished vigil of a love gone wild are the gifts, the grace of the ghazal.

Ghazal verses must be spared the critic's dissecting knife—
Those lovely silver-bodied idols are far more fragile than crystal.

Darshan, when sage Shameem displayed his genius in the world of letters,
Resplendent turned ghazal morning, enchanting and blooming its night.[22:7]

23

My nights of anguish will not see my eyes defiled by sleep—
I would never shame my resolve to keep awake.[23:1]

Carry this message, O zephyr, to my trouble-mongering foes:
I dwell in a realm of peace and contentiousness reject.

But when my fellow-feeling is met with abuse and scorn,
My honor I won't compromise—I have my self-respect.

Worldly woes, body in pain, the sorrows of fortune and love—
Is there a storm that I've not made a sport of?

Listen, impatient lover: there is etiquette to gazing!
It is unseemly to boldly stare at her in a crowded room.[23:5]

A lover—a candle aflame, burning in anguish
Without a word of complaint, enduring fire in silence.

Struck mad with love, when they take to love's path,
Come dust storms and tempests, your lovers walk oblivious.

My friend, those possessing true respect for love's honor
Let tears reach the threshold of their eyes, and no farther.

Unless a tale gives voice to the sorrows of the times,
O Darshan, what is the value in writing a story?

24

Demure and shy, she blushes, showing nascent youth—
Or is it the sun bathing the sky with soft hues at twilight?

From that bewitching houri you have hopes of love, it seems—
Wild imaginings, fantasies, ludicrous dreams!

Afflictions of the world, go on with your tests—
Unflagging is my fortitude, my endurance boundless.

Others revel in the goblet's rounds and the flow of bubbling wine;
The vintage I choose to savor is the blood of my desires.[24:4]

The emptiness of mundane life has driven our hearts to despair;
Every atom is restless for revolution.[24:5]

Life finds happiness in continuous struggle;
Lacking challenge, life feels restless and lost.[24:6]

Just now her veil seemed to quiver, ever so faintly—
Darshan, your efforts in gazing are a success.

25

But for Your pleasure in Your singular beauty in creation,
You wouldn't delight in adorning the world's assembly in myriad hues.[25:1]

Lord, my head belongs bowed at her threshold—
Let fate never force me to beg at another door!

Even in your absence, may your remembrance fill my mind—
May I live in a state where alone, I'm never alone.

When the eye of love regards her in a thousand different ways,
Why wouldn't beauty stay busy adorning herself?

Darshan, when beauty, unveiled, strolls through the garden,
How could even blind narcissus not stare at the sight?[25:5]

26

The blossoms grin mischievously, the breeze begins to tease;
She takes offense—the garden plays pranks and is pleased.

I fear the fire in the garden will blaze up again—
See, the dying flames the wind is stirring.[26:2]

Once, long ago, my eyes would tease her;
Now, teased by modesty, she feels shy.

No tears should be falling now—this is laughter's season;
Why does dawn's breeze bait my heart for no reason?[26:4]

Even victims of cruelty won't leave other victims in peace—
The winds of the world keep lashing at me even in my silence.

O Darshan, every breath is fraught with torment—
Though I live, mortality teases me.

27

I found creation's archetypal beauty nowhere else;
Beauty I've seen, but never a beauty like yours.

They searched but found not a soul to share in their sorrows;
After I was gone, there was no faithful friend.

Time and again I went to temple and mosque,
But where was the succor I get from your wine, cupbearer?[27:3]

Ascetics from a distance, paragons of purity—
Up close you find their virtue leaves something to be desired.

Till my last receding breath I defied every storm;
Thank God my ship had no captain on board![27:5]

This world of Yours, O Lord, may rival paradise in its charm,
But I've never known a moment of peace in this place.

Millions I saw who'd fallen prey to lust and avarice,
But I found none ensnared in love's anguish.

Eyes ecstatic, bubbling over with "Am I not your Lord?"
Saqi, who in this world serves that wine but you?[27:8]

To me alone he gifted all the suffering of the world—
He found no one else who could bear such pain.

If I spoke, to whom should I open my heart, O Darshan?
I find no companion to heed my lament for the world.

28

No goblet of wine, no fragrant night, the garden's doleful face;
She didn't come—spring's caravan stalled in its place.

What happened arose from oblivion when I fell into ecstasy:
I heard her ask from afar—my answer came out bizarre.

Desire to find her grew so intense, I lost all sense of myself—
Time and again she passed by my side—at least, that's what they tell me.

Darshan's grieving voice, though ever so faint,
Still carried like windblown flowers across the silent expanse of his heart.

29

My heart in burning at least gave light to my life;
The garden revived from the weeping of the dew.

Blessed are they who ascend the steps of the gallows—
As martyrs, they gain a life that lasts forever.[29:2]

In the friend's presence, I lost all trace of my self—
But in losing my self, I found bliss.[29:3]

Why grieve at the cold-blooded murder of my heart's desires?
I rejoice that she's earned glory as a beloved!

I cherish one religion—love for all humankind—
For it inspires humanity with the spirit of service.

Leaving mosque and temple, I entered the city of the heart
And exulted to find love's grief transformed into light!

O Darshan, all glory to her for breaking my heart!
A life of love's sorrows has honed my poetic art.

30

If saqi greets me with intoxicating eyes, what then?
Or once more bids me break my vow of abstinence, what then?[30.1]

When the mosque's faithful ask, "Which god do you serve?"
If from my lips her name slips out before God's name, what then?

You're right, I shouldn't speak to her, but please advise me, friend,
If she makes a point of greeting me with beckoning eyes, what then?

Human beings are striving to conquer the moon and sun,
But if the hunter ends up caught in his own trap, what then?

I agree—forgo desire—but please explain to me:
Should she herself come forward with a cup in hand, what then?

The time may come, to keep our love, we'll have to keep apart;
But if our love should ever come to such a pass, what then?[30:6]

O Darshan, now but a favored few enjoy her glance of grace,
But should the times see multitudes arrive at her court, what then?

31

Blessed are you, O drunkards, for by the grace of God
Someone with overflowing cups of bubbling wine has come![31:1]

Tipplers drunk on the ephemeral! Come forward and touch his feet—
The wine in the cup he offers inebriates for eternity.[31:2]

On the path back to God a guide, God's light, and exemplar of virtue—
He has come to the world with the message of the Creator.

Let us be grateful, O sinners, for with the Creator's grace
A message of forgiveness for all our sins has come![31:4]

Once she's fallen captive to your love,
How could the soul-bird ever be caught in a snare?[31:5]

Like drunkards reeling their way to the tavern,
Your lovers go swaying up the gallows steps.[31:6]

Whenever I leave the presence of love's cupbearer, O Darshan,
I come away overwhelmed from receiving something beyond conception.[31:7]

32

Beyond the flight of thought, beyond the reach of mosque
and temple—
How far I have traveled in search of my beloved!

No question, my heart's pain demands that I see you,
But how could I bear to go engulfed in anguish?[32:2]

Listen, ascetic, though this is my heart, it has no concern for itself—
Filled with the world's sorrows, what room is left for its own?[32:3]

Love's sole stock in trade is faithfulness, my friend—
Where does the question of profit and loss come in?

In a true lover's heart this world and beyond stand revealed;
When did the cup of Jamshayd ever reach this stage?[32:5]

In some sort of oblivion I was drawn to this place, saqi!
Otherwise, what have I to do with a tavern?[32:6]

Darshan, despite his thousand showers of grace,
My relentless thirst for his love persists unquenched.

33

The more their heads are kicked, the more they bow them at the door—
Few can break the habit of rubbing their foreheads in the dust.

Love is a passion which springs up irresistibly in the heart,
Like a shower of rain bursting, unforced, from a cloud.

Strange it is, her eyes convey love's secret,
Though not a word of it slips from her lips.

Nothing in this world is more precious than steadfast love,
But where in this world can you find that commodity?

To the moon they flew, and there found dust!
And did that cure their mad obsession to probe the heavens?

What is in a glance of love? Do not ask, O Darshan;
It cannot be explained—you know it when it happens.

34

To whomever but one glance of your grace is sent
Lives estranged from this world, and to the next, indifferent.

Eternal rapture is at hand in this fleeting world—
If you devote your life solely to the tavern.

O my fellow travelers, don't raise such a storm!
I fear you'll overturn our boat and send it to the bottom.

The countless wounds you wrought have made my heart a blooming garden—
How I wish it to become your pathway!

The verse that is truly a verse gives voice to silence—
A wordless message imparted with a glance.

To gauge the ardor of my gaze I've devised a test:
I look at her in silence—she feels my restlessness.

Promise me, my beauty, by the effulgence of your smile
That dawn will one day break in my world of night.

O Darshan, our circle of friends is an enclave of madness;
Whoever joins us here becomes a seer.[34:8]

35

The heart, till it breaks, is but a worthless thing,
But shattering, it transforms into gold.

Just one glance of grace and I'll happily endure
Every cruelty of yours for the rest of my life.

When goblet and flagon break into dance,
Whose is the glance that sparked their reveling?[35:3]

Is that her face reflected in the cup of ruby wine,
Or do I see a star aglow in the crimson twilight?

I've now reached a stage where my sole support
Is the sorrow you bring to my heart.

I have come, as before, from the threshold of the Friend,
Summoned once again by the cries of the times.[35:6]

Battered by the tempest, our ship founders in the waves!
Now we have no hope but our Master.

To fall in love is to accept defeat;
Even in winning at love, you've lost.

Spare one glance of grace for your Darshan, beloved—
He has been broken by the sorrows of life.

36

Off in a corner is my nest, shunned by the face of spring;
The spot where he never casts a glance is my lot in this gathering.

They will gild the sun and moon, adorn the Milky Way!
They are headed for the heavens—heedless of the earth.

Have the winds of the world shifted, or is it you who've changed?
What happened to those enrapturing ways, the glance that lifts my soul?

I've set my sights upon a stage beyond the flight of angels,
While those who claim to know say humans can't attain such heights.[36:4]

The inscriptions engraved on the heart of our age are a precious bequest from the past;
O Darshan, like Khizr, they serve to guide, not swirl up like dust on the path.[36:5]

37

I came away remorseful for venting my complaints—
Why did I cloud the mirror of her heart with the dust of gloom?[37:1]

Those eyes—half-lowered, alluring—and that enchanting face;
You be the judge: beholding you, how can one not fall in love?

Pious ascetics who had boasted of their purity
Left your lane reluctantly, scourged by remorse.[37:3]

Darshan, my only concern is the beauty of the garden—
I long for a spring that has nothing to fear from autumn.

38

To go forth and comfort so many was something impossible—
No one could follow the path I tread in my life.

Gathering storm clouds billow and roll, sweeping aside my vows—
Today let someone pour wine with the heart of an ocean.[38:2]

On others I always saw her lavishing favor;
Whenever we met, she obliged me with a cold shoulder.[38:3]

Only one mad with love could endure what he suffered—
Misfortune never failed to visit his house.

Even your remembrance often left me along the way—
My existence was a journey of despair.[38:5]

I knew but a moment of spring—even that was spattered with blood;
"The calamity in the garden ravaged every bud."[38:6]

Let us speak, O Darshan, of the saqi's wine of love—
Since life must be faced, embrace self-oblivion.

39

Love lends splendor and bliss to this world of pleasure and anguish—
Love is the sound of two hearts beating as one.

If not the bewitching glance from a God-realized man,
What transforms rational life into love's madness?[39:2]

My lonely mornings yearn to hear your footfall,
My anguished nights strain to hear your voice.

Never would my restless gaze dare to be so bold
Were she not beckoning with her alluring glance.[39:4]

An everlasting treasure is love, the wealth of realms divine;
Love sends lovers soaring to ultimate heights beyond.[39:5]

Love is not what is talked of in the marketplace;
Love is unfathomable—absolute mystery.

40

How hard to forgo desire after intimate pleasure!
Better pass over this vale of thorns like a zephyr.

You will pilot my boat of longing to that distant shore!
God protect us! A boatman who claims to be God![40:2]

Beckoning us on every side, an array of enchanting sins;
How hard to pass through this world virtue unscathed![40:3]

How broad and vast the extent of my enlightenment!
Knowing all about the sea, I'm ignorant of the drop.

How can I bear the burning of your absence—now I'm doomed
To be separated from myself, since I'm separated from you.

I should leave your door, saqi—but besides your threshold,
Where would I go, sorely aggrieved and disillusioned by the world?[40:6]

41

I keep talking to my own heart,
Trying to hoodwink my grief at your absence.

No longer does grief over her afford me comfort—
Now I must bear the burden of even this grief.[41:2]

Any path where I even imagine she has walked,
I go there and bow down in devotion.

Now pilgrims in the caravan can travel unafraid—
The thorns infesting the path I've carried away.

Save separation's grief, O Darshan, what do I possess?
I gave her my heart; now only heartache is left.

42

What do they know of laughter's secret, what of joy's mystery?
How can those not steeped in sorrow know the secret of life?

With full consciousness of sorrow, who can bear to be alive?
How can reason grasp my secret of self-oblivion?

To sacrifice myself for someone is my purpose in life.
Why ask me if life has a deeper secret?[42:3]

Voicing hidden grief betrays dignity's self-restraint;
How would the undiscerning know the secret of my silence?

Till one has known the depths of sorrow in all its bitterness,
The sense in perpetual drunkenness remains the tippler's secret.

Your modest reserve in public is proof of our secret intimacy.
How can onlookers understand the motive for your indifference?[42:6]

Those whose creed is cruelty, who stir up discord and strife,
Beyond their grasp is the secret of my fervor for friendship and peace.

All those blind to the beauty of the dawn of democracy,
How can they fathom the secret of the splendor of India?

Love accomplishes everything in this world of possibilities,
Its mysteries fathomed by none but compassionate hearts.

Sincere repentance pleases the heart of the Merciful One;
How can the worldly penetrate the secret of my shame?

O Darshan, to a heart unmoved by humanity's suffering,
Elusive is the secret of my poetry, filled with pain.

43

He did not come to the rooftop and show his effulgent face—
My world this day has not seen a glimmer of light.

Adversity's harrowing storms will never stop me;
My resolve is firm, my love tested by fire.

Your remembrance has broken the bonds of time and space;
You live in my eyes—I see neither sunset nor sunrise.

O friend, a strange anguish overwhelms my being—
My soul is constantly restless, my heart finds no peace.

The eye of the lover has wrought this wonder—bringing his beauty to life!
Even the brilliant rose seems drab when the heart is devoid of love.

I've given myself to the intoxication bubbling from saqi's eyes—
What matter if there are no cups in our assembly?

O Darshan, in truth, devotion is life itself—
Life is wasted if you are not counted his servant.[43:7]

44

I want to reach the bounds of love;
A love-mad guide is what I want.

To awaken consciousness divine,
Your soul-uplifting wine I want.

Dissolve me, absorb me in yourself—
Death in eternity is what I want.[44:3]

Why give voice to the state of my heart?
God is aware of what I want.

O my healer, I am sick for you—
A cure from your hand is what I want.

45

I have no need for Jamshayd's royal chalice or his wine—
The cup of steadfast love is all that I require.[45:1]

How easy to be enamored of the lights in temple and mosque—
What the heart needs is the moth's passion for fire.

Your every word will bring down the vengeance of cross and gallows—
To always speak the truth heroic courage is required.

Call it "Ka'ba," name it "Kashi"—friends,
Our Beloved's house is what we all desire.[45:4]

Rapport between temple and mosque is a simple matter—
The camaraderie of the tavern is required.

O cupbearer, let justice prevail in the tavern!
For all who thirst a goblet is required.

Darshan, I've cast off the bondage of temple and mosque!
The sight of my beloved is all that I desire.

46

Not in tulip or rose, not in moon or twilight—
Nothing I've found has your power to enchant my heart.

My tortured night waits—desperate for a glance of grace;
The stars are already fading—still no light.

The whole world's sorrow and anguish he entrusted to me—
No other heart was imbued with such sympathy.[46:3]

The beloved's glance sent my heart into rapture—
A bliss I'd failed to find in the cup of wine.

Every joy that came was a veil for sorrow—
Alas, living happily was not my lot in life.

Whose radiant visions are these appearing within me!
Even the darkest night is relieved of darkness.

The same air, the same clime, the same garden present,
But the beauty that the roses got, the thorns did not.

O Darshan, not from any instrument have I heard music
That could stir the strings of my restless heart to bliss.

47

Is this the flaming glow of Your face or just a display of Your beauty?
This passing world is enraptured gazing at You![47:1]

Is it the way you speak or the music of your soul
That drives your faithful so mad with love they'd lay down a
hundred lives![47:2]

Just a few looks from the saqi's eyes and drunk were his mad lovers;
How enchanting those glances—how they tugged at the heart![47:3]

Saqi, what to speak of me—ever devoted to you—
Whoever catches a glimpse of you is caught up in love's madness!

Again my thoughts return to you, O life of the world, cupbearer,
"Again each fiber of my being strains to glimpse your face."[47:5]

May Darshan be ever drunk on your radiant visions,
Mind maddened by love, his brow ever pressed to your threshold.

48

How can I believe her message never came?
Her message did arrive—but not in my name.

Dissolved were hopes of bliss from your intoxicating eyes—
Alas, those cups of fortune never came around to me.

Think of his greed, how the gardener plucked the blossoms!
The very essence of the garden was lost to the garden.[48:3]

What joy lies in spring if it descend in a garden
Where reverence for human dignity is forgotten.

What an irony about the tavern master's presence!
Those who thirst, O Darshan, gain no entrance!

49

Who ever bid you to drink alone, in secret?
This is wine, so serve it to others and drink![49:1]

Worldly sorrows, bitter trials—forget them all and drink;
Humming stirring songs of love, raise your cup and drink.

Even as you reach for the cup, hold fast to the hem of devotion—
First bow your head in worshipful love, then drink.

If your longing cools, then what hope is there for bliss?
All those stars that lie asleep—awaken them and drink![49:4]

The remedy for life's sorrows is to drown them in tears of love;
Friends, a dark night has fallen—light up the lamps and drink.

Whatever wine the saqi wills becomes your destiny;
Even if he pours you poison, smile, my friends, and drink.[49:6]

Seeing my true devotion, the venerable sheikh exclaimed,
"Since drink you must, O Darshan, better come to the
mosque and drink!"[49:7]

50

You are the enemy of my life and you, my savior;
As you have inflicted this pain, provide a cure!

I've reached such a stage of respect for my self
That to seek any help would put my resolve to shame.[50:2]

A single ray of light sent to relieve my life's darkness—
This hint of borrowed light I could not bear.[50:3]

How would I have known the splendor of your court?
Did you ever call me—even by mistake?[50:4]

Bemoaning your lot, cursing fate's cruel decrees,
You commit a great sacrilege against the lover's creed.

How, O Darshan, could you find distinctions in love's world?
Here—be they humble or exalted—all are one.

51

I come bearing the immortal wealth of love—
I come to offer up my life at your feet.

No pearls or silver have I to lavish upon you—
I come to offer the gift of streaming tears.[51:2]

In lieu of domain or dominion, my ambition is hearts;
I come to create a new order of rule.

O Lord of the Judgment, ask whatever you will—
I come before you with nothing but my silence.[51:4]

52

Whose threshold is this where my head irresistibly bows?
O my proud heart, now your conceit is undone!

While youth yet blooms the heart's desire comes to dust—
Alas for the candle snuffed out with night just descending.

A drink from your eyes and fully quenched is my thirst;
How can thirst be appeased with wine from a cup?

Who knows, O life of spring, why one glimpse of you
And the closed bud of my heart has suddenly bloomed!

O saqi, just look at my eyes flowing with tears!
This, too, is a way my eyes drink in your tavern.

Why take offense, my love, when I voice a just complaint?
What needs to be said must not remain unsaid.

As a bud bursts in bloom, the garden echoes with warning:
See how life is drawing closer to death.[52:7]

The arias of the intellect are unbearable noise,
A din that drowns out the human voice.

Make your way quickly to the tavern, O Darshan!
Your share will go into the cups of your rivals.[52:9]

53

The assembly of master artists revealed a world of radiant beauty;
I gazed enraptured on that circle of mystic seers.

Rent by creeds, they embraced as one, overcome by love—
The tipplers shared the tavern master's cloak.[53:2]

The lights of God's attributes are reflections of His essence;
Whether Sheikh or Brahman, in truth, there is no difference.[53:3]

O cupbearer, pour self-absorbed Darshan a cup of your wine—
The vintage that frees the heart from all sense of me and mine.

54

The visionary eye ranges beyond the Ka'ba and Sinai—
God is not veiled from those with the eye to see.[54:1]

Whose house is not effulgent with his visions?
Just one—the world of my heart is bereft of his presence.

By my own efforts alone will I reach the goal of my longing—
No help from anyone will I accept.

Should I drive her from my mind, the anguish of love forget?
O torments of fate, I am not so helpless yet![54:4]

Is this how you value my love? Is this all my due?
Love's etiquette, apparently, does not apply to me?

To sink this world and the next in a glass of wine—
What can perform this feat but the saqi's eyes!

Though you're not here, a throng of your memories surrounds me—
I'm not alone or forsaken—I feel no despair.

As night gathered, gloom enveloped your lovers—
Without you the assembly is barren of joy and light.

I have the mettle within to contain the secret—
My vessel is secure, my nature not Mansoor's.[54:9]

The vast reaches of time and space can never come between us—
You may be far from my eyes, but not from my heart.

O Darshan, I was preordained to see his radiant visions—
A thousand thanks my world is not in darkness.

55

When affliction assails them, they simply laugh it away!
Wondrous are your mad lovers, steeped in wisdom divine!

Sparing no thought for themselves, indifferent to their own pain,
Consumed are your mad lovers by the suffering on the earth.[55:2]

How would they even notice what is laughable in others?
Their own state suffices to keep your mad lovers amused.[55:3]

Amidst a flood of tears they pour the cup to overflowing—
This is how your mad lovers defy the assaults of fortune.

Who knows what came over them as soon as spring arrived!
Your mad lovers, as if fighting themselves, were tearing their own collars![55:5]

Once in a while, at least, bestow a glance that revives!
Your mad lovers are perishing of unfulfilled desire.

I've watched Darshan pass through times of joy and affliction—
Your mad lovers are cheerful, no matter their condition.

56

The effulgence of the sun and moon, the splendor of creation
Merely reflect the sublime beauty of my beloved's face.

Ah, what she thought but a flower and tossed aside—
Someone should ask me about this blossom's worth.

Now it lies blighted by autumn, O heart, but how long can this last?
Tomorrow these ruins of a garden will rival paradise.

Through how many terrifying stages they must have passed,
Traveling evolution's path to this human birth![56:4]

Pushing cup and decanter aside, he walked out of the tavern—
Nothing but your radiant presence would satisfy his thirst.[56:5]

57

What escape has humankind from the prison of sorrow,
Condemned to a night of pain which has no dawn.

A lover finds only the path to the beloved worth taking;
Otherwise, one path is as good as another.

O devotees of intellect, come live in the city of the heart!
No other place is so charming or beautiful.

I'm certain of your grace, though to me it's obvious
My cries fail to reach you, my sighs have no effect.

Please don't ask me to describe the grief of fruitless waiting—
That is a long story, not simple in the telling.

Our hearts were plundered—even so we reached our destination;
On the path of life, no guide avails but love.

Losing awareness of self, I awoke to the secret of life—
A boon of self-oblivion, not the fruit of discernment.

Love is a treasure transcendent, enduring beyond the crush of time,
A flame of eternal fire, not a flash in the dark.

Meet enraptured Darshan—he'll reveal the secrets of consciousness,
Though now he's in a place where he's unconscious of himself.[57:9]

58

The time has come for someone to offer prayers from the heart—
Let someone render up the dues of love.[58:1]

God forbid that others know such suffering—
This writhing and tossing of my tortured heart.

I offered up my heart and soul in sacrifice to him—
If he will not accept them, what more can anyone do?

My restless heart yearns to tell its story once again—
I pray that someone have the heart to listen.

May my saqi pour again from his intoxicating eyes,
For someone, thirst aroused, should be drinking![58:5]

I, too, crave the wine of enlightenment—
Let someone open up the tavern door!

My heart yearns, O Darshan, to gaze into those eyes—
Heed my prayer, O Lord—let someone come![58:7]

59

How could you fathom, dear traveling companion, my journey is
different from yours—
I shun any stations along the way, my path is not of this world.[59:1]

There's no need to ask about my wishes—I've received far more than
I ever hoped for;
My story is wondrous indeed, my condition unique in this world.[59:2]

These people are slaves of lust, my faithful friend—how can they
understand what I desire?
The one I love is utterly unlike them—my beloved is not of this world.

The apparent zeal of my devotions belies the constant turmoil
in my heart—
At every turn I find myself dismayed that my goal still lies
far beyond.[59:4]

Compassionate and gracious is my Lord, always merciful
and forgiving;
Seeing the plight of the world, I am certain the god it worships is a
different sort of god.[59:5]

Where I set out from is a mystery, my existence a journey from the
womb of time,
Somewhere inconceivable my origin, my ultimate abode not of
this world.

I am known by all as feeble Darshan, yet my heart is radiant with
someone's light;
Oblivious to all else, there I seek him—while I am sought by someone
not of this world.[59:7]

60

The eyes of love imbue all things with beauty—
The world of love is beauty without end.

My eyes concede the glories of paradise,
But after all, one's homeland is one's home.[60:2]

Enchanting garden, pageant of blooms, enrapturing spring breeze—
If you withdrew, where is the point in these?[60:3]

Only they are worthy to talk of the ultimate goal
Whose certainty is drawn from firm resolve and strenuous effort.

Sometimes I remember you, sometimes you appear—
Both are gifts of grace from you, dwelling within my heart.

My temple—constancy in love, my Ka'ba—constant love,
My faith and my religion—only constant love.[60:6]

Better than the feast at a tyrant's table
Is the barley loaf earned by a poor man's toil.[60:7]

This earthly abode of human beings, who are the pride of angels,
To me is as sublime as paradise.[60:8]

Once it was idols I adored, convinced by my eyes;
Now I've fallen in love with God, for I see Him clearly within.[60:9]

61

At times this path runs through gardens, at times through deserts—
Life is both marriage bed and battlefield.

What has become of humanity's zeal to embrace martyrdom?
We now find the gallows forsaken and desolate.[61:2]

By joining with others to drink, your thirst will be quenched—
Close flow the Ganges and Jamna and then merge as one.[61:3]

Now no tulips are pinned to scarves, no one tears his collar—
Desolate is the garden, forsaken is the forest.[61:4]

I'm not the only one roaming, feet blistered, through mountains
and wilderness—
Many a tulip-like beauty I've met, their heads covered with dust.[61:5]

Once anguished by yearning, my heart is no longer empty—
I was blessed with devotion, O Darshan, and love for my homeland.[61:6]

62

Immune now is my heart to life's sorrows and worldly cares—
The pain of love for you cures all afflictions.

Where am I to bow my head? How to find Your door?
All I see before me are temple, mosque and church.

No one I met denied the supremacy of the goal,
But not a one had any inkling of the path to take.[62:3]

This is no spring breeze moving gracefully through my garden—
It's an invitation to madness addressed in my name.[62:4]

This enchanting spell of life is nothing new to me,
But "a dream I've dreamed over and over again."[62:5]

Who knows what moment in time may prove propitious?
Go bow your head at the crossroads—why do you wait?[62:6]

O grief of love, may you prove a balm for my heart,
Lying gravely wounded by the beguiling charms of the world.

Blossoms have begun to bloom everywhere in my heart!
How blissful the breeze that blows in my garden!

As yet these drops know not their immensity—
Within each drop lies concealed the sea.[62:9]

When I looked with the eye of love, it stood revealed—
Within each sand grain spreads a boundless desert.[62:10]

How could I deny that You exist?
I see Your beauty at work in everything.

What to say of those dear ones now bent on my demise—
Those who are as kin to me, thirsting for my blood![62:12]

O Darshan, why dread sorrow's gathering darkness?
Your heart is lit by a flame of eternal light.

63

From every scene of life his gaze withdrew with indifference—
In this world of bustle and pageant the seer stood alone.

In this age what chance is there for hearts to truly meet?
Even mingling with a crowd, one remains alone.

Every thought of you brings new intimate revelations—
My nights are never lonely, at dawn I'm not alone.

The tortures of love and beloved, the sorrows of life and the world—
Till self-oblivion is attained, who can be alone?

Every stage sees more wayfarers falling by the wayside—
Alas, I fear our guide may end up all alone.[63:5]

My eyes met his and flowers blossomed around me—
My eyes were autumn stricken so long as they remained alone.[63:6]

No traveling companion, no guide appeared, O Darshan—
I fought and won the battle of life alone.

64

The fervor of my love will never weaken—
My world of desire will not crumble.[64:1]

The ecstasy of grief turned into song—
Now my heart will never feel bereaved.[64:2]

The effulgence of my world will only grow—
The lamp of burning grief will never dim.[64:3]

Even beyond this plane of earth and water,
The pain of love for you will never wane.[64:4]

This show of anger is just for appearance' sake—
I'm certain that, at heart, she's not displeased.[64:5]

Once one's head is bowed at your threshold,
The days of bowing down to the world are over.

Darshan, I will defy the shocks of fate—
My zeal to accomplish my work will not abate.

65

Flowers in blossom, lamps aglow, the air humming with song;
Under her fragrant veil, evening smiles.[65:1]

Desires flare up in the heart without end,
As if someone kept rubbing time's cheeks again and again.

To utter a word of passion is trespass, to mention love is a sin—
Just look at the mischance where fate had us meet!

O friend, my search in temple and mosque has drained me—
I found no Hindu or Muslim anywhere.[65:4]

Make your steps on devotion's path worthy of remembrance,
The guiding signs you've left marking every turn in life.

Such color and fragrance overflowing in the tavern of the heart!
O cupbearer, keep your cup moving around the assembly![65:6]

A new style of song Darshan sang today, so filled with love,
His voice lit new lamps that burn with melodious light.[65:7]

66

Fellow artists of the world, heed my appeal:
Let your masterworks bare human suffering.

Ever hostile to progress, bitter foes of love's madness—
"What can one say to diehards who worship tradition?"[66:2]

The sorrows of love have freed them from both worlds.
What can we say to those who are caught in his tresses?[66:3]

How pristine their appearance—but how foul their hearts!
Even sinners like us are pure next to those holy ones.

Mad lovers have watered the garden with their blood—
This spring the rose beds give off a different scent.[66:5]

The atmosphere of a crystal palace enshrouds the soul in darkness;
I found rays of mystic light streaming through a cavern.[66:6]

Laughing for joy, they mounted the steps to the gallows.
O Darshan, what else would she expect of her lovers?[66:7]

67

What I need most of You, God—how to put that in words?
Your grace in its ultimate measure is what I want.

I wish to be done with ego, so to be one with the God;
To follow a love-mad guide is what I want.

What could grant me the gift of life everlasting?
A life-infusing glance is what I want.

From all eternity I have stood at Your door and begged—
The alms I seek are more than what others want.

Why resort to words to voice the plight of my heart?
You already know exactly what it is I want.

I've no idea what I should ask from you—
Whatever is right for me is what I want.

O Darshan, my sins are endless, so always overhead
The grace of your sacred protection is what I want.

68

How wondrous the harmony emerging from love—
From two hearts arises an identical song.[68:1]

Infinite, indefinable its ultimate state;
All we can know is life has a beginning.[68:2]

Only yesterday my heart overflowed with music;
Now it lies silent, a broken instrument.[68:3]

Look not on me as a beggar in the tavern—
The range of my flight is to the highest heaven.[68:4]

O Darshan, I am lost in remembrance of my friend—
Exulting in my self-oblivion!

69

Show me the miracle of Christ, for my breath is nearly gone;
Spread your mantle of mercy, which cures all human ills.

To be drunk on the wine of oneness is the essence of faith;
That is the wine every Hindu and Muslim craves.[69:2]

Full of perils, littered with thorns is the valley of love, O heart,
But we are sure to reach the goal—our Master will protect us.

Reveal the secret of "Die before death!" my divine confidant,
Then make the mystery of " 'Be!' and it was," now veiled,
an open book.[69:4]

Minstrel, make music—sans strings or reed—in the presence of
supreme beauty!
Every beat of your heart is an enrapturing melody.[69:5]

O Darshan, let not love's labyrinthine pathways cause alarm—
The goal itself will call you, love's madness keep you safe.

70

Ever mindful of the world's eyes, she had to preserve her honor.
Prudence at times demands strange tacks—she couldn't return
my love.[70:1]

She robbed me of my hopes, then left my heart to die;
A lamp of love she lit just to extinguish it.

She stands in the idol temple, testing my love and faith—
O friend, do I worship the idol or gaze upon her face?[70:3]

When the night of separation comes, I'll have to bear it—but why
grieve now
When he's given the gift of gazing on him, lavishing
visions resplendent.

Gone is her heart's old restlessness; vanished, those quivering tears—
All the signs indicate she must have forgotten me.[70:5]

Had she severed me from the world and made me her own,
I'd be in ecstasy,
But Darshan, she still is not mine, yet severs everyone from me.

71

When the long-lost straggler turned up at the caravanserai,
His friends happily cried, “Look! The heedless one came
to his senses!”[71:1]

When she removed her veil, all were dazzled
By the vision of Sinai’s lightning in their midst.[71:2]

Tossed about by raging waves, I despaired of life
When suddenly I spied the shore—my heart resumed its beat.

When in the twilight she appeared on the rooftop,
It seemed the moon had risen full in the sky.

Her stunned consternation attested to her crimes
When that murderess was led in irons to her Reckoning.[71:5]

Whenever any caravan reached a way station,
The wayfarers looked everywhere, but saw no sign of Darshan.[71:6]

72

When amidst a flood of woes my grief-drowned house I recalled,
A moth locked in the burning embrace of a candle came to mind.

Worldly afflictions had misted over the mirror of my heart;
When I saw you a long-forgotten story came to mind.[72:2]

How stirring was your sermon, preacher, on paradise and houris!
Sometimes I thought of my tavern and sometimes of my saqi.[72:3]

I told the tale of my heartbreak, but no carouser listened;
Even the saqi took no notice that my cup was broken.

A waft from a bank of flowers and my collar is in shreds—
One step in your lane and my heart is struck mad again.[72:5]

Remembering someone, Darshan slipped into self-oblivion—
Who could then recall the Ka'ba or the idol house?[72:6]

73

My beloved, they say, is angry with me. For what reason?
Can someone explain the caprice that moves her heart?

Let him first have a look at her—who sparks the tumult of doomsday—
Then inquire of the reverend sheikh what he has to say.[73:2]

What is death but glad tidings of eternal union!
What people call "death" is the herald of true life.

The days of dancing in delirious love have returned!
Once more the season's breeze fans our madness.

The heart, till it breaks, is but a silent stone,
Yet from its shattering arise anguished melodies.

"Sublime is beauty's every word! Love's talk is folly!"
Of course, what you say is right! I repeat, absolutely right![73:6]

Bearing the pain of countless hearts, Darshan has left this world;
Desolate and lonely now lies the assembly of lovers.[73:7]

74

When we fall into conversation, I speak of all manner of things,
But what is in my heart I dare not impart.

Lest her intoxicated pride of beauty exceed itself,
I deliberately do not call that idol "God."

Your intoxicated stumbling is but an alluring pose—
To us no slip of yours is a fall from grace.[74:3]

Unless from the beloved's lane the evening breeze comes blowing,
Her lovers don't consider it air to breathe.[74:4]

O martyrs for the homeland, you have won eternity!
This is glad tidings of life—why call it "death"?[74:5]

Your habit of cruelty attests to our intimacy—
We connoisseurs of love can't brand you "treacherous."[74:6]

Unless those clouds make even puritans rise up in dance, O Darshan,
We cannot call them rain clouds of God's grace.[74:7]

75

The death of a jovial heart is a calamity!
Flowers withering in autumn—a tragedy![75:1]

Someone in this world who could bear to listen
To my tale of separation—an impossibility!

Should our guide's vigilance slacken but for a moment,
The caravan would be plundered—a catastrophe![75:3]

It was I who offered my nest to the lightning's fire;
I did this to myself—sheer insanity![75:4]

How could sympathetic souls endure it—
The clamor of sighs and wailing like doomsday misery![75:5]

To forsake the love of flesh and blood houris
In the vague hope of paradise? Absurdity![75:6]

Now to find that Darshan has been anointed
The master of the tavern—God have mercy![75:7]

76

The sum of all light, the play of the garden's colors—
Your face, the radiant moon; your body, the flowers.

My footsteps never faltered, though the path of love at times
Wound through jungle, wound through desert, wound around my neck like a rope.

A thousand revolutions have altered the face of the world,
Yet unchanged still is beauty's complexion and the demeanor of love.

A human being must be resolute and endure life's bitter sorrows—
In times of grief and affliction, let no furrow disfigure the brow.

The world may blindly dismiss it as something worthless,
But what the artist's chisel has carved the world cannot efface.

A cradle of love and kindness is my country—
But love's foes find only hatred's grave.

However lofty the sentiment, if divorced from reality,
How is that wisdom, art or poetry?

Each soul in this world holds nothing so dear as life,
But even more precious to me than life is my homeland.[76:8]

So much have I heard made of the world's joys and charms,
But I've known nothing here but troubles and sorrow.

The very soul of beauty and delicacy, He does appear
Through spring, infusing every bud; through zephyr, every garden.

A thousand times, O Darshan, I've passed the test of love—
Who knows why beauty puts no trust in me?

77

From the moment you cast your evil eye, O hunter,
The world of my nest has lain in ruins around me.[77:1]

From the day You commanded creation into being,
Evils untold have appeared and plagued the world.

Humankind fell prey to myriad sorrows
The day this thing called "love" was invented.

How unexpected is your visit—and to ask of my condition!
What new ingenious torture prompts you now, my dear?

Only when the earth is plowed can a plant strike roots—
The basis of the making always lies in the breaking.

O candle, you gave the moth not even a thought—
Now the poor thing lies charred, bereft of a shroud.

Day and night for days on end he hasn't said a word—
What strange affliction has befallen Darshan?

78

Who knows what state I was in when our eyes met!
All awareness of my existence was gone.

For you that moon and sun are enchanting snares—
Beware lest your gaze be caught and you rise no higher![78:2]

Is spring's beloved, who I long to reach, annoyed with me today?
Why else would my path to her seem bleak and lonesome?

O audacious tipplers, have regard for the goblets and cups!
While passing through the world of hearts, move gently.[78:4]

My madness knows why, nightlong, desperate with sorrow,
With tearful eyes I rushed about embracing shadows.

I follow no pathway or guide—just an urge to move forward;
I feel the tug at my heart leading me onward.

Friends, we must not let darkness enshroud us again!
So many have kissed the gallows that we might see dawn![78:7]

What a thrill when beauty herself compels us to look!
Were she not waiting restlessly, how would she capture our eyes?[78:8]

O Darshan, life is the confluence of reality and dreams;
In this union lies the exaltation of human beings.

79

Life—unfathomable in ages past, shrouded in mystery now;
At the dawn of time only conjecture, and even today.

Once the voice of awakening was paid for with brickbats and stones,
As that song of peace and friendship is still dear today.[79:2]

Day and night through our hearts we spoke of a thousand different things—
Still I long to speak to him in the flesh today.

Though the blood Your martyrs shed was soaked up by the earth,
"The horizon glows with a red mist even today."[79:4]

Love grows languid, its fervor bedimmed by time,
Still the sun burns like noon on the plains of my madness today.[79:5]

Far beyond time's reach lies the realm of reverie;
Though my face is worn, still vivid are my memories today.

Not once has my life's countenance bloomed with the joy of youth—
Life's spring at its dawn was like autumn night, and still is today.

Times past saw the outspoken face the terror of spear and sword;
A critical voice fears arrows even today.

Bestow on thirsty Darshan your glance, for parched is his throat, saqi!
In the past his words burned with passion, and still burn today.[79:9]

80

I do not walk alone—love's mad zeal is my companion;
Out of the vortex of night's gloom I'll distill the light of dawn.[80:1]

How lucky I was to escape the highway robbers—
Just so my guide could lead me far astray.[80:2]

Were my musings on her loveliness to be mirrored in the cup,
Her beauty's scintillation would add potency to my drink.

My every slip from virtue without fail You condemn,
Yet You are the one who adorned every path I take with sins![80:4]

She promised me "tomorrow," but I could not wait—
The life that I'd been granted proved far too brief.[80:5]

As our age turns its back on the way of love,
This world of enchanting beauty confronts the abyss.

The more I long for his darshan, the more he feels disdain—
My anguished prayers are impotent, my weeping goes in vain.[80:7]

Translations of Persian Ghazals

81

Around the flaming candle pours
A swarm of moths in frenzied flight,
Rushing to their beloved's door
To give up their lives in fiery light.

Insipid seem the garden flowers,
The moonlit night as overcast,
Their charms are naught but signs of sorrow
Until the beloved appears at last.

Someone staggers toward the pub,
So contagious his ecstasy that
Swept up in dance are cask and cup
And even the tavern sways blissfully.

When the cupbearer cast a glance,
Such rapture in my soul it bred
That blissfully drunk I watched entranced
As the tavern reeled around my head!

No doubt, preacher, the path of love
Is bewildering and perilous,
But when a tippler is daring enough,
He finds the way not arduous.

If like a renunciate you live,
Remembering him exclusively,
His love, O Darshan, will make him restive
And draw him to you helplessly.

82

From the cups of his eyes spills ravishing wine,
Lifting my soul in ecstasy;
With the tavern master ever in mind,
My heart exults in his bounty.

If aught but love for the true friend
You've built upon as your life's base,
Be not deceived! When you meet your end,
Your entire life will appear a waste.

Not all who take a pick in hand
Are Farhaads desperate for Sheereen,
Not all who cut through mountains can
Convey through them a milky stream.[82:3]

Just look at how this garden's grown
So lush with crimson tulip blooms,
In whose wondrous splendor's shown
My whole heart, raw with wounds.

Whence comes my silent misery?
Ask her, who's so compassionate;
She's seized my heart, I'm on my knees,
Waiting for her sword blade to hit.

83

This tale has no words—listen with your heart!
What it relates cannot be described.[83:1]

Alas for the tipplers' hapless plight!
The gracious saqi is nowhere in sight.[83:2]

Like a fish out of water I am desperate
Till the friend appears and I gaze in his eyes.

On those enrapturing eyes I'm drunk—
Of goblet and wine what need have I?

Call them not lovers unless, like Mansoor,
They mount the gallows and the noose is tied.[83:5]

Sit carefree in the shadow of a saint—
No burdens remain where devotion resides.[83:6]

With myriad afflictions this world snares the soul—
There's no escape without a master to guide.[83:7]

84

How pristine are these drops raining down from springtide clouds!
How enchanting the blossoms floating down from lofty boughs!

Of what use to me are the goblet and carafe
When bubbling wine is pouring forth from my beloved's eyes!

Such a marvelous garden is now blooming in my breast!
A thousand crimson tulips spread across my wounded heart.[84:3]

Be not a slave to the lures of greed and lust—
Welling passions overwhelm the unripe with each breath.

Take your cup and come to the tavern, O Darshan!
Behold! Wine is raining down from the springtide clouds!

Translations of Urdu Sonnets

85

A Memory

O breath of life, do you remember when you stole my heart?
A thousand woes lay concealed in your alluring walk.
Soon you were flowing in my every vein, O life of spring—
You looked at me, you smiled—remember?[85:1]

My love, you were the bare necessity of my life—
Now you've cast me aside, and in grief I languish.
Tell me the truth—do you ever spare me a thought?
Alas for life's caravan so mercilessly plundered!

Who was it that instructed you so well in ways perverse?
What fault of mine deserves such punishment that leaves me sighing?
Is it now a sin just to love someone?
Just what have you gained from your treacherous game?

Still I live; still in grief; still raw, my heart's wounds;
Come to me now! Love's lamp is flickering!

86

In Separation from the Beloved

My nights pass in longing for you, without a glimmer of light.
My love, your tantalizing charms still torment my thoughts.
Your word you broke—that memory too haunts me without respite,
Leaves me stone silent, heart restless, eyes ever weeping.[86:1]

A caravan of grief crawls across my desert heart—
I, madman moth of love, am barred from happiness
As I go on burning—but in my own fire.
Your nights are overflowing goblets, mine are overflowing eyes.

In glorious hues contemplation paints desire's abode;
The moonlit night begins to sing a melody of love,
A song of reverent kindness, the tale of faithful lovers;
But you, O radiant beauty, alone endow the assembly with splendor.

Break through the bounds of perception and draw near—
Suffuse my world with enchanting sonorous light.

87

Why Spurn Me Now?

Why spurn me now, O life of my desire—
My whole world dances at the sight of you;
Your sweet smile is my life's sustenance;
My fate, bewitching houri, hangs on you.[87:1]

Though you're aloof, your memory, like a friend, cheers my heart, till
Despair overwhelms, I long to behold you, nights last forever,
A caravan of yearning, hope, dismay and grief, a tinge of trust—
then hopes dashed—
My heart, now made of pain, once laughed.

Your eyes—brimming cups of scintillating ruby wine,
Your lips—sweet with the subtle savor of the vintner's nectar,
Your cheeks—as soft and delicate as the petals of a rose:
All these entrust forever to your humble poet.

Come back to me, beloved—we'll again sing songs of love—
Once more we'll draw sweet music from the strings of life.

A Bouquet from Darshan's Garden

Miscellaneous Verses from

***Talāsh-e Nūr* (Quest for Light)**

***Manzil-e Nūr* (Abode of Light)**

***Jādah-e Nūr* (Pathway of Light)**

88

From *Talāsh-e Nūr* (Quest for Light)

All I remember is a sudden glimpse of him—
Then I was lost—to him and myself.[88:1]

Now the whole panorama of eternity stretches before me,
Revealed when you lifted the veils that confine consciousness.[88:2]

For that one smile I'm grateful, which swelled like a wave
And flowed onward as a sea of a thousand lights.[88:3]

In the wilderness of exile, you will sustain me;
Your love will fill my heart as I mount the gallows.[88:4]

If your body is dragged through thorns, let it go!
The soul is a flower that autumn cannot ravage.[88:5]

From *Manzil-e Nūr* (Abode of Light)

In pulsating dance sins beckon and tease on the dance floor
of the heart;
Every human being is wrapped tight in the arms of desire.[88:6]

Were we to reflect your virtue in our lives,
We would make this garden the cynosure of spring.[88:7]

To the garden you revealed the secret: spring knows but one color;
The flowers you infused with the scent of oneness.[88:8]

From *Jādah-e Nūr* (Pathway of Light)

All living creatures seek a life of peace,
So pass your days on this earth humanely.
Even the heart that beats in an animal's breast
Knows sympathy, brims with love.

So look on all living creatures with loving compassion—
Bring to humanity's night the light of dawn.[88:9]

Commentary on the Poems

1

Verse 1

This verse expresses the tragic irony that human beings, for whose sake God brought creation into being so that they would realize Him, fail to fulfill that purpose by seeking God everywhere but where He resides—within themselves. The verse recalls a famous tradition or saying (*ḥadīth*) of the prophet Muḥammad often quoted by one of the most influential Sufi mystic-philosophers, Ibn 'Arabī (1165–1240):

> *qāla kuntu kanzān makḥfiyyān fa-aḥbabtu an 'urafa fa-ḳhalaqtu'l-ḳhalqa likai 'urafa.*[126]
>
> God said, "I was a hidden treasure; I desired to be known, so I created the creation so that I could be known."

In another related hadith, the Almighty says,

> *lā yasa'unī ardhī wa-lā samā'ī wa-yasa'unī qalbu 'abdī'al-mu'mini.*[127]
>
> Neither My earth nor My heavens can contain Me, but I am contained in My faithful servant's heart.

The great Sufi poet-saint Jalālu'ddīn Rūmī (1207–1273) has written a number of verses on the theme of this latter hadith.

goft peiġhāmbar keh ḥaq farmūdeh ast
man nagonjam hīch dar bālā o past
dar zamīn o āsmān o 'arsh nīz
man nagonjam īn yaqīn dān ei 'azīz
dar del-e mo'men begonjam ei 'ajab
gar marā jū'ī dar ān delhā talab[128]

"Thus spoke the Lord," the Prophet declared:
" 'I cannot be contained above or below,

In the earth, in the heavens, even in the empyrean.
Have no doubt, O noble one, I am contained
In a true believer's heart. Oh, what a wondrous thing!
If you wish to find Me, seek in those hearts.' "

negah kardam andar del-e ḳhwīshtan
dar ān jāsh dīdam degar jā nabūd[129]

I gazed within my own heart—
There I saw Him—nowhere else.

delā jostīm sar-tā-sar nadīdam dar to joz delbar
maḳhwān ei del marā kāfer agar gūyam keh to ū'ī[130]

O heart, I searched from end to end, but in you I saw just the Friend.
Call me no heathen if I say, my heart, that you are He.

Verse 4

This verse contains a play on two Persian words: *ḳhwud-shināsī* (self-knowledge, self-realization) and *ḳhudā-shināsī* (God-consciousness, God-realization).

Verse 6

This verse contains a play on words between *ḳhudā*, meaning "God"; *nā-ḳhudā*, meaning "atheist, infidel"; and *nāḳhudā*, meaning "ship's captain, boatman, seaman," the latter two terms being spelled the same in Urdu.

2

Verse 1

The lover hides his love, but his unusual silence in the beloved's presence gives away his secret. The Urdu poet Mo'min Ḳhān Mo'min has expressed it thus:

kho'e ga'e ham aise kĕh aġhyār pā ga'e[131]

I was so lost even strangers could fathom my secret.

Verse 2

The second line of this verse quotes a hemistich from a ghazal by Iqbal.[132]

Verse 3

The beloved in Urdu poetry is traditionally fickle. Because of her changing moods, the lover can never be sure of his bliss. As Sant Darshan said in one of his discourses,

> there are many states on the spiritual journey. At first it appears to be easy. It is a path strewn with roses and filled with joy, beauty and ecstasy. We receive glance after glance of grace until we become quite oblivious of our own self and of the world. In the initial stages we usually do receive much attention from the Master, and this almost spoils us. But as we progress on the path, we begin experiencing the pain, anguish and restlessness of love. Our Beloved starts playing hide and seek with us. Sometimes we get more attention; sometimes we get less. Sometimes we are in bliss, and sometimes we are in pain.[133]

Verse 4

The gardener, lightning, and wind are the bird's traditional enemies in Urdu poetry. The gardener, always a selfish, villainous figure, picks the rose with which the nightingale (the lover and, here, the poet) is in love. The lightning and wind destroy the nightingale's nest.

4

Verse 4

The second clause of the first line of the Urdu verse literally reads, "I'll see/experience the stage of elucidation/interpretation," and thus, "clear understanding."

When the spiritual master opens the inner, spiritual eye of his disciples, they awaken from the delusory dream of worldly life. Thus enabled to experience the spiritual realms beyond the material plane of existence, they gain a true perception of reality and an accurate perspective on the perplexing happenings in their lives.

Verse 5

These darners have been enlisted to mend the collars and cloaks of distraught lovers during the night of waiting for the beloved. Conventionally in Urdu and Persian poetry, a lover feels so suffocated by overwhelming passion for his beloved that, to seek relief, he rends his collar, tears off his shirt, and goes off wandering distractedly in the forest. Here the poet declares he tore his cloak in the grief of separation from God at the dawn of creation, the dawn of the night of waiting. This tear can be mended only by their reunion.

Verse 6

Sant Darshan contrasts the easy and sheltered existence of worldly benefactors (chandeliers in beauty's sleeping chamber) with the life of a God-realized spiritual master, who undergoes unending trials and tribulations and sacrifices all comforts to guide seekers after truth back to their divine home.[134]

6

Verse 1

"Both worlds" signifies this world and the spiritual realms beyond the physical plane.

Verse 2

The Ka'ba, located in Mecca, is the holiest shrine in Islam.

Verse 3

The moth suffers the grief of separation from its beloved flame; the poet, from his beloved spiritual master. Their intense longing ultimately leads to *fanā'*—the annihilation of their individual existences in the fire of love and eternal union with their beloveds.

Verse 5

Sant Darshan has written, "After we have gained a certain degree of concentration [in meditation] we begin hearing the Sound Current.

It has an indescribable beauty and magnetic power and pulls us up irresistibly. It is a Music which is unstruck and unending. We may tire of the finest music composed by human beings, but the divine Harmony enraptures us and fills us with divine bliss."[135]

Verse 7

According to Sant Darshan, "The primal creative principle is resounding within each one of us. . . . This Music pulsating within us is beyond time, being endless and eternal. . . . [T]he music of this world is produced by some action of our own. . . . But Divine Music, the Music of God, is unstruck. It was, it is, and it shall ever be without end. . . . If we can learn to hear it, we will drink of the Nectar of eternal life."[136]

7

Verse 1

The humble holy men the poet is referring to may well be his spiritual masters, Hazur Baba Sawan Singh and Param Sant Kirpal Singh.

Verse 3

Here the poet speaks of Ḳhwājah Mu'īnu'ddīn Chishtī (c. 1141–1236), a saint from Ajmer in Rajasthan who introduced the Chishti order of Sufis into India, and of Guru Nānak (1469–1539) from Punjab, who was the first guru of the Sikhs.

Verse 5

Darshan uses the word *ḳhirad* (intellect, reason) in the second line of the Urdu original, but we have translated the word here in the broader sense of "mind." Sant Darshan himself appeared to use "intellect" and "mind" in a general sense interchangeably. In one public talk he stated, "We are constituted of soul and intellect. . . . It is the soul which animates and enlivens our body and intellect."[137] In another talk he says, "The union of soul and mind in our body has made us human, yet we are so enveloped by maya that we regard ourselves merely as a body."[138] In any case, seekers must through all-consuming love subdue and still their minds or intellects to gain access to the inner spiritual realms and attain union with God. Sant Darshan wrote, "According to Kabir Sahib and Guru Nanak, the supreme challenge before the seeker is that of conquering his *manas* (mind), and according to the Sufis it is that of mastering *nafs* (mind). Both insist that the mind is not easy to subdue."[139]

8

Verse 1
The event occasioning this verse may have been the passing of the poet's spiritual master, Hazur Baba Sawan Singh, on April 2, 1948, just at the height of spring. The poet's spring was thus plunged forthwith into autumn. As Sant Darshan said in one of his discourses, "It was an irony of fate that the beloved of spring was taken away from us at a time when spring was in full bloom. . . . So, in that hour of jubilation, in that hour of joy, in that hour normally attended with intoxication and inebriation, the greatest tragedy on earth befell us."[140]

Verse 2
Sant Darshan, as an erudite man of letters educated at Government College, Lahore—the premier college in India at the time—was hardly one to disparage the acquisition and value of intellectual knowledge. His verse suggests that such knowledge is limited to the material realms of existence and incapable of providing the true perception of reality gained from mystical transcendence of the mind and senses.

Verse 4
See 4:6 and note for a verse with a similar theme.

9

Verse 2
The spiritual master wishes to lead spiritual seekers on the mystic journey into the beyond. Most, however, are so wedded to traditional religious doctrines and ritualistic devotional practices that they fail to follow him on the inner way.

Verse 3
This verse was included in the version of this ghazal found in *Talāsh-e Nūr* but omitted from the version in *Matā'-e Nūr*. The Urdu reads,

bahut hai nigāh-e karam phir bhī kam hai
ham ahl-e na<u>*z*</u>*ar haiṅ na*<u>*z*</u>*ar dekhte haiṅ*[141]

Verse 4
In Urdu poetry the true lover is a doomed person. Traditionally, he complains that his love is always spurned, while the beloved lavishes her love on others—here on those whose sincerity has not even been tested.

10

Verse 1
It is only by diving in meditation to the depths of their being, far beneath the churning seas of worldly desires and attachments, that spiritual seekers can discover their true nature and find God.

Verse 2
"The empyrean" (*'arsh-e 'a*<u>*z*</u>*īm* or *'arsh-e a'*<u>*z*</u>*am*) in Sufism marks that stage of the soul's spiritual progress where it enters the highest heaven and reaches the throne of God. According to Sant Darshan, when the soul "reaches its true Home . . . [and] arrives in the presence of its Creator, it is enfolded in the process of becoming one with its source."[142] Further, "the journey from our limited physical condition to our True Home may be described in linear terms, much as one describes a journey from a valley to the top of a mountain. But there are no terms for describing what follows: the progressive merging of the soul with its Creator."[143]

The great Persian Sufi poet-saint Farīdu'ddīn 'A<u>tt</u>ār (c.1145/46–1221) mentions *'arsh-e a'*<u>*z*</u>*am* in the following verse:

ei żarreh-ī az nūr-e to bar 'arsh-e a'<u>*z*</u>*am tāfteh*
az 'arsh-e a'<u>*z*</u>*am dar gużar bar har do 'ālam tāfteh*[144]

Oh, a single particle of Your light shone upon Your exalted throne,
And then reflecting off of it illuminated both worlds.

Verse 5
This verse describes what often happens to the teachings of enlightened beings after they leave the world. Those who come after them and have

had no direct experience of their mystical practices make a zealous, well-meaning attempt to preserve their teachings. Unfortunately, however, these teachings then stagnate into formalized rites, rituals, conventions, and doctrines, while the mystical essence is diluted and lost.

Verse 6

The lover is grieving over his once-faithful beloved's fickle rejection of him and her callous wish to expunge all trace of their love. For Sant Darshan's discussion of his suffering during Sant Kirpal Singh's periods of public indifference toward him, see Darshan Singh, *Love Has Only a Beginning*, 119–21.

Verse 8

True martyrs are those who have "died" to themselves, sacrificing their own will to embrace the will of the divine beloved. The love and faith that they retain are, in reality, the source of life everlasting.

Verse 10

The second hemistich of this verse comes from a ghazal by Mir Taqi Mir.[145] Mir witnessed the sacking of Delhi and vicious massacre of its inhabitants by the Afghan king Aḥmad Shāh Abdālī in January 1757 and again, according to Mir's account, by Abdali's soldiers in January 1760, after which Mir left the city.[146] Upon his return, shortly after the Afghans' defeat of the occupying Marathas in January 1761, he again confronted scenes of desolation caused by further Afghan looting.[147] Mir wrote several poems on his impressions of these events, with the line Darshan has borrowed coming from the following couplet:

kin nīndoṅ ab to sotī hai ai chashm-e giryah nāk
mizhgāṅ to khol shĕhr ko sailāb le gayā

O my weeping eyes, what kind of sleep do you sleep?
Open your eyelashes: a flood has swept the city away!

By using this line in his own verse, Darshan implies that we are being swept away from our true purpose by the lure of worldly desires and pleasures, asleep to the inner desolation wrought by wayward living. Perhaps the allusion to Mir's verse also suggests some parallel between our own spiritual deficits and the moral catastrophes we witness in the world.

11

Verse 2

For verses with a similar theme, see 27:2, 27:9, 32:3, and 55:2.

Verse 8

Having transcended the regions of the inner moon and sun in meditation and reached the radiant form of his spiritual master, the poet is wonderstruck that the moon and sun are paying homage to him when it is he who is bowing before his master. It then dawns on the poet he has no conception of whom he is bowing to or how exalted he is.

Verse 11

The *Shāh-nāmeh* (Book of Kings), Iran's voluminous national epic written by the Persian poet Abo'l-Qāsem Ferdowsī in the late tenth and early eleventh centuries, tells of a fabulous, seven-ringed wine cup filled with the elixir of immortality and owned by the ancient mythological Persian emperor Jamshayd (pronounced "Jamshayd" in Dari, Tajik, and Urdu, and "Jamsheed" in Iranian Persian). This cup, called the "Jām-e Jam" (cup of Jamshayd), was a *jām-e jahān-nemā*, a cup that has been variously described as revealing what was transpiring anywhere in this world or in the seven heavens.[148]

12

Verse 6

Ghalib has two famous verses on the cure for grief:

'ishrat-e qaṯrah hai daryā meṅ fanā ho jānā
dard kā ḥad se guzarnā hai davā ho jānā[149]

The ecstasy of the drop is to be lost in the sea;
When pain transcends its limit, it becomes its own cure.

ranj se ḳhūgar hu'ā insāṅ to miṭ jātā hai ranj
mushkileṅ mujh par paṛīṅ itnī kĕh āsāṅ ho ga'īṅ[150]

When grief becomes a habit, the suffering disappears;
So many woes I've had to face that sorrow has become easy.

Verse 8

This verse is in the Urdu tradition of *ḳhẉudī*, or "self-respect." The poet doesn't want to be indebted to anyone, for that would entail subservience and dependence. In a well-known verse in this tradition, Iqbal writes about the royal falcon, his symbol of dignity and self-respect:

gużar auqāt kar letā hai yĕh koh o bīyābāṅ meṅ
kĕh shāhīṅ ke liye żillat hai kār-e āshyāṅ-bandī[151]

Midst wilderness and mountains he is content to pass his days—
For the falcon to build himself a nest amounts to self-disgrace.

In another verse he goes so far as to say,

ḳhẉudī ko kar baland itnā kĕh har taqdīr se pĕhle
ḳhudā bande se ḳhẉud pūchhe, batā terī reẓā kyā hai![152]

I've raised my self-respect to such a height that even God
Before bidding this servant do something must ask,
"What is your will?"

See also 50:2, and 54:3 for verses with a similar theme.

Darshan's attitude in his verse is fully in line with the teachings of the Sant Mat saints. The great medieval Indian poet-saint Kabir Sahib (1440-1518), who is often referred to as "the father of Sant Mat," speaks in no uncertain terms about the destructive effects of dependency on others.

māṅgan maraṇ samān hai, mati ko'ī māṅgo bhīkh
māṅgan te marnā bhalā, ye satguru kī sīkh[153]

Begging amounts to death—extend not your hand for alms;
This is the satguru's teaching: it is better to die than to beg.

Another *dohā* (couplet) of Kabir's in the same vein is as follows:

āb gayā ādar gayā nainan gayā saneh
ye tīnoṅ tab hī gaye jab'hiṅ kahā kachhu deh[154]

Gone are dignity and respect, affectionate looks from others;
These three vanish from your life once you start saying "give me."

13

Verse 3
Only worship at the door of the beloved—a living, God-realized mystic who embodies the ideal lives of the enlightened founders of the world's great religions and experientially reveals the esoteric mysteries at the heart of the founders' teachings—can satisfy the poet's spiritual longings.

Verse 7
The poet envisions a world of eternal spring ushered in by love and peace. He deprecates doctrines and movements that advocate rebuilding the world through violence and destruction, maintaining that "the new age will come about through a change of hearts."[155] Sant Darshan further writes, "We are witnessing the dawn of a spiritual revolution. By definition, such a revolution, unlike political, social or economic ones, cannot be enforced from without. It is an inner revolution which centers on a change of consciousness. We cannot convert others, we can only convert ourselves."[156]

Verse 9
This verse has a mystical dimension. By turning inward to experience visions of the Divine (the moon and sun being preliminary inner experiences of the Light of God on the mystic path), seekers develop their spiritual consciousness, which affords them strength and solace during troubling times and contributes to illuminating the darkness inundating the world.

14

Verse 1

The change of season from winter to spring depicted in this verse is a metaphor for the spiritual life of any lover of God trying to attain union with the Lord. Just as the breeze must make a long, tiring journey to usher in the spring season of rebirth, mystic lovers must spend long, "austere" nights in disciplined meditation before they are blessed with the "dawn" of resplendent divine revelations within.

Verse 3

The idols of deities in Hindu temples are lavishly adorned with crowns, diadems, necklaces, jewels, peacock feathers, garlands, and other ornaments. In this verse, as is common in Persian and Urdu poetry, the poet looks on his beloved as an idol compelling no less devotion than that given to God.

Verse 4

The lover in Darshan's poetry attains mystical union with the beloved in meditation only during the night of longing. In this verse the heart of the lover, shedding tears like a dripping candle, shares the suffering and self-sacrifice of the lamp, for both are fated to spend the entire night on fire. However, the dawn harbors no such sympathy for the lamp or the lover—with the great, gathering light of day, it sardonically overpowers the lamp's flickering efforts and puts an end to the night before the beloved has appeared. Thwarted in his desire to meet his beloved within, the anguished lover must wait for the next night to come.

15

Verse 3

Trying to apprehend spiritual reality through intellect is wasted effort, comparable to seeking a vision of God by worshiping idols of stone. A ray of Divine Light appears only by abandoning oneself to love.

Verse 4
The world has experienced such spiritual decline that now even the desire to find God has departed from people's hearts.

Verse 5
Darshan laments the passing of a world that once had all the loveliness of a flourishing garden but now presents a scene of utter desolation. The flowers have been pulled up and the land lies barren. Even the thorns that gave protection to the flowers have withered.

What the garden symbolizes, however, is open to a variety of interpretations. We do not have sufficient context to say whether the poet's comments on the garden's desolation reflect despair over a devastating personal experience (for example, the passing of one of his spiritual masters); the disappearance of love from the world (the previous and following verses are on this theme); the moral and spiritual degradation that afflict humankind (in which the flowers of moral principles and spiritual ideals have been uprooted, leaving a barren land of selfishness and widespread suffering); or some other possibility.

Verse 6
The gallows is the symbol of lovers' self-sacrifice for the sake of the beloved. Whether the beloved cruelly rejects them or ignores them or orders them to do what is contrary to their desires and causes them great suffering, their love remains constant and they willingly obey. This verse is saying that the darkness is so heavy and overwhelming that even the gallows—the one place one would surely find the light of love burning—is now abandoned. There are no true lovers to sacrifice themselves.

16

Verse 2
This verse brings to mind the scene of what in past times was a typical wedding night in India. With marriages generally arranged, the couple's first intimate meeting traditionally took place only on that night. The

bride would be both expectant and bashful before her new husband as he gradually approached to lift her veil.

Verse 3
Usually it is the beloved who robs the lover of his heart. In this case, the lover has spiritually evolved such that his heart has voluntarily surrendered itself to the beloved and, in so doing, robbed itself of itself, for now it is lost in love for the beloved.

Verse 4
Only one caught in the tresses of the beloved can truly understand what love is.

Verse 6
In this vein, Ghalib has a verse that says,

mĕrī ta'mīr meṅ muẓmar hai ik ṣūrat ḳharābī kī
hayūlá barq-e ḳhirman kā hai ḳhūn-e garm dĕhqāṅ kā[157]

In my construction is concealed the plan of its destruction—
The lightning that destroys the crop is the heat of the farmer's blood.

(The "heat of the farmer's blood"—the sweat by which the farmer grows the crop—lays the ground for the lightning to strike.)

Verse 7
The lure of the world is so compelling that our minds resist renouncing it; either worldly pleasures ensnare us or we ourselves seek them out.

17

Verse 1
The poet implies that all worldly attainments are ultimately worthless if one has not through meditation experienced God during one's lifetime. Darshan has used the word *mehrbān* in the second line to refer to the compassionate Lord in the same way its equivalent (*miharvān*, *miharvāṇ*) has been used in the Ādi Grant'h of the Sikhs:

jā tūṅ tusĕhi miharvān tā Nānak sach samāhi[158]

When You are pleased, O compassionate Lord,
Nanak merges with Truth.

miharvān rakh la'ī'an āpe[159]

The compassionate Lord is the one who liberates.

Mehrbān could be translated equally well as "kind, compassionate people," as in 17:5. (See Hariśhchandra Chaḍḍhā's commentary in Darshan Singh, *Matā'-e Nūr* (Hindi, 2016 ed.), 169 (poem 47, verse 1).[160]

Verse 2
The poet is having a déjà vu experience, perhaps of an inner spiritual realm seen in meditation or an experience from a previous life.

Verse 8
Sant Kirpal Singh used to declare, "Feelings, emotions and drawing inferences are all subject to error, seeing is above all."[161] The person who talks glibly of spiritual matters without actually having experienced divinity only causes confusion.

18

Verse 2
When their longing in meditation for their spiritual master becomes unbearable, the master blesses his disciples with a vision of his radiant form in the inner heavens. This experience comforts and elates them and encourages them to persevere in their devotion.

Verse 5
Darshan may well be writing about his father, Sant Kirpal Singh, in this verse, although the verse could apply to any true lover of God. In this age when human beings have gone mad in materialistic pursuits and sunk to the depths of social and moral depravity, seekers who develop spiritually to the extent that they transcend the physical world

in meditation and gain access to the highest spiritual regions are rare. The sun and moon referred to here may be either the inner heavenly bodies one finds at the frontier of the astral plane, or symbols of the entire inner spiritual cosmos. As Jalalu'ddin Rumi has written,

chūn betāzand āsmān-e haftomīn meidān shavad
chūn bekhospand āftāb o māh rā bālīn konand[162]

When he runs, the seventh heaven is his playing field;
When he sleeps, the sun and moon are pillows for his head.

Verse 8

Neither comforts of this world nor paradise hereafter holds any attraction for those endowed with the riches of communion with God. Jalalu'ddin Rumi writes of these spiritual monarchs in this vein:

to cheh dānī keh mā cheh morghānīm
har nafas zīr-e lab cheh mī-khwānīm

gar beṣūrat gadā-ye īn kūyīm
beṣefat bīn keh mā cheh solṭānīm[163]

How could you know what bird I am,
What under each breath I warble!

Though I appear a beggar of the streets,
Look to my nature—I am a king!

Verse 11

Darshan has written that, in his poetry, a "crystal palace" symbolizes "a life of luxury and comfort" while a "prison" symbolizes "a life of hard work," which might be "connected with home, family, societal obligations, the cares of earning a living, or some other domain." Further, it is only by leaving the life of luxury and comfort "that we can perform service to humanity."[164]

19

Verse 1

This verse can be read as either a universal condemnation of apathy in the face of suffering or the poet's complaint there is no one to understand his suffering in love and apply balm to his lacerated heart. Ghalib also has a verse with this latter sense:

yĕh kahāṅ kī dostī hai kĕh bane haiṅ dost nāṣiḥ
ko'ī chārah-sāz hotā ko'ī ġham-gusār hotā[165]

What kind of friendship is this when the friend does nothing but give advice?
Were there but someone to cure my ills, someone to sympathize!

Verse 2

Similarly, Iqbal has complained about God:

bāt kĕhne kī nahīṅ, tū bhī to harjā'ī hai[166]

It's absurd to speak of Your faithfulness—You visit every house.

Verse 4

In Urdu poetry "someone" often obliquely refers to the beloved. Here, the thought of the beloved continually replaces the thought of God in the lover's prayers.

Verse 6

Darshan here is echoing a hadith of the prophet Muhammad that recounts how the Prophet defined "the greater holy war" (*al-jihādu'l-akbar*) as "the struggle to subdue the lower self" (*mukḥālafatu'n-nafs*),[167] the lower self thus being the greatest "infidel." For the spiritual masters in the Sant Mat tradition, *nafs* refers to the mind, which must be purified of lust, anger, greed, attachment, and ego before the soul can be truly free to return to its divine source.

20

Verse 1

The divine garden, our original home of ecstasy and eternal spring, has been buried beneath the dust of our relentless efforts for material gains in the world; hence, only the shadowy sense of this garden remains in the human consciousness. This verse recalls the biblical story of Adam and Eve's expulsion from the Garden of Eden.

Verse 3

Only their arrival in their long-lost divine home (Sach Khand, or Muqam-e Haq) can dispel "the dark night of the soul" for sincere seekers after truth.

In the second line Darshan uses the word *vaṯan* for the divine homeland. Sant Ravi Dās in a shabad in the Adi Granth likewise uses it to refer to the divine abode.

begam purā sĕhar ko nā'o
dūkh aṅdohu nahī tihi t'hā'o

. . . .

ab mohi khūb vatan gah pā'ī
ūhāṅ khair sadā mere bhā'ī
kā'im dā'im sadā pātisāhī

. . . .

mĕhram mahĕl na ko aṭakāvai[168]

Begampura ["City without Sorrow"] is the name of the town.
There is no suffering or anxiety there.

. . . .

Now I have found my wonderful home.
There one finds lasting well-being, my brethren.
Firm and stable, God's kingdom is forever.

. . . .

All there know God's palace, no one blocks their entrance.

See also endnote 55 for a prose passage of Sant Darshan's regarding the exiled soul longing for its homeland.

Verse 6

The Ganges and the Jamna (Yamuna) are the two most sacred rivers for Hindus, a dip in either of which is claimed to give salvation of the soul. The two rivers flow south from the Himalayas separated by an average distance of about sixty miles and a maximum distance of about one hundred miles, with the distance between them gradually narrowing until they meet at Prayag (Allahabad). The confluence of these two rivers and the invisible Saraswati River is known as Triveṇī Saṅgam and considered as one of the holiest Hindu places of pilgrimage. Mystics speak of the Ganges and Jamna of the inner, spiritual regions, a bath in whose confluence washes away all sins.

21

Verse 2

A Persian poet has similarly said,

harcheh bīnī sū-ye aṣl-e ḳhwod ravad
jozv sū-ye kol-e ḳhwod rāje‘ shavad[169]

Whatever you see is traveling back to its source—
The part is finding its way back to the whole.

In Darshan's verse, the "part" represents the individual soul in a state of separateness from the Oversoul, or God, here symbolized by the "whole." "Death" in this sense is the end of the soul's separation from the Lord through the shedding of individual existence and "dying in the Creator"—a state that the Sufis have referred to as *fana fi'llah*. Sant Darshan has emphasized that this state does not result in the annihilation of the soul: "This death is not death, for it is to die in the very Source of life; it is to become one with that Source. From then on one is part of the Ocean of consciousness, of all that was, is, and shall be."[170]

22

Verse 2
In India, rooftops often consist of open terraces. People sleep there on summer nights, and friends assemble there for talk and recitation of poetry.

Verse 4
The houris are the beautiful virgins of the Qur'anic paradise.

Verse 7
In this verse Darshan pays homage to his poetry mentor, Janāb Shamīm Karhānī.

23

Verse 1
True lovers of God are so driven to meet the Lord that they spend their nights in meditation; they cannot bear to cease remembering their divine beloved, even for a moment of sleep. As Guru Amar Das has written,

ik pal khin visrahi tū su'āmī jāṇa'u baras pachāsā[171]

To forget You for even an instant, O Lord, is for me a parting of fifty years!

Verse 5
Looking directly at the beloved would be indiscreet, as it would give away the lover's secret and embarrass the beloved when she is in the company of others.[172]

24

Verse 4

To gain the pleasure of his spiritual master and develop spiritually, the poet painfully sacrifices his worldly desires and ironically begins to find intoxication in those sacrifices.[173]

Verse 5

For Darshan such a revolution was a spiritual one (see 13:7 note).

Verse 6

This verse was incorporated from ghazal 13 of *Matā'-e Nūr* (beginning "jab kabhī sāqī-e madhosh kī yād ātī hai").

25

Verse 1

In the Hindu Vedas, God says, "I am one and wish to be many" (eko'ham bahu syām), thereby bringing the creation into being; yet God remains the ever-changeless one behind the phenomenal world. Sufis like Jalalu'ddin Rumi have said that God manifested the creation in order to be loved by and have union with His separated souls:

hīch 'āsheq ḳhod nabāshad vaṣl-jū
keh nah ma'shūqash bovad jūyā-ye ū[174]

Not a single lover would seek union
Were the beloved herself not seeking it.

God achieved this object of being loved by investing the whole creation with divine beauty, which compels the love of all sentient beings.

Verse 5

In Urdu and Persian poetry, the narcissus symbolizes the eye, but one without vision.

26

Verse 2

This verse is open to a number of interpretations. The poet may be addressing communal riots that would periodically break out in India which, once they had erupted, were difficult to quell. The garden could symbolize an Indian city that had experienced such rioting and managed to suppress it. Darshan, as a great humanitarian, would certainly have feared that even a slight provocation could reignite the fires of trouble.

The garden might also symbolize the lover's heart, in which the painful fire of separation had been burning but began to abate. The lover fears that the breeze coming from the beloved's direction could rekindle the dying flames and his agony. This interpretation seems less plausible, however, because, in both Urdu poetry and Sant Mat, the love of true lovers is constant in even the most adverse, unpromising circumstances, and their longing, no matter how painful, would never decrease. Such lovers would find sweetness and comfort in the anguish of love, and would not trade it for anything in the world; rather, they would fear the diminishing of their anguish far more than its increase. See endnote 115 for a passage by Sant Darshan on the pain of love and separation.

Verse 4

The morning breeze, by wafting the fragrance of the beloved to the lover, appears to be rubbing salt on the lover's wounds, for her fragrance reminds him that during the joyful, romantic spring season the beloved has ignored his affections, leaving him to pine alone in anguish.

27

Verse 3

The poet finds spiritual support and solace only in the cupbearer's eyes, which are bubbling over with the wine of God-intoxication.

Verse 5
A captain would have retreated from the storms and led the ship to an easily accessible haven. With the strength to defy the storms, however, the poet trusts in God to deliver his ship to the remote port he wishes to reach—the mystic abode of the Divine. The poet's resolve to depend on no one for help in his quest to realize God is reminiscent of Iqbal's philosophy of *ḳhw̤udī* (see 12:8 and note).

In the following contrastive verse, Darshan claims that he does rely on his spiritual master, Hazur Baba Sawan Singh, for intervention, instead of on God:

ḳhudā gar nāḳhudā hogā to hogā, mujh se kyā ma̱tlab!
merī kishtī kā Sāwan nāḳhudā ma'lūm hotā hai[175]

If God is the captain, so be it—what have I to do with Him!
The captain of my ship is none other than Sawan.

For the pun on the words *ḳhudā*, *nāḳhudā*, and *nā-ḳhudā*, see 1:6 note.

Verse 8
"Am I not your Lord?" (alastu bi-rabbikum) refers to Qur'an 7:172 and describes the primal covenant between God and humankind:

wa-i̱th aḳhatha rabbuka min banī Ādama min Thuhūrihim thurrīyyatahum wa-ash'hadahum 'alá anfusihim alastu bi-rabbikum qālū balá shahidnā.

When your Lord brought forth descendants from the loins of Adam's children and made them testify concerning themselves, the Lord said, "Am I not your Lord?" They replied, "We bear witness that You are."

In this verse, the glances of the cupbearer, who is God incarnate, inspire the same kind of submission.

29

Verse 2

For a discussion of the image of the gallows in Urdu poetry, see 15:6 note.

Verse 3

So long as the soul has consciousness of its individual existence, it cannot rise into divine consciousness and is deprived of lasting bliss.

30

Verse 1

Urdu poetry developed in the Islamic milieu, where wine is forbidden, so poets frequently play on the themes of drinking and abstinence in their verses. Darshan's wine is the intoxicating divine love that radiates from the eyes of the saqi—the spiritual master—and uplifts his tipplers into inner spiritual realms where they experience mystic visions and revelations.

Verse 6

The experience depicted in this verse finds illustration in the agonizing period in Darshan's life when, to counter the jealousy and propaganda of others, Sant Kirpal Singh for a year and a half coldly ignored Darshan in public (though he was affectionate to him in private).[176] Another example, where the separation of the master and disciple was voluntary, is found in the story of how the fourth Sikh Guru, Rām Dās, sent his youngest son, Arjan, away from him for an extended period in order to establish beyond doubt Arjan's credentials as the disciple most fit to carry on Ram Das's spiritual work.[177]

31

Verse 1

Ironic felicitations are in order because drinking, which is forbidden by *sharī'ah*, or Islamic law, has now been sanctioned by the Lord. The cups referred to are the eyes of the spiritual master overflowing with the intoxicating wine of God-consciousness.

Verse 2

A *janamsākhī* (anecdotal account of Guru Nanak's life) relates how Guru Nanak recited the following verse when declining some bhang offered by the first Mughal emperor, Bābur.[178]

post mad afīm bhang utar jā'ī parbhāt
nām khumārī Nānakā chaṛhī rahe din rāt[179]

Poppy, liquor, opium, hashish—their intoxication ends by morning;
The inebriation of Naam, O Nanak, envelops me day and night.

Verse 4

A divinely anointed spiritual master affords forgiveness for the sins of his disciples by burning up the *sañchit* (accumulated stored) karmas they have contracted in their innumerable births since separating from the Creator;[180] eliminating, diluting, or adjusting the *prālabhd* (fate) karmas they are destined to undergo in their present birth;[181] and taking their karmas on himself through vicarious suffering, which absolves them of reactions to those karmas.[182]

Verse 5

The snare referred to here signifies the enchantments and temptations of *māyā*—the world of mind, matter, and illusion.

Verses 6 and 7

These verses were incorporated from ghazal 75 of *Matā'-e Nūr* (beginning "haiṅ aur voh apnoṅ se jo katrā ke chale haiṅ").

32

Verse 2

It's not clear from the verse why the poet cannot bring himself to see the beloved when he's in such a state of agitation and distress. Perhaps he feels he should go to the beloved with happiness and gratefulness in his heart rather than risk infecting the beloved or others in the assembly with his despair and gloom. For a verse expressing that sentiment, see 37:1. At any rate, the irony of the verse is he's so agitated from not seeing her that he can't go to see her.

Verse 3
The ascetic renounces the world to gain freedom from its suffering and peace for his heart, while true lovers of God renounce their hearts and embrace the suffering of the world as their own.

Verse 5
For Jamshayd's cup, see 11:11 note

Verse 6
Theological creeds reject the tavern, which is the favorite haunt of the Sufis. A strong intuition for finding the truth has unwittingly led the poet there.

34

Verse 8
Ironically, the madness that possesses love-struck devotees in the company of an enlightened spiritual master opens their inner vision to an undistorted perception of reality.

35

Verse 3
As wine is forbidden in Islam, no one would have touched it had the beloved not quietly given the go-ahead with an approving look in her eyes (literally, *nazaroṅ kā ishārah*). This verse recalls a verse by the great Urdu poet Jigar Morādābādī (1890–1960):

pītā baġhair-e iżn yĕh kab t'hī mĕrī majāl
dar pardah chashm-e yār kī shĕh pā ke pī gayā[183]

Would I have dared to drink without permission!
What of her prompting eyes behind the veil?

In the context of Darshan's mysticism, however, it is his spiritual master's intoxicating glance of love that sets the revelry in motion.

Verse 6

In a similar verse, Swāmī Śhiv Dayāl Siṅgh (1818–1878) writes of God's response on seeing humankind plunged in unrelieved suffering:

tab satpurush dayā chit āī
kali meṅ saṅt rūp dhar āyā
sab jīvan ko diyā saṅdesā
sattlok kā bhed janāyā[184]

Then Sat Purush, moved by compassion,
Took birth in Kal Yuga as a saint.
To all humankind He gave his message
And revealed the secret of Sat Lok.

(Sat Purush is a name of the Almighty used in the Sant Mat tradition. Kali Yuga or Kal Yuga is the Dark or Iron Age, the fourth of four ever-recurring time cycles in the manifestation of the universe, in which life is short and hard, justice is minimal, evil predominates, and spiritual awareness is at its lowest ebb.[185] Sat Lok is the Region of Truth, another name for Sach Khand.)

36

Verse 4

Many look on angels as closer to God than humans and capable of protecting them. The poet's view, however, is more in line with that of the prophet Muhammad, who, during his *mi'rāj*, or "ascent to heaven," could be accompanied by the angel Gabriel only part of the way, beyond which the angel's wings would have burnt. In Jalalu'ddin Rumi's *Maśnavī*, the angel Gabriel says,

gar yekī gāmī neham sūzad marā[186]

If I take even one more step, I'll burn up.

goft bīrūn zīn ḥad ei ḵhẉush-farr-e man
gar zanam parrī besūzad parr-e man[187]

Said [Gabriel], "Were I to fly beyond this point,
My wings, illustrious friend, would burn up.

Rumi's contemporary, Sheiḵh Sa'dī Shīrāzī (c. 1213–1291), in his Persian poem *Būstān* (*The Garden*) writes,

agar yek sar-e mū'ī bartar param
forūġh-e tajallī besūzad param[188]

If by even a hair's breadth I fly higher,
His dazzling light will set my wings on fire.

Moreover, God ordered the angels to bow down to Adam after creating him, for God had blessed Adam alone with the knowledge of the nature of things, of which the angels admitted they had none. (Qur'an 2:30–34)

Verse 5

Khizr, identified in Qur'an 18:64–82 as the mysterious companion of Moses who consciously carries out the will of God, is the patron saint and guide of travelers. Legend has him discovering the Fountain of Eternal Life in the Land of Darkness. As a perfect saint and prototypical Godman imbued with divine consciousness, he has the ability to impart esoteric knowledge to mystics and bring about their mystical union with God.[189] Here the poet takes issue with modern thinkers who dismiss the spiritual wisdom that has come down from the past as beclouding the truths revealed by science.

37

Verse 1

For a related verse, see 32:2.

Verse 3

A brief sitting with a spiritual master brings a deeper sense of spiritual fulfillment than a lifetime of the pieties and austerities prescribed by religious orders. The puritans in this verse are filled with awe that, leading an ordinary life in the world, the master has achieved God-realization, which puts their asceticism to shame and proof.

38

Verse 2

For people scorched by the heat of summer in North India and Pakistan, the clouds and rains of the rainy season are a great blessing, rejuvenating both the earth and people's hearts. When the clouds roll in like drunkards to quench the parched, thirsty earth, the inviting weather and romantic atmosphere is, in the Urdu poetic tradition, too much for poets to resist, and they, like Faiz, express their celebration of life and exultation of love by drinking:

ā'e kuchh abr, kuchh sharāb ā'e
us ke ba'd ā'e jo 'aẓāb ā'e[190]

When clouds begin gathering, break out the wine!
For now, forget what calamities may follow.

In such an atmosphere, the poet expects the beloved (here obliquely referred to as "someone") to be generous with wine and her favor. In Darshan's verse, the "someone" he alludes to is likely his munificent spiritual master, Hazur Baba Sawan Singh—"Sawan" being the Hindi and Punjabi name for the summer month of monsoon rains in northern India.

Verse 3

Sant Darshan explained that his father, the great spiritual master Sant Kirpal Singh, was most loving toward him in private yet, in public, so reserved as to seem indifferent.[191]

Verse 5

Remembering God or his spiritual master with every breath of his life is an article of faith for the poet. On occasion, however, he was so beset with affliction that even that remembrance left his mind. The poet shows an appreciation of the human condition: faced with life's deepest suffering, people are often unable to keep their faith.

Verse 6

The second line of the verse is a quotation whose source we were unable to locate. For verses with a similar theme, see 14:2 and 52:7. In his Hindi commentary on this verse, Harishchandra Chadda writes about how fleeting is the life of a bud, for no sooner does it bloom into a majestic flower than the process of its destruction begins, whereby its petals fall off one by one or a gardener plucks it.[192]

39

Verse 2

In the first line of the verse, Darshan uses the term *mard-e mu'min* (literally, man of faith), a term originally used by Muhammad Iqbal in his poetry to signify the Perfect Man, or a God-realized mystic. Other terms with essentially the same meaning used by Iqbal were *mard-e ḥaq* or *mard-e ḳhudā* (literally, man of God). Iqbal's concept of the Perfect Man was influenced by Jalalu'ddin Rumi, who also used the terms *mard-e ḥaq* and *mard-e ḳhudā*, as well as the term *insān-e kāmel* (perfect man). The transformative power of the glance of the *mard-e mu'min* in Darshan's verse echoes that in a verse of Iqbal's:

ko'ī andāzah kar saktā hai us ke zor-e bāzū kā!
nigāh-e mard-e mu'min se badal jātī haiṅ taqdīreṅ[193]

Who can even guess at the strength of his arm!
The glance of a Perfect Man even changes destiny.

In a note on the section on "Divine Vicegerency" in his translation of Iqbal's Persian poem *Asrār-e Ḳhwudī* (*Secrets of the Self*), Professor Reynold Nicholson writes, "Here Iqbal interprets in his own way the Súfí doctrine of the *Insán al-kámil* or Perfect Man, which teaches that every man is potentially a microcosm, and that when he has become spiritually perfect, all the Divine attributes are displayed by him, so that as saint or prophet he is the God-man, the representative and vicegerent of God [*nāyeb-e ḥaq*] on earth."[194]

Iqbal portrays some of the characteristics of the Perfect Man as follows:

nāyeb-e ḥaq hamchū jān-e 'ālam ast

. . . .

dar jahān qā'em be-amr-e'llâh bovad

. . . .

naġhmeh zā tār-e del az meẓrāb-e ū
bahr-e ḥaq bīdārī-ye ū ḳhẉāb-e ū

. . . .

mī-barad az meṣr esrā'īl rā
az qum-e ū ḳhīzad andar gūr-e tan
mordeh jān'hā chūn ṣanowbar dar chaman
żāt-e ū towjīh-e żāt-e 'ālam ast
az jalāl-e ū najāt-e 'ālam ast
ẓarreh ḳhorshīd-āshnā az sāyeh'ash

. . . .

hasti-ye maknūn-e ū rāz-e ḥayāt
naġhmeh-ye nashīndeh-ye sāz-e ḥayāt[195]

God's vicegerent is as the soul of the universe,

. . . .

He executes the command of Allah in the world.

. . . .

Heart-strings give forth music at his touch,
He wakes and sleeps for God alone.

. . . .

He leads Israel out of Egypt.
At his cry, "Arise," the dead spirits
Rise in their bodily tomb, like pines in the field.
His person is an atonement for all the world,
By his grandeur the world is saved.
His protecting shadow makes the mote familiar with the sun.

. . . .

His hidden being is Life's mystery,
The unheard music of Life's harp.[196]

Verse 4

For a contrasting verse on a similar theme, see 23:5.

Verse 5

The Urdu in the first hemistich contains the word *lāhūtī*, a Sufi term meaning "divine." In the context of this verse, *lāhūtī* alludes to the highest plane of spirituality—beyond the realms of mind, matter, illusion, and ego—where the ascending soul experiences the state of *fana fi'llah*, or absorption in God.

40

Verse 2

The original Urdu verse contains a pun on the words *ḳhudā*, *nāḳhudā*, and *nā-ḳhudā* (see 1:6 note).

Verse 3

In this vein, a well-known Persian verse sometimes attributed to the great Persian lyric poet Ḥāfeẕ Shīrāzī (1325/26–1389/90) says,

dar mīyān-e qa'r-e daryā taḳhteh bandam karde'ī
bāz mī-gū'ī keh dāman tar makon hūshyār bāsh[197]

You bind me to a raft, cast me into the raging sea,
And then admonish me: "Take heed, lest your clothes get wet!"

Verse 6

Despondent from waiting long at the door of the saqi (his spiritual master) without receiving any attention or wine (spiritually uplifting divine love), the lover nevertheless realizes that it is futile to leave and face the world that has already caused him profound disappointment and sorrow. Moreover, as Mir has written, he would be committing a sacrilege in love that would expose him as faithless and worthy of contempt:

baiṭ'hne kaun de hai phir us ko
jo tĕre āstāṅ se uṭ'htā hai[198]

Who would accept him in their midst—
The one who walks away from your door.

41

Verse 2

This verse of Darshan's is reminiscent of a verse by Jigar Morādābādī:

hā'e kyā ho gayā ṯabī'at ko
ġham bhī rāḥat-fazā nahīṅ hotā[199]

Alas, to what condition I am reduced
When even grief has ceased to give me comfort.

42

Verse 3

From the poet's standpoint as a disciple of Hazur Baba Sawan Singh and Param Sant Kirpal Singh, the word "someone" in the first line would refer to his spiritual beloveds; from his standpoint as a spiritual master, "someone" would refer to anyone under his spiritual care and protection.

Verse 6

For a verse with a similar theme and its background, see 30:6 and note.

43

Verse 7

To emphasize that from devotion (*bandagī*) one receives life (*zindagī*), Sant Darshan used to relate an anecdote from the life of Guru Gobind Siṅgh's beloved court poet Bhā'ī Nand Lāl Goyā. When Goya presented his long Persian poem *Bandagī-nāmeh* (Book of Devotion) to his spiritual master, the guru slightly altered the spelling of the title, changing it to *Zindagī-nāmeh*, or "Book of Life."

44

Verse 3

When a God-realized spiritual master's disciples become attuned to their master in meditation, the master is able to absorb their consciousness into his God-consciousness, thereby enabling them to "die" to their individual existence, "become conscious co-workers of the divine plan,"[200] and attain union with the Almighty (*fana fi'llah*) and life everlasting (*baqā'*).

45

Verse 1

See 11:11 note for Jamshayd's cup.

Verse 4

The Ka'ba, located in Mecca, is the holiest shrine in Islam. Kashi, the modern day Varanasi, is the most sacred city and place of pilgrimage for Hindus.

46

Verse 3

This verse brings to mind Qur'an 33:72:

> *innā 'aradhnā'l-amānata 'alá's-samāwāti wa'l-'ardhi wa'l-jibāli fa-abaina an yaḥmilnahā wa-ashfaqna minhā wa-ḥamalahā'l-insānu innahu kāna Thalūmān jahūlān.*
>
> We offered the Trust [of divine responsibilities] to the heavens and earth and mountains, but out of fear they refused to bear it; but man took on the burden, proving himself unjust [to himself] and ignorant [of what he was undertaking].

Mir has expressed a similar sentiment:

sab pĕh jis bār ne girānī kī
us ko yĕh nātavāṅ uṭ'hā lāyā[201]

The load that all others found burdensome
This feeble one came forth to shoulder.

47

Verse 1

The Persian phrase *'ālam-e imkān* (or *'ālam-e mumkināt*) in the second line is one used by Ghalib, Iqbal, and Islamic philosophers over the centuries to differentiate the contingent existence of the perishable, transitory creation (*'ālam-e fanā, dunyā-e fānī*, or *fānī dunyā*)—dependent on the power of God to endow it with being—from the Necessary Being of God, the sole reality.

Islamic scholar Seyyed Hossein Nasr has written,

> For Islamic thought . . . the world is not synonymous with wujud [being]. There is an ontological poverty (faqr) of the world in the sense that wujud is given by God who alone is the abiding Reality, all "other" existents coming into being and passing away. . . . Everything in the created order in fact participates in the condition of contingency so that the universe, or all that is other than God (ma siwa'llah), is often called the world of contingencies ('alam al-mumkinat).[202]

Verse 2

The great Urdu mystic poet Aṣġhar Gonḍvī (1884–1936) has a beautiful verse that describes the power of the beloved's call:

hamah tan hastī-e ḳhwābīdah mĕrī jāg uṭ'hī
har bun-e mū se mĕre us ne pukārā mujh ko[203]

My sleeping self was shaken into wakefulness—
From the root of each hair of mine she called out to me.

Verse 3

In the first line the poet has used the word *ishārah*, which, in this context, means "amorous look or glance." The great Urdu poet Akbar Allâhābādī (1846–1921) has similarly used the word *ishārah* in this sense in the following verse:

bas ik ishāre meṅ le gaʾī tū diloṅ se īmān o ṣabr o taqwá
batā tū ai chashm-e mast-e kāfir yĕh kyā hai gar sāḥirī nahīṅ hai[204]

With one glance you rob the heart of its faith and
endurance on piety's path;
O infidel with intoxicating eyes, what is this if not magic!

Verse 5

The second line of the verse is a quotation whose source we were unable to locate.

48

Verse 3

This verse is open to a number of interpretations. The poet may be condemning leaders (symbolized by the gardener) who, instead of working for the welfare of their nations and the world (the garden), are driven by greed to engage in exploitative pursuits (such as wars) that destroy the lives or well-being of citizens (plucking the flowers) and rob the garden of those who could make vital contributions to it.

The verse can also be interpreted as a condemnation of those for whom all objects of beauty are but commodities for sale or who compromise their ideals for worldly gain. As the Urdu poet Sāḥir Ludhiyānvī (1921–1980) has written,

maiṅ ne jo gīt tĕre pyār kī ḳhāt̲ir likhe
āj in gītoṅ ko bāzār meṅ le āyā hūṅ[205]

The songs I wrote out of love for you
I've put up for sale in the marketplace.

49

Verse 1
The wine Darshan refers to is the wine of divine love.

Verse 4
At the outset, disciples may enter the spiritual path with great enthusiasm, but under the strain of worldly affairs their zeal begins to wane and their spiritual practices lapse into a formality. By making communion with God the ruling passion of their lives, they can revive their spiritual longing and hopes for divine ecstasy.

Verse 6
A competent spiritual master takes charge of working out his disciples' karmic accounts. Thus, even when they must undergo misfortune or suffering, they should accept it happily, as a gift from their master, knowing that he is dispensing it in the best interests of their spiritual growth. Sant Darshan has written,

> if we have full faith in the Master, if we have fully surrendered ourselves to him, we will naturally have confidence in him, as our destiny lies solely in his hands. . . . Our Beloved Master [Sant Kirpal Singh] always used to tell us that our destiny is controlled by the Master the moment he initiates us into the Mysteries of the Beyond. Our account with the Angel of Death is at that moment torn to pieces. From that moment on we are entirely in the care of the Master. One initiated into the Path of the Masters knows that henceforth the arbiter of his fate is the Master; the Master is his only benefactor.[206]

Verse 7
Drinking is forbidden in Islam as an impediment to devotion to God. By inviting a tippler like Darshan into the mosque, the sheikh ironically is

violating his own principles. This verse subtly suggests, however, that narrow-minded religious dogmas are transcended when a person is imbued with passionate love for God and enjoys mystical communion with the Lord.

50

Verse 2

Realizing that his essential self (*ḳhẉudī*) is divine, the poet, like Iqbal, rejects all outside support in his quest to realize God. See 12:8 note.

Verse 3

Nothing provides solace to true lovers in the throes of love's grief except the grace coming directly from the beloved.

Verse 4

The Urdu word *bazm* (assembly) evokes the scene of a beautiful, sophisticated, and cultured lady holding court over a salon filled with her admirers.

51

Verse 2

On many occasions, Sant Darshan stated that flowing tears of love for God or the spiritual master are actually "pearls" of far greater value than those from the sea.[207]

Verse 4

According to the teachings of Sant Mat, at the time of initiation, a God-realized spiritual master, who has attained spiritual heights far beyond the realm of the Lord of Judgment, takes over the karmic accounts of his disciples and becomes the arbiter of their destinies (see 31:4 note and 49:6 note). Guru Arjan Dev (1563–1606), the fifth guru of the Sikhs, says in one of his hymns,

chitar gupat kā kāgad fāri'ā jamdūtā kachhū na chalī[208]

He tears up the record of Chitr and Gupt, and Jamdūt is helpless before him.

(Chitr and Gupt are angels that record all of a person's thoughts, words, and deeds and present the record to Dharam Rāj (or Dharam Rāi), the Lord of Death (or the Lord of Judgment). Jamdūt (the Messenger or Angel of Death) takes the soul from the body at the time of death and brings it before Dharam Raj for judgment.)[209]

The celebrated Persian poet Ṣā'eb Tabrīzī (1592–1676) has likewise written,

torā beh rūz-e ḥesāb īn soḵhan shavad maʻlūm
keh būdeh salṯanat bī-ḥesāb darvīshī[210]

On Judgment Day you'll realize the truth of these words:
For the kingdom of mystics there is no reckoning.

Thus, Darshan's silence before the Lord of Judgment is perhaps a display of his confidence in the protection of his spiritual master—he has no fear of the Lord of Judgment and knows that this deity has no power over him.

Our translation of this verse follows the version found in the Urdu edition of *Matāʻ-e Nūr* (1988) and the Hindi editions of *Matāʻ-e Nūr* published prior to 2016.

52

Verse 7
Reaching its prime, the flower itself gives warning of what inevitably follows—decay and death. The great Persian poet Sheikh Saʻdi echoes a similar sentiment:

gol berīzad bevaqt-e sīrābī[211]

Petals scatter when they reach their bloom.

Verse 9
This verse exhorts seekers after truth to remain ever vigilant and not give in to spiritual lethargy, lest the moment of grace arrive and find them absent.

53

Verse 2
This verse alludes to a story related about the end of Guru Nanak's life. It is said that after the guru had passed away, a quarrel broke out among his Hindu and Muslim disciples because the Hindus wished to cremate his body while the Muslims insisted on its burial. In the end, it was decided that each group would place its own flowers upon his body and, the next morning, the group whose flowers were less withered would take custody of it. When morning came, the flowers of both groups were still blooming and fragrant. When they removed the sheet, they discovered that the guru's body had vanished. Each group then took half of the sheet, the Muslims burying theirs and the Hindus consigning theirs to the flames.[212]

Verse 3
A Sheikh is a Muslim holy man; a Brahman, a Hindu priest. References to them, which occur frequently in Urdu poetry, symbolically represent the tenets of Islam and Hinduism.

54

Verse 1
One whose third or spiritual eye is open does not search for God at the Ka'ba, Islam's holiest shrine, or on Mt. Sinai. A person with inner vision is not bound by formal religions and may not even follow one. A Persian poet has written,

masjed-e kūrān ze-āb o gel bovad
masjed-e ṣāḥeb-delān rā del bovad[213]

Only the blind deem a building of clay as the mosque;
Those with spiritual hearts see the mosque is the human heart.

Verse 4

This verse appears in *Talāsh-e Nūr* but was omitted from *Matā'-e Nūr*. The Urdu reads,

ġham-e jānāṅ ko bhulā dūṅ, nah karūṅ dost ko yād
itnā maiṅ, ai ġham-e daurāṅ, abhī majbūr nahīṅ[214]

Verse 9

Manṣūr al-Ḥallāj was a late-ninth-century Sufi mystic from Baghdad who was executed for heresy. In popular tradition, the cause of his martyrdom was his publicly exclaiming at the height of divine intoxication, "Anā'l-Ḥaqq" (I am the Absolute Truth, or, I am God).[215] Since he reputedly showed no care in the least as he was being executed, he is known as a symbol of suffering for love. At the same time, by revealing his mystical union with God, he is considered to have committed the greatest sin of a lover. Hence, in this verse, the poet indicates that, by keeping silent, his strength and love are even superior to those of Mansoor.

55

Verse 2

This verse was included in *Talāsh-e Nūr* but omitted from *Matā'-e Nūr*. The Urdu reads,

nah apne hosh kī parvā, nah apne dard kā fikr
ġham-e zamīṅ se pareshāṅ haiṅ tere dīvāne[216]

Verse 3

Sant Darshan has written that, through self-introspection, those who are keen to meet the divine beloved become so intent on eradicating their own faults that they have no time to criticize others and no heart to look at others' failings.[217]

Verse 5
For the poetic convention of mad lovers tearing their collars, see 4:5 note.

56

Verse 4
The "evolution" referred to here is not biological but karmic. According to the teachings of Sant Mat, the incarnation of the soul into a human form is a rare phenomenon occurring only after eons of torturous experiences in the lower forms of creation.[218]

Verse 5
Harishchandra Chaddha in his Hindi commentary on *Matā'-e Nūr* states that this verse refers to the early days of Sant Darshan Singh's spiritual mission when, after the passing of Sant Kirpal Singh, he withdrew from satsang affairs and went into seclusion—just as Sant Kirpal Singh had done following the passing of Hazur Baba Sawan Singh in 1948. The verse implies that Sant Darshan did so to commune with his spiritual masters in meditation.[219]

57

Verse 9
Ghalib has expressed a similar idea in the following verse:

ham vahāṅ haiṅ jahāṅ se ham ko bhī
kuchh hamārī ḳhabar nahīṅ ātī[220]

I am now in a state where even I myself
Have no awareness of myself.

58

Verse 1
In this verse, along with verses 4, 6, and 7, "someone" obliquely refers to the beloved.

In the first verse, the suffering lover declares that his unwavering devotion at least obligates his beloved to sincerely pray for his tortured soul—an irony in that it is the beloved's aloofness and cruelties that have caused his suffering in the first place.

Verse 5
The divine wine from the saqi's eyes inflames rather than quenches thirst—the more one drinks of divine love, the more one needs to drink.

Verse 7
The verse contains an implied irony: the lover seeks not God but rather God's help to encounter his beloved.

59

Following Sant Darshan Singh's passing, a folded sheet of paper containing Sant Darshan's handwritten changes in Urdu to three of this ghazal's verses was found in a pocket of his by Mātā Harbhajan Kaur Jī, Sant Darshan's wife and the mother of Sant Darshan's spiritual successor, Sant Rajinder Singh. She had reportedly recommended that the Master make some changes to the poem, some of whose verses were written for her, because she felt people would have difficulty in understanding what he had intended by the verses.[221] Darshan appears to be addressing his wife directly in verses 1–3, and referring to her as "someone" in revised verse 2 and "someone else" in revised verse 4 (see 59:4 note below).

Verse 1
The poet's final destination is Sach Khand or Muqam-e Haq—the Region of Truth, where he will attain *fana fi'llah*—union with the Almighty.

Sant Darshan's revision of this verse reads as follows:

tujhe kyā ḳhabar mere ham-safar, merī us maqām par hai naẕar
merī manzileṅ, mere marḥale, merā rāstah ko'ī aur hai[222]

How could you fathom, dear traveling companion, my aim's a transcendent abode;
My destination, the stages I cross, my path are not of this world.

Verse 2
Sant Darshan's revision of this verse reads as follows:

merī chāhatoṅ ko nah pūchhiye, jo milā ṯalab se sivā milā
maiṅ hūṅ āsre kisī aur ke, merā āsrā ko'ī aur hai[223]

There's no need to ask about my wishes—I've received far more than
I ever hoped for;
Someone looks to me for support, while my support is not
of this world.

Verse 4
Sant Darshan's revision of this verse reads as follows:

mĕrā żauq-e sajdah o bandagī, kĕh hai kashmakash meṅ yĕh zindagī
ko'ī aur hai mĕrā naẕar meṅ, mujhe chāhtā ko'ī aur hai[224]

My zeal for worship and devotion belies the turmoil in my heart—
I gaze with love on someone, all the while adored by someone else.

Verse 5
According to the teachings of Sant Mat, God the Creator (Sat Purush) is an ocean of love that the soul may experience in fullness in the fifth spiritual plane (Sach Khand or Muqam-e Haq) and merge with entirely in the eighth and highest spiritual region (Anami Desh). The lower three planes of creation, however—the physical, astral, and causal regions (Piṇḍ, Aṇḍ, and Brahmāṇḍ in the terminology of Sant Mat, and Kaṡīf or Mādī, Laṯīf, and Laṯīfu'l-Laṯīf or 'Ālam-e Jabrūt in Sufism)—the planes of mind, matter, and illusion, are under the sway of Kāl, "the Negative Power," or the power that is responsible for maintaining the lower three regions. Unlike Sat Purush, who is all love, compassion, and forgiveness, Kal is the agent of the system of karmic justice, according to which every thought, word, and deed creates a reaction that ultimately manifests in the physical world as a reward or a punishment that affords no mitigation. As the karmic system is based on the principle of "an eye for an eye, a tooth for a tooth" and is devoid of any compassion, the physical plane—the arena of karmic reactions—is one of untold suffering and misery for most

of its denizens. Thus, Darshan in this verse contrasts the God of the enlightened mystic with the god worshipped by those in deep ignorance of reality, who in pursuit of their own selfish desires treat others in the cruelest and most merciless ways and ultimately reap the fruits of their actions unmitigated, as just deserts.

Verse 7

Guru Amar Dās, the third Sikh guru, affirms that finding the Light of God within is the true purpose of human life:

e sarīrā meri'ā har tum mĕh jot rakhī tā tū jag mĕhi ā'i'ā

. . . .

e netrahu meriho har tum mĕh jot dharī har bin avar
na dekhahu ko'ī[225]

O my body, the Lord planted a light in you—for its sake did you come into the world.

. . . .

O my eyes, the Lord infused His light in you; look not upon another save the Lord.

In connection with Darshan's theme of God and His lover mutually seeking each other, Muhammad Iqbal has a Persian verse in which the poet, addressing Moses, says,

gadā-ye jelveh raftī bar sar-e ṯūr
keh jān-e to ze-ḳhwod nā-maḥramī hast
qadam dar jostojū-ye ādamī zan
ḳhodā ham dar talāsh-e ādamī hast[226]

Seeking a vision, you went to the summit of Sinai,
For your soul was a stranger to itself.
Go off in search of someone truly human—
God too is in search of a human being.

In the same spirit, Kabir Sahib describes how God has fallen in love with him for having cultivated a heart of godly purity:

Kabīr man nirmal bha'ī'ā jaisā gaṅgā nīr
pāchhai lāgo har phirai kahat Kabīr Kabīr[227]

Kabir, my heart has grown pure as Ganges water;
God now follows me about, calling, "Kabir! Kabir!"

60

Verse 2
The spiritual homeland of the mystics in the Sant Mat tradition—Sach Khand or Muqam-e Haq—lies far beyond the paradise idealized by adherents of the world's religions. For a passage from the Adi Granth by Sant Ravi Dās on the spiritual homeland, see 20:3 note.

Verse 3
The poet is addressing his beloved.

Verse 6
For the Ka'ba, see 6:2 note.

Verse 7
This verse may have been inspired by a moving story from the life of Guru Nanak. Refusing the invitation to a feast from a high-caste local official, Malik Bhāgo, the guru stayed with a poor but pious carpenter named Bhā'ī Lālo. When Bhago angrily took him to task for rejecting his food, the guru took the food offered by him in one hand and the simple bread prepared by Lalo in the other and squeezed. Blood dripped from Bhago's offering and milk from Lalo's. The guru thus demonstrated that Bhago had enriched himself by squeezing the blood of the poor.[228]

Verse 8
For the affinity of Darshan's view on angels with that of Jalalu'ddin Rumi, Sheikh Sa'di, and the Qur'an, see 36:4 note.

Verse 9
According to Sufi philosophy, there are three levels of certainty: *'ilmu'l-yaqīn*, intellectual certainty; *'ainu'l-yaqīn*, visual certainty; and

haqqu'l-yaqīn, experiential certainty.[229] *Haqqu'l-yaqīn* has also been defined as "seeing Almighty God with the eyes of the heart."[230] Sant Darshan has written, "the heart spoken of by the Saints is not a muscle in our chest, but the center of our very being between the two eyebrows behind the eyes. That is where the real heart of the Saints lies, because that is the seat of the soul."[231] Darshan has used the term *'ainu'l-yaqīṅ* in the first line of this verse and *haqqu'l-yaqīṅ* in the second.

Darshan also uses the Persian and Urdu word *but* in the first line of this verse. *But* in Urdu poetry is used to mean the statues of deities in Hindu temples, enchantingly beautiful women, or the poet's beloved. In the context of this verse, the word may also symbolize all the attractions of the material world. Regardless of how the word is interpreted, Darshan is saying that the beauty of the world experienced through sense perception lacks reality. Only the experience of God gives an insight into the unchanging, absolute truth.

61

Verse 2

Nowadays few have the divine passion to practice true spiritual martyrdom: sacrificing sensual and material gratification, pride, and limited judgment on the altar of the spiritual master's (the beloved's) behests, while enduring the challenges of developing spiritual love. The theme of martyrdom is a traditional one in Urdu poetry. Faiz has written,

maqām, Faiz, ko'ī rāh meṅ jachā hī nahīṅ
jo kū-e yār se nikle to sū-e dār chale[232]

Faiz, on the path I found no other place to my liking—
When I left the beloved's lane, I walked straight to the gallows.

In another verse he says,

aise nādāṅ bhī nah t'he jāṅ se guzarne vāle
nāṣiḥo, pand-garo, rāh-guzar to dekho[233]

Those who gave up their lives were truly not fools—
O counselor, O preacher, just look at the path they took!

Jalalu'ddin Rumi has echoed this sentiment in one of his verses:

ei basā Manṣūr-e penhān ze-e'temād-e jān-e 'eshq
tark menbarhā begofteh bar shodeh bar dārhā[234]

Many an unknown Mansoor, moved by faith and the spirit of love,
Rejected the pulpit and ascended the steps of the gallows.

For Mansoor al-Hallaj, see 54:9 note.

Darshan speaks of the martyrdom of love in another of his verses as well:

dayār-e 'ishq meṅ tum kyoṅ khaṛe ho ahl-e havas?
yahāṅ to dār o rasan ke sivā kuchh aur nahīṅ

O men of lust, beware of entering this land of love,
Here you will find only the cross and the gallows.[235]

Verse 3
Just as the coming together of the Ganges and Jamna is said to increase their holiness and provide salvation, the gathering of devotees of the master in the spiritually charged atmosphere of his satsang quenches their spiritual thirst and paves the way toward their spiritual liberation. For more on the Ganges and Jamna, see 20:6 note.

Verse 4
The poet laments the disappearance of the ideals of true lovers as portrayed in such tales as *Laila and Majnoon* and *Farhaad and Sheereen*. The beloved is the paragon of beauty, whose world is symbolized by the garden. The impassioned lover who could not gain her favor tore his collar and took to the forest (see 4:5 note).

Verse 5
This verse depicts the shared experience of suffering that love brings to both lover and beloved. Burning equally in love's fire, their restlessness and distraction making it impossible for them to engage with anyone

or anything except the one they love, they go off wandering in the wilderness. "Heads covered with dust" not only conveys the sense of ordeal but presents, from the eastern point of view, a rather shocking image of the desecration of the beloved.

Verse 6

For "homeland," see 20:3 note.

62

Verse 3

For Sant Darshan, the supreme goal of human life was attaining union with the Creator.[236] Only a spiritual master who has attained this goal can truly extend the assurance of God's existence and show the way to realize the divine.

Verse 4

What for others is merely the intoxicating spring breeze is, for the poet, an irresistible incitement to frenzied love, for it imitates the beloved's graceful, coquettish gait and, as is traditionally the case in Urdu poetry, comes from the beloved's lane carrying the sweet fragrance of her tresses.

Verse 5

The second line of this poem is a quotation whose source we were unable to locate.

Verse 6

One must be ever vigilant on the spiritual path; the beloved may pass one's way unexpectedly, "like a thief in the night," and the beloved's grace could come at any time.

Verses 9 and 10

Even the minutest particle in creation reflects a greater reality. Developing the eye of love, one acquires vision to see the whole world as a mirror house of God—the drop containing the ocean, the sand grain containing the desert, everything reflecting God's beauty. The Sufis call this view *waḥdat al-wujūd* (the unity of all existence)—"the knowledge that there is nothing existent but God, or the ability to see God and creation as two aspects of one reality, reflecting each other and depending upon each other"[237]—which is characterized by the Persian phrase *hameh ūst*, or "All is He." In a verse similar to Darshan's, Iqbal has written,

ġhavvāṣ-e muḥabbat kā allâh nigah-bāṅ ho!
har qaṯrah-e daryā meṅ, daryā kī hai gahrāʾī[238]

May God watch over the diver in love's sea!
Every drop of the sea has the depth of the sea.

Likewise, Ghalib says,

qaṯre meṅ dajlah dikhāʾī nah de aur juzv meṅ kul
khel laṛkoṅ kā huʾā dīdah-e bīnā nah huʾā[239]

Not finding the Tigris in the water drop or wholeness in the part,
You play a childish game, lacking the eye that sees.

William Blake, in his "Auguries of Innocence," finds an indissoluble connection between the multifarious phenomena of nature:

To see a World in a Grain of Sand
And a Heaven in a Wild Flower,
Hold Infinity in the palm of your hand
And Eternity in an hour.[240]

Verse 12
Regardless of whether the poet is reflecting on a personal experience, historical event, or universal condition, the verse means that the same blood runs in the veins of all humankind, yet because of personal hostility or communal strife, people are at each other's throats and, in a sense, shedding their own blood.

63

Verse 5
The poet is distressed that so many have been unable to surmount the difficulties of the spiritual path and apprehensive that the rest

of the wayfarers—including himself—could themselves suffer the same fate.

Verse 6

Here "alone" connotes not only physical isolation from the spiritual master but also egocentricity and lack of motivation to raise spiritual consciousness.

64

Verse 1

Here the poet speaks of his love for his spiritual master and his desire for union with God.

Verse 2

Mir has said in one of his verses,

'umr bhar ham rahe sharābī se
dil-e pur-khūn kī ik gulābī se[241]

I remained drunk for the whole of my life—
It took just one cupful of blood from my heart.

Sant Darshan has written, "If we are really waiting for our Beloved to arrive, . . . for somebody who has caused us poignancy and grief, yearning and pining, longing and torture, then waiting has its own charm, waiting has its own bliss. . . . [A]t times it appears that its intensity is going to drain all life out of us, yet that same waiting can be transformed into bliss and tranquility and result in the ultimate communion of the soul with the Creator."[242] And as this verse implies, in such a state, one may begin to hear the inner sound current resounding, which assuages one's pain even as it fans the flames of love.

Verse 3

The lamp in the second line could represent the poet's sharing in others' suffering rather than his grief over separation from his beloved. However, as every verse but the last involves his relationship with the beloved, the lamp of sympathy seems a less likely interpretation.

Verse 4
One can read this verse to mean the poet's suffering continues after death or after transcending the physical realm in meditation and entering the inner spiritual realms.

Verse 5
For a verse with a similar theme and its background, see 38:3 and note.

65

Verse 1
Verses 1, 2, 6, and 7 come from Poem 70 in *Matā'-e Nūr* (beginning "gungunātī hai havā, phūl khile, dīp jale"); verses 3, 4, and 5 come from Poem 71 in *Matā'-e Nūr* (beginning "hai sharṯ dil se dil mile aur jāṅ se jāṅ mile").

Verse 4
According to Sant Darshan, "Spirituality . . . is nothing but personal experience of the Divine; no one has ever acquired it only through reading books or attending weekly congregations. Spirituality starts where belief ends. There is a world of difference between belief and spirituality—spiritual experience."[243] And as for who can be considered true adherents of their faiths, Sant Kirpal Singh has written,

> The highest objective of Sikh religion is to turn out *Khalsas*. A Khalsa is one who witnesses within him the *Pooran Jyoti* (the supreme Light of God in full effulgence). Similarly, a Hindu is one who makes manifest in him the *Jyoti* of Ishvara [the Light of God] and listens to the unending and unstruck music of the soul (*Anhad* and *Anhat Nad*), the symbols of which he adores and worships outside in his temples and shrines by lighting candles and striking bells. A true Muslim is one who sees the *Noor* of Allah or the Light of God and hears the *Kalam-e-Kadim* (the Voice of God, the most ancient music or song ceaselessly going on within him). A true Christian likewise is one who bears testimony to the Light of God and hears the Sound of God

which transforms him into an awakened spirit at the mount of transfiguration.[244]

Verse 6

The tavern symbolizes the spiritual master's satsang either in this world or in a spiritual region within. The exhilarating color and fragrance pervading the atmosphere comes from the wine of divine love overflowing the cups of the master's eyes and filling the eyes of his devotees.

Verse 7

In India the singing of the Dīpak Rāga (Music of Illumination) is said to ignite lamps spontaneously. The lamps in this verse are hearts that, under the inspiration of the poet's song, begin to resonate with new fervor. On a mystical level, the verse signifies the mystic adept's manifesting the inner "sonorous light" to his disciples at the time of spiritual initiation.

66

Verse 2

The second line of the verse is a quotation whose source we were unable to locate.

Verse 3

By subjecting them to the sufferings of love, the spiritual master frees his disciples from attachment to this world and the desire for heaven, both of which block the soul's ascension into divine consciousness. At the same time, lovers thus caught in the beloved's tresses, which symbolize the master's spiritual influence and grace, are given to divine ecstasy and are oblivious to anything but the beloved. Their state leads onlookers to consider them out of their minds and senses. As Harishchandra Chadda remarks in his Hindi commentary on this verse, we can only envy the sufferings of such lovers, not offer words of sympathy.[245]

Verse 5

In the same vein, Hafez has written,

bā ṣabā dar chaman-e lāleh saḥar mī-goftam
keh shahīdān keh and īn hameh ḳhūnīn kafnān[246]

I asked the breeze at daybreak in a garden where tulips bud:
"Tell me, whose martyrs are these, appareled in shrouds of blood?"[247]

Verse 6

Darshan used the image of crystal palaces to symbolize a life of luxury and comfort (see also 18:11 and note).[248] In this connection, Sant Kirpal Singh wrote that "luxuriant abundance and opulence [and] the licentious sensualism of ease and affluence . . . contribute to the imbalance of the unsophisticated mind. These are the thorns and thistles that mar the beauty of the undisturbed state of mind, which is the soil best suited for the dawn of Divinity."[249]

The image of the cave in the second line of this verse can be interpreted on two levels. On an outer level, a cave can refer either figuratively to a life of humble simplicity or historically to the caves in which holy men meditated and achieved spiritual enlightenment. On a mystical level, a cave signifies the eye-focus within the body where one concentrates with unwavering attention in meditation.

Verse 7

The beloved in Urdu poetry is generally portrayed as an aloof, tyrannical murderess. Here, despite rejecting her lovers and ordering them to the gallows, she has full faith that they are happy to have gained her attention and the chance to fulfill her wishes, which they will carry out without questioning or raising objections. Amir Khusro, the great Delhi court poet and disciple of the Sufi saint Nizāmu'ddīn Auliyā, has taken up this theme in one of his Persian verses:

shād bāsh ei del keh fardā bar sar-e bāzār-e 'eshq
mozhdeh-ye qatl ast garcheh va'deh-ye dīdār nīst[250]

Rejoice at the happy news, my heart! She's ordered that tomorrow
You'll be slain in love's bazaar—with no promise you'll get
her glance.

After presenting this verse as a story in a satsang talk, Sant Kirpal Singh adds, "This is what love demands from the lover [as well as] complete submission to the will of the beloved without any rhyme or reason. Love is just a one-way traffic so far as the lover is concerned. It knows no bargaining. All it connotes is implicit obedience. Not my will, but thine, cries the true lover. A Persian poet has defined love thus: 'What is Love? It is to be a bondsman of the beloved. And to go wandering and offering one's heart.' "[251]

68

Verse 1

Amir Khusro writes in a Persian verse,

man to shodam to man shodī man tan shodam to jān shodī
tā kas nagūyad ba'd az'īn man dīgaram to dīgarī[252]

I am now you, you are now me, I am the body, you are the soul;
Thus, hereafter, none can say, I am the one; you, the other.

Verse 2

Life is a continuum of consciousness, extending from the various degrees of limited material and mental consciousness of the physical world up to the ultimate stage of all-consciousness in the wholly spiritual realm of Anami (*be-nishāṅ*, *be-nām* in this Urdu verse)—the nameless, formless absolute.

Verse 3

This condition of having a broken heart is ultimately not unfortunate. Comparing the heart to a mirror, Iqbal has written,

tū bachā bachā ke nah rakh ise, tĕrā ā'inah hai voh ā'inah
kĕh shikastah ho to 'azīztar nigāh-e ā'inah-sāz meṅ[253]

Don't try to protect it! You have that kind of mirror
Which, broken, is more precious in the mirror-maker's eyes.

That is, one whose heart has been made tender, softened by love's agonies, is more pleasing to God than one untouched by love.

Verse 4

For other verses by Darshan and Jalalu'ddin Rumi with a similar theme, see 18:8 and note.

69

Verse 2

In the first line the poet uses the Arabic word *tauḥīd*, which denotes the oneness of God and constitutes the first part of the *shahādah*, the Islamic profession of faith—*lā ilâha illā-'llâh* (There is no god but God—a concept echoing the Jewish affirmation of faith, *sh'mā yisrā'el ādonāī eloheinu ādonāī echād*—Hear, O Israel, the Lord our God, the Lord is one.) The Sufis expand this concept to include the divine nature of the entire creation, a view reflected in the Hindu Vedas when, at the time of creation, God declares, "I am One and wish to be many" (eko'ham bahu syām), and in the Ish Upanishad, which, in the words of Sant Darshan, "tells us that the world we see is an aspect of God. In the Gurbani it is said: *The world you see is the form of the Lord; Behold the Lord in all His forms.*"[254] Sant Darshan would often declare that those souls who have merged with the Creator see the Light of God shining in all creation and in every heart.[255]

Verse 4

The first line refers to the tradition of the prophet Muhammad that says "Die before you die" (mūtū qabla an tamūtū).[256] The mystery of " 'Be!' and it was" (kun fa-yakūn), which describes God willing the cosmos into existence, is found in Qur'an 2:117, 16:40, 36:82, and 40:68. The Hindu sacred texts describe the act of creation as "I am One and wish to be many" (eko'ham bahu syām). By "dying while living," or rising above physical body-consciousness, one comes into contact with the hidden Word of God, the divine power that brought the entire creation into existence.

Verse 5

Just as Darshan often portrays the satguru by the image of the divine cupbearer who pours out the wine of Shabd through his eyes, the poet also depicts him as the divine musician who, as the embodiment of the Shabd, radiates its "Unstruck Melody" (Anhat Shabd) from his very being to receptive souls longing to hear its strains. As Sant Darshan said in one of his public talks, "God sends saints and masters to awaken humanity. They are the divine musicians who help us become attuned to the Celestial Melody so that we can return to our source."[257]

For passages by Sant Kirpal Singh and Sant Darshan Singh referring to this divine Music, see 65:4 note and endnotes 53 and 72.

70

Verse 1

Commenting on this verse, Sant Darshan has written about Sant Kirpal Singh's indifference to him in the presence of jealous people. See 30:6 and note.

Verse 3

A well-known verse attributed to Punjabi Sufi poet Bullhe (Bulleh) Shāh (1680–1757) says,

namāz paṛhāṅ kĕh tudh val dekhāṅ
mainūṅ ka'bah bhul gayo'ī[258]

Should I say my prayers or gaze upon your face?
Where the Ka'ba lies I have forgotten.

Verse 5

The first line of the Urdu verse contains no nouns or pronouns to indicate whether it is the lover or the beloved whose restlessness and tears have vanished.

It is possible to interpret Darshan's assertion to mean that he was so telepathically attuned with the beloved that his own restlessness and tears stopped when the beloved began to forget him. However, that would amount to an admission that he was not a true lover in that his anguished longing was dependent on the beloved's love for him.

While one would not expect the traditionally cruel and aloof beloved in Urdu poetry to express love for the lover, the beloved is also proverbially fickle, so she might have previously expressed some feelings for him that have now apparently dried up. In this connection, as previously noted, Sant Darshan in his autobiography mentioned several periods when his beloved father, Sant Kirpal Singh, who was very affectionate with him in private, publicly showed indifference to him, and that during one such period of a year and a half, his torment grew so great that he could barely sleep.[259] In light of such painful experiences, we have interpreted that the restlessness and tears in the verse belong to the beloved.

71

Verse 1

This verse refers to a seeker who had wavered from the path of spirituality and then recovered his faith.

The word *manzil* in the first line of the Urdu verse, which means a place for accommodating travelers, a caravanserai, or an intermediate stage of a journey (*marḥalah*), can also mean the final destination or goal.[260] A translation of this verse using the latter sense of *manzil* might read,

> When the long-lost straggler finally found his way to the goal,
> His friends happily cried, "Look! The heedless one came to his senses!"

Verse 2

The many references in Urdu poetry to Mt. Sinai allude to Qur'an 7:143:

> *wa-lammā jā'a Mūsá li-mīqātinā wa-kallamahu rabbuhu qāla rabbi arinī anThur ilaika qāla lan taránī wa-lâkini'nThur ilá'l-jabali fa-ini'staqarra makānahu fa-saufa taránī fa-lamma tajallá rabbuhu lil-jabali ja'alahu dakkān wa-ḳharra Mūsá ṣa'iqān.*

> And when Moses came to the place appointed by us and his Lord addressed him, he said, "O my Lord! Show Yourself to me, that I may behold You!" The Lord said, "You shall not see Me; but behold the mountain—if it stays fast in its place,

> then you shall see Me." And when his Lord appeared to the mountain, it crumbled to dust; and Moses fell down in a faint.

Verse 5

To answer for the crimes of committing atrocities on the hearts of all her lovers, the poet imagines his beloved dragged before the judgment seat of God on the Day of Resurrection, a time, according to the Qur'an, when no evil deed remains hidden and the wicked are dismayed to be confronted with all their sins. (See Qur'an 18:49, 30:12, 52:45, 81:10–14, 82:1–5, 99:6–8.)

Verse 6

As in the first verse of this poem, the poet uses the Urdu word *manzil*, meaning either "way station" or "final destination." By translating *manzil* as "way station," or "stage of a journey" (*marḥalah*), the verse reflects the meaning of 59:1 in which the poet "shun[s] the stations along the path." Thus, the wayfarers in the present verse find no sign of Darshan because, in his fervent dedication to reach the final goal, he never even stopped there.

If one translates *manzil* as "destination," however, the meaning of the verse becomes obscure. One might interpret from a mystical standpoint that the wayfarers who reached the end of the journey—the court of the Lord in the fifth spiritual plane, Sach Khand—found no sign of Darshan because he had been fully absorbed into the Ocean of Divine Love in the eighth and highest spiritual region, Anami Desh, but such a reading seems to strain the bounds of sense.

72

Verse 2

According to Harishchandra Chadda in his Hindi commentary on *Matā'-e Nūr*, the "long-forgotten story" refers to God's promise to the souls He was exiling to temporal realms at the dawn of creation (*rūz-e azal*) that He Himself would come down to them in the form of a sant satguru to bring about their reunion with Him. Chadda Sahib's interpretation was based on Sant Darshan's explanation to him of the following verse:

bandagī terī karūṅ mujh ko taufiq tū bakṣh
va'dah-e rūz-e azal yād dilāne vale

If my devotion is to bear fruit, bestow your help and grace,
Fulfilling the promise made at the dawn of creation.

Verse 3
While the Muslim imam promises a paradise to come with rivers of the purest, most delightful wine (Qur'an 47:15, 76:21, 83:25–26) and beautiful houris (maidens with big, lustrous eyes) as companions (Qur'an 44:56, 52:20), the only paradise Darshan longs for is the tavern he already frequents and the companionship of his saqi, from whose enrapturing eyes he drinks the mystic wine of enlightenment.

Verse 5
For the poetic convention of mad lovers tearing their collars, see 4:5 note.

Verse 6
In this verse "someone" obliquely refers to the beloved.

73

Verse 2
The sheikh constantly preaches that all will have to render account on the Day of Judgment for succumbing to temptations that distract from the worship of God. The true test of whether the sheikh can follow his own advice is for him to see the beauty of the poet's beloved, which itself has the power to bring about the Resurrection.

Verse 6
The lover tauntingly gives in to the beloved's claim that she is always right. Ghalib has a verse along the same lines that reads,

kahā tum ne kĕh kyoṅ ho ġhair ke milne meṅ rusvā'ī
bajā kĕhte ho sach kĕhte ho phir kĕhyo kĕh hāṅ kyoṅ ho[261]

You say your meeting my rival would bring me no disgrace!
Oh, you're right! Perfectly true! How could it be wrong! Say it again!

Verse 7
See 5:2 for a verse with a similar theme but using the image of the tavern.

74

Verse 3
This verse presents us with a scene from the tavern, where the beloved is stumbling in her drunken ecstasy. The poet, however, suggests that this stumbling is in reality a coquettish pose adopted by the beloved to entice and captivate the hearts of her lovers.

The poet's comment in the second line reflects the angle of vision of a spiritually awakened disciple, who sees that the apparently inadvertent mistakes of a perfect spiritual master are not mistakes at all. Sant Darshan has talked about how God-realized spiritual masters adopt the pose, as it were, of being ordinary human beings just to enable those they meet to identify with them and feel encouraged to pursue their spiritual development. He writes, "The wonder of wonders is that the Godman comes down from his [divine] pedestal and sits with us at the same dimension we are sitting. . . . He talks with us, he eats with us, he works with us, and sometimes he even jokes with us to establish that homogeneity. Unless that homogeneity is established, we do not get a confirmation in our heart of hearts that we can also do what he has done."[262]

Verse 4
After the scorching heat of a summer day in India, people come out to enjoy the refreshing evening air. To the lover, however, the sultriness of the day is not relieved unless the breeze has passed through the beloved's lane, carrying her fragrance.

Verse 5
This can certainly be read as a patriotic verse, but the word "homeland" (*vaṯan*) may also have a mystical significance (see 20:3 note).

Verse 6
Ghalib has a verse that reads,

qaṯa' kīje nah ta'alluq ham se
kuchh nahīṅ hai to 'adāvat hī sahī[263]

Please don't break your relationship with me!
If nothing else, keep up your hostility.

Verse 7
The massing of dark clouds during the hot, dry summers in northern India and Pakistan makes people dance with joy over the impending arrival of cooling, revitalizing rains, and is thus a symbol of divine grace. In this verse, Darshan may also be alluding to a story Hazur Baba Sawan Singh often related in his satsangs about the Punjabi Sufi poet-saint Bulleh Shah, in which Bulleh's own father, a puritanical Muslim religious judge, was swept up in dance in spite of himself through the power of God-intoxicated Bulleh's glance of grace.[264]

75

Verse 1
The *radīf* (refrain) of this ghazal is the phrase *qiyāmat hai*, which can mean "It's the Day of Judgment, the doomsday, a great upheaval, the end of the world, a calamity." The phrase also connotes a sense of great astonishment, which is expressed variously according to the context in which it appears.

Verse 3
This verse shows the immensity of the spiritual master's responsibility toward his disciples, whose souls he is bound to protect. Without his intercession, the disciples would be vulnerable to temptations and attacks from negative forces on the inner way, which would spell their spiritual downfall. As Jalalu'ddin Rumi has said,

pīr rā bogzīn keh bī-pīr īn safar
hast bas por-āfat o ḳhauf o ḳhaṯar
ān rahī keh bārhā to rafte'ī
bī-qalāvūz andar ān āshofteh'ī
pas rahī rā keh nadīdastī to hīch

hīn maro tanhā ze-rahbar sar mapīch
gar nabāshad sāyeh-ye ū bar to gūl
pas torā sar gashteh dārad bāng-e ġhūl
ġhūlat az rah afkanad andar gazand
az to dāhītar darīn rah bas bodand[265]

Choose a mystic guide, for without a guide this journey
Is beset with untold fear, peril, and calamity.
Even on a road that you've traveled many a time,
Without an escort you are left in utter bewilderment.
So, venture not alone on a road you've never seen,
On no account forsake the company of the guide!
Without his protective hand overhead, O fool,
You will be bewildered by the call of vicious ghouls;
They will lead you off the path to your destruction;
Oh, many savvier than you have trod this path and perished.

Verse 4

The poet could foresee the calamities that would befall his heart (his nest), yet he could not resist surrendering it to the cruel, fickle beloved (symbolized by the lightning).

Verse 5

For a verse on a related theme, see 7:4.

Verse 6

The poet refuses to embrace the puritanical believers' ideal of postponed gratification, for neither does he accept that the charms of the houris (maidens of paradise) will be superior to those of the beauties of this world, nor is he sure that such houris even exist. In a mystical sense, no paradise to come or the beauties that inhabit it could compare with the paradise the poet has found in the company of his enrapturing beloveds—his spiritual masters.

Verse 7

It is a shocking irony and an unimaginable turn of events that lowly Darshan has been anointed tavern master (*pīr-e muġhāṅ*) with the responsibility of pouring out the wine of mystic love to all. In his Hindi commentary on this verse, Harishchandra Chadda writes, "God save this tavern! Considering the squandering habits of these profligate wastrels [the spiritual tavern masters], the entire store will be brought to ruin at his hands."[266]

76

Verse 8

For "homeland" see 20:3 note.

77

Verse 1

Here the "hunter" is the beloved and the "evil eye" her bewitching glance. The nest symbolizes the nightingale-lover's heart.

78

Verse 2

According to Sant Darshan's teachings, seekers of God on their mystical ascent cross the inner stars, moon, and sun before reaching the threshold of the truly spiritual planes.[267] Iqbal has used the image of stars to symbolize an elementary stage on the journey of love:

sitāroṅ se āge jahāṅ aur bhī haiṅ
abhī ʻishq ke imtiḥāṅ aur bhī haiṅ[268]

Beyond the stars are other worlds—
Still to come, more tests of love.

Verse 4

The poet advises the tipplers that the world of hearts is like a china shop whose contents are as fragile as the wine goblets they cherish. In a similar strain, Mir has compared this world to a glassworks:

le sāṅs bhī āhistah kĕh nāzuk hai bahut kām
āfāq kī is kārgah-e shīshah-garī kā[269]

Breathe gently! Delicate are this world's relations,
Fragile as blown glass in a glassworks.

Verse 7
Prophets and mystics, at great sacrifice, even martyrdom, broke the shackles of conventional religious observances and through their mystical teachings lighted humanity's way to God-realization. The poet warns us against letting their message become diluted and reverting to the darkness of formal rituals and practices.

Verse 8
Sant Darshan was fond of quoting the Persian proverb that says,

'eshq avval dar del-e ma'shūq peidā mī-shavad

Love first emanates from the beloved's heart.

For the entire verse, see endnote 56.

79

Verse 2
Great leaders and reformers who boldly call for reconciliation and amity between antagonistic peoples have always encountered the hatred and fierce opposition of their fearful and less enlightened contemporaries. A prime example is the assassination of Mahatma Gandhi in 1948 for preaching communal harmony in India.

Verse 4
Although the martyrs' blood has disappeared in the earth, the sky still bears witness to their sacrifice with a red glow on the horizon.

The second line of the verse is a quotation whose source we were unable to locate.

Verse 5
The phrase *apne junūṅ ke dasht* (the plains/desert/forest of my madness) indicates that the lover has not yet gained the favor of or had

union with his beloved and, in the throes of his mad passion for her, has taken to wandering the wilderness.

Verse 9
This verse calls to mind two couplets from Jalalu'ddin Rumi's *Maṡnavī*:

ātesh ast īn bāng-e nā'ī va nīst bād
har keh īn ātesh nadārad nīst bād
ātesh-e 'eshq ast k'andar nei fotād
jūshash-e 'eshq ast k'andar mei fotād[270]

This cry of the flute is fire, not wind;
May whoever is bereft of this fire become naught!
'Tis the fire of love that burns in the flute,
'Tis the fervor of love bubbling up in the wine.

80

Verse 1
A ruling passion for the beloved enables seekers on the mystic path to endure the grief ("vortex") of the long night of separation and ultimately achieve effulgent union ("the light of dawn") in meditation.

Verse 2
This verse depicts the tragic plight of many seekers after truth. Even if they manage to avoid the worldly temptations that beset the spiritual path, often the guides they choose—themselves spiritually blind people ruled by worldly cravings or lost in the exercise of occult powers—lead them away from their divine goal. As Sant Darshan himself commented, "If we look around us, we find that those who set themselves up as our pathfinders are often the ones who lead us astray. Those who should help us to resolve the problems of life are the very ones who serve to lead us into confusion."[271]

Verse 4
For a verse in this vein attributed to Hafez, see 40:3 note.

Our translation of the second line of the verse is based on the version in the 1991 Hindi edition of *Matā‘-e Nūr* rather than on the line from the original Urdu version (published in 1988).

The Hindi version reads "aur sajā dī hai gunāhoṅ **se** mĕrī har rahguzar," while the Urdu version reads "aur sajā dī hai gunāhoṅ **ne** mĕrī har rahguzar," which we would translate as "Yet it was these acts of sin that filled my path with beauty!"[272] (The 2016 Hindi version reverts to "**ne**" in the transliteration of the poem itself but retains the comment on the verse based on "**se**" from the 1991 edition.[273]) While we cannot say with certainty that this powerful and compelling line from the 1988 edition contains a typographical error, or that the poet changed the line after it was published, the thought conveyed in the line is not at all characteristic of the poetry of Darshan, who was not wont to speak with an irreverent voice defying conventional morality, as Ghalib does in the following verse:

nākardah gunāhoṅ kī bhī ḥasrat kī mile dād
yā rab agar in kardah gunāhoṅ kī sazā hai[274]

O Lord, if there be punishment for my sins,
Reward me for those I regretfully couldn't indulge in.

Verse 5
In this context, Mir has written,

us ke īfā'-e 'ahd tak nah jī'e
'umr ne ham se bevafā'ī kī[275]

I didn't live to see her fulfill her promise—
My life in the end proved unfaithful to me.

Likewise, Ghalib did not take any stock in his beloved's promises:

yĕh nah t'hī hamārī qismat kĕh viṣāl-e yār hotā
agar aur jīte rĕhte yahī intiẕār hotā

tĕre va'de par jīye ham to yĕh jān jhūṭ jānā
kĕh ḳhwushī se mar nah jāte agar i'tibār hotā[276]

It was not my destiny to have union with my beloved;
However long I'd lived, there would still have been this waiting.

You think I lived on your promise? I knew that it wasn't true,
For wouldn't I have died of joy if I had really believed you?

Verse 7

The Hindi word *darshan* generally means to behold a loved one and enjoy his or her elevating presence. In a mystical sense, it means to receive the soul-uplifting glance of the spiritual master, or to lovingly absorb one's attention into the master's eyes so fully that one becomes completely and ecstatically lost in him, forgetting the world outside and one's individual existence.

82

Verse 3

Here Darshan alludes to the story of the architect-sculptor Farhād and the Armenian princess Shīrīn, the most famous version of which appears in the epic romance *Ḵhusrow o Shīrīn* (Khusrow and Sheereen) by the great Persian narrative poet Neẕāmī Ganjavī (c.1141–1209). In Nezami's telling of the story, Sheereen has become estranged from her lover, the young Sasanian king Khusrow II (reigned 590–628). Responding to Sheereen's desire for milk from her mountain herds, Khusrow's friend and go-between, Shāpūr, enlists the immensely strong Farhaad to cut a stone canal through solid mountain rock to deliver the milk to Sheereen's palace. When Farhaad eventually comes into Sheereen's presence, he falls hopelessly in love with her, but she does not requite his love.[277] When Khusrow learns of Farhaad's intense passion for Sheereen, he attempts to persuade the commoner Farhaad to abandon his love for the princess. Ultimately, however, Farhaad prevails in their verbal duel, about which Professor Heshmat Moayyad writes, "the dialogue is the culmination of the clash between two conflicting codes and concepts of love, [Khusrow's] heroic and sensual, regarding the beloved as a prize or booty to be conquered and possessed, [and Farhaad's] unrequited and all-consuming, relishing the very notion of the annihilation of the self through love."[278] Having failed to discourage Farhaad, Khusrow commissions him to cut a road through the rocks of Mount Bīsotūn, promising to give up his own claim to Sheereen as a reward if he succeeds. Farhaad carves a relief of Sheereen on the mountain to inspire him as he works, and Sheereen goes out to encourage him in his unrelenting labor. Learning that this supposedly impossible task is nearly complete and enraged with jealousy, Khusrow sends Farhaad the false news that Sheereen has died, on hearing which, Farhaad, in utter despair, leaps from the rocks to his death.[279]

83

Darshan composed this ghazal in Persian. The poem appeared in *Talāsh-e Nūr* at 146 but not in the Urdu version of *Matā'-e Nūr*. The Persian text is as follows:

be-del beshnow ḥadīṡ-e bī-zabānī
keh eẓhārash begoftārī nabāshad

faġhān bar rūzgār-e bādeh-ḳhwārī
keh sāqī nāz-bardārī nabāshad

meṡāl-e māhī-ye bī-āb hastam
agar dīdār-e ān yārī nabāshad

manam maḳhmūr az ān do dīdeh-ye mast
be-jām o mei marā kārī nabāshad

man ūrā 'āsheq-e ṣādeq nagūyam
keh chūn Manṣūr bar dārī nabāshad

neshīn fāreġh be-ẓell-e pīr-e kāmel
keh dar ṭā'at torā bārī nabāshad

darīn donyā keh dām-e har balā ast
be-joz morshed madad-gārī nabāshad

Verse 1
The story referred to here is the inexpressible Word of God reverberating within the mystic heart, the door to which is the third or inner eye.

Verse 2
For Sant Darshan's comments on the spiritual master's aloofness from the disciple in the higher stages of love, see 2:3 note.

Verse 5
For Mansoor, see 54:9 note.

Verse 6
The original Persian uses the term *pīr-e kāmel,* meaning "perfect saint" or "perfect spiritual guide."

Verse 7
The original Persian uses the word *morshed,* meaning "spiritual guide or master."

84

This poem appeared in *Talāsh-e Nūr* at 148 but not in the Urdu version of *Matā'-e Nūr*. The Persian text is as follows:

cheh qaṯr-hā keh ze-abr-e bahār mīrīzad
cheh ġhoncheh-hā ze-sar-e shāḵhsār mīrīzad

marā beh jām o ṣorāḥī cheh kār ei sāqī
keh bādeh az negah-e ān negār mīrīzad

cheh golshanīst shegofteh darūn-e sīneh-ye man
hazār lāleh del-e dāġhdār mīrīzad

mabāsh ḥalqeh beh gosh-e kamand-e ḥerṣ o havā
ze-har nafas, havas-e ḵhām-kār mīrīzad

begīr jām o beh meiḵhāneh ei beyā Darshan
bebīn! keh bādeh ze-abr-e bahār mīrīzad

Verse 3
For a verse with a similar image, see 82:4.

85–87

Verse 1
The Urdu originals of poems 85–87 were written as quasi sonnets containing three stanzas of four lines with the rhyme scheme *abba cddc effe*, and a concluding rhymed couplet *gg*. The translations do not incorporate the sonnets' rhyme scheme.

88

Verse 1
Darshan Singh, *Talāsh-e Nūr*, 150 (fourth couplet):

bas itnā yād hai ṭakrā gaʾī kisī se naẕar
phir us ke baʿd nah us kī ḳhabar nah apnī ḳhabar

Verse 2
Darshan Singh, *Talāsh-e Nūr*, 68 (fourth couplet):

maẕāhir-e abadī ab mĕrī nigāh meṅ haiṅ
taʿīyyunāt ke parde uṭ'hā dī'e tū ne

Verse 3
Darshan Singh, *Talāsh-e Nūr*, 68 (sixth couplet):

us ek mauj-e tabassum kā shukrīyah, jis se
hazār nūr ke daryā bahā dī'e tū ne

Verse 4
Darshan Singh, *Talāsh-e Nūr*, 94 (lines 9–10):

tū hameṅ wādī-ye ġhurbat meṅ sahārā degā
tere jażbe rasan o dār pĕh yād ā'eṅge

Verse 5
Darshan Singh, *Talāsh-e Nūr*, 58 (first couplet):

jism kāṅṭoṅ se guzartā hai guzar jāne do
rūḥ voh phūl hai jis par nah ḳhazāṅ ā'egī

Verse 6
Darshan Singh, *Manzil-e Nūr* (Urdu), 86 (lines 9–10); *Manzil-e Nūr* (Hindi), 152 (stanza 39, lines 3–4):

t'hirak rahe haiṅ gunah dil kī raqṣ-gāhoṅ meṅ
jakaṛ gayā hai bashar ārzū kī bāhoṅ meṅ

Verse 7
Darshan Singh, *Manzil-e Nūr* (Urdu), 78, lines 17–18; *Manzil-e Nūr* (Hindi), 119 (stanza 16, lines 5–6):

isī 'amal ko agar iḳhtiyār kar lete
to ham chaman ko nigār-e bahār kar lete

Manzil-e Nūr is a long poem on Guru Nanak's life and teachings for which the poet received an Indian-government academy award in 1972.[280]

In this verse, Darshan speaks of Guru Nanak's *sadāchār*, whose importance Nanak poetically summed up as *sat ūpar āchār* (True living is higher than truth).[281]

Sant Kirpal Singh translated "sadachar" as "righteous living," explaining that

> it does not imply any rigid code or set moral formulae, but suggests purity and simplicity, which radiate from within and spread outwards, permeating every action, every word, every thought. It is as much concerned with one's personal habits, good and hygienic, as with one's individual and social ethics. And on its ethical side, it is concerned not merely with one's relation to one's fellow men but to all living things, i.e., harmony which is the result of recognition that all things are from the same Essence; and so a worm is as much a part of Brahman as the mightiest of gods, Indra.[282]

Regarding the spiritual master's influence on the development of sadachar and the relationship between sadachar and inner spiritual ascent, Sant Kirpal writes,

> [Sadachar] is a way of life, and in such matters only heart to heart can speak. It is this that makes Satsang, or association with a true Master, so important. It not only serves as a constant reminder of the goal before the seeker, but through the magic touch of personal contact, gradually transforms his entire mode of thinking and feeling. As his heart and mind under this benign influence grow gradually purer, his life more fully centers in the divine. In short, as he increasingly realizes in practice the ideal of sadachar, his thoughts, now scattered and dissipated, will gain equipoise and integration till they arrive at so fine a focus that the veils of inner darkness are burnt to cinders and the inner glory stands revealed.[283]

Verse 8
Darshan Singh, *Manzil-e Nūr* (Urdu), 82, lines 17–18; *Manzil-e Nūr* (Hindi), 137 (stanza 28, lines 5–6):

chaman ko maḥram-e yak-rangī-ye bahār kiyā
guloṅ ko nakhat-e waḥdat se mushkbār kiyā

In this verse the poet addresses Guru Nanak, who preached the message that the people of India and the entire world (the flowers of the garden), despite their diversity of color, were all united as children of the same Creator in the oneness of God (the one color of spring), and that it was this underlying divine unity that made them fragrant.[284]

Verse 9
Darshan Singh, *Jādah-e Nūr* (Urdu), 229, lines 3–8; *Jādaye Nūr* (Hindi), 170 (lines 11–16):

har jān-dār amn kā t̲ālib hai dĕhr meṅ
insāniyat ke sāt'h basar kījī'e zindagī
jo dard-mand bhī hai, muḥabbat bharā bhī hai
ḥaiwāṅ bhī apne sine meṅ rakhte haiṅ dil vohī

ḥaiwān par bhī luṯf o karam kī naẕar kareṅ
is ṯaraḥ shām-e nau'-e bashar kī saḥar kareṅ

This verse is an excerpt from "Jāndār kā Lahū" (The Blood of the Living), a poem on vegetarianism.

Table of Correspondence between Translated Poems and Urdu Originals

English	Urdu/ Hindi*	English	Urdu/ Hindi*
1	4	27	52
2	12	28	22
3	6	29	56
4	10	30	23
5	8	31	44 & 75
6	14	32	41
7	2	33	24
8	1	34	25
9	26	35	57
10	7	36	28
11	27	37	45
12	15	38	29
13	46	39	58
14	11	40	30
15	36	41	48
16	19	42	31
17	47	43	59
18	38	44	32
19	37	45	60
20	16	46	33
21	49	47	74
22	18	48	34
23	51	49	61
24	20 & 13	50	40
25	39	51	9
26	21	52	53

53	3	71	77
54	54	72	84
55	63	73	85
56	35	74	86
57	64	75	78
58	76	76	87
59	65	77	82
60	43	78	62
61	66	79	42
62	69	80	68
63	67	81	88
64	80	82	89
65	71 & 70	83	X/90†
66	72	84	X/91‡
67	79	85	92/94
68	81	86	94/96
69	73	87	93/95
70	83	88	X/X§

Note: verse numbers in *Love's Last Madness* do not always correspond to the verse order in *Matā'-e Nūr* as verses that Sant Darshan Singh himself translated have not been included in this book.

---

* Darshan Singh, *Matā'-e Nūr* (Urdu), 1988, and *Matā'-e Nūr* (Hindi), 2016. Exceptions in the following notes:
† Darshan Singh, *Talāsh-e Nūr*, 146, and *Matā'-e Nūr* (Hindi), 255.
‡ Darshan Singh, *Talāsh-e Nūr*, 148, and *Matā'-e Nūr* (Hindi), 257.
§ See Commentary on Poem 88 for Urdu and Hindi sources of miscellaneous verses.

Notes

Preface to the Revised Edition

1. Note that diacritics are used in spelling foreign words and names for the most part only on first mention.
2. Gonḍvī, *Kulliyāt-e Aṣġhar*, ed. Kānt, from "Nishāt-e rūḥ" 11 (from the *na't* (eulogistic poem written in praise of the prophet Muhammad) entitled "Na't ḥaẓūr sarūr-e kā'ināt ṣallá'l-lâhu 'alaihi wa sallama"), verse 6, line 2.

Introduction
Sant Sarshan Singh (1921-1989)

3. Darshan Singh, *Love Has Only a Beginning*, 130.
4. Darshan Singh, *Love at Every Step*, 26.
5. Darshan Singh, 82.
6. Darshan Singh, *Wonders of Inner Space*, 169.
7. Darshan Singh, *Love Has Only a Beginning*, 89.
8. Kirpal Singh, *Heart to Heart Talks*, 2:277–78; Darshan Singh, *Love Has Only a Beginning*, 50.
9. Darshan Singh, *Love Has Only a Beginning*, 92.
10. Darshan Singh, 92.
11. Kīmtī Lāl Aroṛa (chief of security for Sant Kirpal Singh, Sant Darshan Singh, and Sant Rajinder Singh from 1958 to 1994), interview by translators Barry Lerner and Harbans Singh Bedi, July 5, 2015, Potomac Falls, Va. Mr. Arora reported that he saw staff members at Sant Darshan Singh's office weeping the day before Sant Darshan Singh's retirement in 1979, and that the following day, the officer in charge of the office security gate also wept, stating that he had never met any officer who loved his staff as much as Sant Darshan Singh had.
12. Darshan Singh, *Love Has Only a Beginning*, 23–24.
13. Darshan Singh, 87.
14. Darshan Singh, 84.
15. Darshan Singh, 140–41.
16. Darshan Singh, late-night group meeting attended by translator Barry Lerner at Sant Darshan's house, Kirpal Ashram, Delhi, India, Spring 1981.
17. Darshan Singh, *Love Has Only a Beginning*, 149–50.
18. Arora, interview.
19. Nanavati, *Justice Nanavati Commission*, 1:43–58.
20. Dr. Darshan Singh, MD (cardiologist from Ontario, Canada, who treated Sant Darshan Singh during the 1980s). Personal interview with translator Barry Lerner at Sawan Kirpal Meditation Center, Bowling Green, VA., June 28, 1996.
21. Singh, MD, interview.
22. Singh, MD, interview.
23. Darshan Singh, *Love Has Only a Beginning*, 32.

24. Darshan Singh, 122–26.
25. Darshan Singh, 43–44.
26. Darshan Singh, 128.
27. Aḵhtar, *Hindostān Hamārā*, vol. 1, Table of Contents, "Navāṅ adhyāy—hamāre dhārmik netā," and Introduction, 42. Five of the six poems of Darshan's in volume 1 (poems on Lord Mahāvīra, Lord Jesus, Prophet Muḥammad, Ḵhwājah Mu'īnu'ddīn Chishtī, and Ḥaẓrat Niẓāmu'ddīn Auliyā), were taken from Darshan Singh, *Talāsh-e Nūr*, 99–100, 109–110, 123, 133–135, 137; the single poem in volume 2 (on Subhāśh Chandra Bos) was taken from *Talāsh-e Nūr*, 89–90. Darshan's poem on Guru Nānak Dev Jī in volume 1 of the anthology consisted of stanzas of what was published four years later as a substantially longer poem, *Manzil-e Nūr*, for which he won an academy award from the government of India in 1973. Darshan Singh, *Love Has Only a Beginning*, 129–30. These stanzas on Guru Nanak can be found in Darshan Singh, *Manzil-e Nūr* (Urdu), 73 (stanza 1), 74 (stanza 3), 75 (stanza 3), 77 (stanza 3), 78 (stanza 2), 79 (stanza 3), 80 (stanza 2), 85 (stanza 1), 88 (stanza 1), 89 (stanza 2), 96 (stanza 3), 102 (stanza 3); and *Manzil-e Nūr* (Hindi), 97 (stanza 1), 103 (stanza 4), 107 (stanza 7), 115 (stanza 13), 117 (stanza 15), 124 (stanza 19), 128 (stanza 21), 144 (stanza 35), 161 (stanza 44), 167 (stanza 48), 196 (stanza 70), 222 (stanza 88).
28. Lāl, *Naġhmah-e Rūḥ: Ṣūfiānah Ġhazaloṅ kā Intiḵhāb*, 3–6. Lal's dedication reads, "Dedicated to Sant Darshan Singh, composer of great poetry and preceptor of spiritual values" (Shĕ'rī adab ke ḵhāliq aur rūḥānī aqdār ke ḥāmil Saṅt Darshan Siṅgh ke nām). The poems of Darshan included in Lal's anthology originally appeared in *Talāsh-e Nūr* or later in *Matā'-e Nūr*. Most of Darshan's verses from Lal's book are translated in poems 1, 53, and 54 of *Love's Last Madness* and in Sant Darshan's book *Love at Every Step* at 81–97.
29. Darshan Singh, *Love Has Only a Beginning*, 142.
30. Ahmad, *Intellectual History of Islam*, 91–111.
31. Darshan Singh, *Love Has Only a Beginning*, 125.

Sant Mat—The Theory of the Mystic Path

32. "What I am telling you is not anything new. It is all there in the scriptures. I simply had the good fortune to sit at the feet of a Master in India who was a practical and perfect Saint. At his feet I learned not only the theory but also the practice—seeing the truth for myself. . . . These scriptures . . . were produced by the holy Masters who found God within themselves. Whatever experience they had, they recorded for our guidance and help." Kirpal Singh, *The Night Is a Jungle*, 59–60, 62.
33. "It is said that God in His formless state was all alone. He was an ocean of all-consciousness, all bliss, all love. He had no form and no name. Then He decided to become many from One. With this thought came a vibration which manifested in two principles: the Light of God and the Music of the Spheres or the Sound Current. . . . This God-into-expression Power was the cause of all creation. As it descended, it brought forth realm after realm of creation—the supracausal, the causal, the astral, and the physical planes." Darshan Singh, *Streams of Nectar*, 15–16.

34. "Soul is the essence of God. . . . It is a drop of the Ocean of All-consciousness. But, unfortunately, our spirit is identified with the body at the sensual plane, so much so that we have lost our identity." Kirpal Singh, "A Grand Delusion," *Sat Sandesh* 2, No. 7 (Aug. 1969), 10.

"[The Masters] say you are conscious entities, drops of the ocean of all-consciousness, but environed by mind and matter so much so that you have forgotten your self." Kirpal Singh, ". . . and the Darkness Comprehended It Not."

35. "[The drama of life] is all an expression of the inexorable Law of *Karma*. Desire is the root-cause of all bondage and rebirths." Kirpal Singh, *Spiritual Elixir* 2:36.

"It is only karma born of desire or Kam that leads to bondage." Kirpal Singh, "The Law of Karma."

> Each thought, each word and each deed has to be accounted for and compensated for in Nature. Every cause has an effect and every action brings about a reaction. Uproot the cause and the effect disappears. This has been done by the Masters who have transcended these laws, but all others are bound by the bonds of Karma, which is the root cause of physical existence and the clever device of Nature to maintain this existence. . . . The mind contracts Karma, puts a covering on the soul and rules the body through the organs and the senses. . . . Karma is the cause of rebirth and each birth is in turn followed by death. Thus the cycle of enjoyment and suffering, which are concomitants of birth and death, continues. . . . All Karma must be wiped out completely before permanent salvation can be had. Kirpal Singh, *Man! Know Thyself*, 15–17.

"When one begins to see the Spirit and Power of God, he at once becomes an agent, a mere cog or an insignificant instrument in the divine set-up. Then he is *Neh-karma* [karma free] and all his seeming acts are acts of the invisible Power and he is only a *sakshi* or a witness thereof. This is figuratively called becoming [a] conscious co-worker of the Divine Plan. Once this delusion of doership is dispelled, there remains nothing to bind the individual." Kirpal Singh, "Delusion of Doership," 5.

36.

> However hard we labor, however sincerely we yearn to return to our Creator, we are compelled to realize our own helplessness, the impossibility of our situation.
>
> When a soul realizes the impossibility of its plight, it cries out to the Lord . . . [and] prays to Him to come to its rescue and save it from certain destruction [at the hands of desires and temptations]. . . . When this cry bursts from the soul, God hears it and heeds it. . . . When we surrender ourselves completely to His protection, accepting our vulnerability, He takes charge of us. Taking the rags of the human being, He comes down among us to help us return to our Home. . . . God Himself does come in the form of saints . . . for our salvation. They are embodiments of the Absolute, the Supreme Father. They are human mouthpieces of the Lord. Darshan Singh, *Spiritual Awakening*, 95–96.

37. In Sant Mat, the word "saint" (*sant*) does not simply mean a holy or virtuous person, or someone canonized by the Church. Rather, it is a technical term

denoting a definite level of spiritual attainment. Sant Darshan Singh's spiritual predecessor, Sant Kirpal Singh, discussed the different gradations of spiritual mastership as follows:

> A *Sadh* is one who has gone beyond the region of *Trikuti* (*Onkar*) which is the same as *Lahut* in Sufi terminology and *Hu* in Islamic theology. He has witnessed the spirit in its pristine glory, after having rid it of all coverings, and is now *Trigunatit* (*beyond* the three gunas: *Satva*, *Rajas*, and *Tamas*, in which all human beings work according to their natural and native instincts); *beyond* the five elements (earth, water, fire, air and ether, of which the physical world is composed); *beyond* the twenty-five *Prakritis* (the subtle forms in varying degrees of the elements); and *beyond* also mind and matter.
>
> In short, he is an adept in self-knowledge, or the art and science of spirit, and can, at will, disengage the spirit from the various *koshas* (sheaths or caskets) in which it is enclosed like a priceless gem. . . .
>
> By a process of self-analysis, he (a *Sadh*) has known the self or spirit in its real form—to wit, that it is of the same essence as God; and now he strives for God-knowledge.
>
> A *Sant* is one who is adept not only in self-knowledge but in God-knowledge as well. He far transcends the material, materio-spiritual, and spirituo-material realms. Master of Truth as he is, his abode is in the purely spiritual region, technically called *Sach Khand* or *Muqam-i-Haq*, the Realm of Truth.
>
> A *Param Sant* is the Grand Master of Truth beyond all description and hence ineffable. He is at one with what is variously known as *Anami* (The Nameless One) of Kabir; *Nirala* (Indescribably Wonderful), *Mahadayal* (Boundless Mercy) or *Swami* (The Great Lord of all).
>
> There is no material difference between a *Sant* and a *Param Sant* except in nomenclature.
>
> But none of them, whether a *Sadh*, a *Sant*, or a *Param Sant*, can act or function as a Guru or Master unless he is competent to impart spiritual instructions and he has been commissioned from above to do this work. Whoever holds this authority for spiritual work becomes a *Sadh Guru*, *Sant Guru*, or *Param Sant Guru*, as the case may be.
>
> There may be a number of *Sadhs*, *Sants*, or *Param Sants*, but none of them can of himself assume Guruship or spiritual preceptorship without being commissioned for the work. Kirpal Singh, *Godman*, 18–20.

38. When a person is accepted by the Master he takes a second birth, as it were, into the Master's house. He comes into the Master's fold full of worldly attachments and dyed in the darkest shades of mind and matter. He is so identified with his body and bodily relations that he can never think that he is something apart from them. . . .

> With [the disciple's] birth in the Master's house, the Master takes upon himself an immense load of responsibility. By individual instruction and attention, [the Master] gradually weans the jiva [embodied soul] from sense pleasures. He tells the disciple that he is neither body nor mind nor

intellect, but something more glorious—soul or spirit . . . . By spiritual discipline, the Master enables him to free his mind of mental oscillations. Now he develops a state of equipoise, and . . . a consciousness of spirit dawns in him. . . .

[The disciple] has to be pulled up from his senses, mind and intellect, and this no one but a Master can achieve.

To stop the course of the mighty rush of sensory currents flowing headlong into the world, and to hold them at one center, is a gigantic task in itself. The next job of the Master is even more important than this.

After the preliminary cleansing process, he pulls scales from the inner eye and gives it vision and Light; and he breaks the seal on the inner ear, making the jiva hear the inner music of the soul. By his individual attention and care, he makes an adept out of trash and scrap—capable of understanding and enjoying the unspoken language and unwritten law of God, and of doing actions without the aid of outer organs and faculties. . . .

He takes in his own hands the entire process of winding up the karmic impressions of the jiva. Kirpal Singh, *Godman*, 160–62.

39. The outer expression of the soul is known as the attention. Presently our attention is scattered throughout our body and goes out of our body into this world through the five senses. . . . We have to withdraw our attention from the world outside and collect it at the seat of the soul, located between and behind the two eyebrows. This point is referred to in different scriptures as the single eye, the third eye, the tenth door or *daswan dwar*, the *divya chakshu*, or the *ajna chakra*. . . . This is the point at which we concentrate our attention in order to see the inner Light and hear the Celestial Sound. Rajinder Singh, *Inner and Outer Peace through Meditation*, 21.

"This same current of the Light and Sound that flows out from God also returns to its source. Our soul is of the same essence as God, and is a drop of the ocean of all-consciousness. If we can come in contact with that current of Light and Sound within us, our soul can travel upon it back to its source. Then we can attain knowledge of who we really are. We can attain self-knowledge and God-realization." Darshan Singh, *Streams of Nectar*, 16.

So the Master teaches us this art [of dying while living], helps us in rising above body-consciousness, and helps us in crossing the inner realms of the stars, the moon, and the sun. Then we come face to face with the radiant form of our Master. The form of our Master at that stage is so enrapturing, so captivating, so enticing that we gradually lose ourselves into that form. Then, the Master takes us under his own protective wings through the higher spiritual realms. . . . Unless we get the guidance of a perfect living Master we cannot traverse through the higher planes. Darshan Singh, "True Freedom," 4.

40. We gradually go beyond the first three planes. There we shake off the shackles of mind and matter, and our soul becomes completely purified

of all the human sins. It is only when we have crossed the supracausal plane that our soul starts realizing that we are of the same essence as God, and there it cries out "Sohang," which means "I am that," or "Tat Twam Asi," which also means the same thing. The mystic word for this stage is "Anal-haq," which means "I am God." . . . [The soul] continues traversing the higher planes, and first merges in the Master. That is the first stage of mysticism, which is known as fana-fil-Sheikh, or merger with the Master. Then through the Master's grace and God's blessings, the soul enters our eternal home, Sach Khand. Darshan Singh, 4.

41. "After crossing the stages beyond Sach Khand, ultimately [the soul] attains communion with the Creator. That is the stage where our soul attains lasting happiness, lasting peace and lasting salvation. This ultimate stage is known as fana-fil-Allah, or merger in God." Darshan Singh, 4.

When Baba Sawan Singh once wrote that he did not even yearn for Sach Khand but only prayed that he had "love and faith at the Satguru's holy feet," Baba [Jaimal Singh] Ji was extremely pleased and replied that such self-surrender was "indeed the highest *karni* (discipline)" and assured him that "he who had such a love for the Master would certainly reach Sach Khand, and passing through the Alakh, Agam, [and] Anami-Radhasoami, get merged in the Wonder Region." Kirpal Singh, *Baba Jaimal Singh*, 99–100 (quoting from a letter written by Bābā Jaimal Siṅgh to Baba Sawan Singh dated September 11, 1897).

The Mystic Path through Darshan's Poetry

42. From the moment we open our eyes in this world, we are nourished by love. A newborn baby is not interested in toys or playthings; he only craves his mother's affection. As we grow, love for parents and family remains the primary force in our life. Later, we seek the love of friends. And by the time we reach adulthood, we are in search of a life-companion to cherish. We crave love in all aspects of life. We seek affection and acceptance from those with whom we associate. And when these are denied, we feel despondent, even depressed. It is the lack of love which accounts for so much pain and unhappiness in this world. . . . It is only love which can bring about peace, harmony, and bliss. Darshan Singh, *Wonders of Inner Space*, 155–56.

43. "Although it is our natural impulse to seek lasting, permanent love, we have been unable to find it. The reason for this is that we are under a grand delusion. . . . We crave lasting love in an ephemeral world." Darshan Singh, 157.

Ever since our soul was separated from God, we have become identified with the mind, body, and the physical world. We have become so lost in them that we have forgotten that we are soul. Our body and mind are material, but the soul, which is of the same essence as God, is spirit. Because it is a purely conscious entity, it can experience happiness only from that which is conscious, not from that which is material. . . . That which is material can only provide temporary comfort to the physical body. . . . The soul can only be happy when it comes in contact with that which is all-consciousness, that which is lasting. Darshan Singh, *Streams of Nectar*, 15.

"We pursue one pleasure after another, one desire after another, in quest of happiness. But this quest is doomed to failure, for how can the soul which is spirit find rest or bliss in that which is material and not of its essence?" Darshan Singh, 68.

44. "The outer expression of our soul is attention. If we were to direct our attention to God, the source of love, we would be reconnected to a regenerative Power that is infinite and everlasting." Darshan Singh, *Wonders of Inner Space*, 157.

45. The verse in its entirety reads as follows:

muḥabbat ibtidā o intihā hai har do 'ālam kī
yĕh naẓrānah matā'-e lā-makānī le ke āyā hūṅ

Love is the beginning and the end of both worlds—
This divine treasure is the gift I've brought for all.

(All translations from Urdu, Hindi, Punjabi, Persian, and Arabic in this book were done by Barry Lerner and Harbans Singh Bedi, unless otherwise noted.)

Although the *qāfiyah* (repeating internal rhyme) and *radīf* (refrain) of the second line of the Urdu verse quoted above are the same as those of poem 9 in the Urdu and Hindi versions of *Matā'-e Nūr* (poem 51 in *Love's Last Madness*), we were unable to locate this verse in any of Darshan's published Urdu poetry collections. Sant Darshan would quote it in his satsang talks, but the verse appears to have been published only in his Urdu essay "Merā Naẕarīyah-e Shā'irī" (Hindi version "Kavitā ke bāre meṅ Merā Drishṭikoṇ") ("My Concept of Poetry"), in Darshan Singh, *Matā'-e Nūr* (Urdu), 38; *Matā'-e Nūr* (Hindi), 30; Darshan Singh, *Manzil-e Nūr* (Urdu), 30; *Manzil-e Nūr* (Hindi), 72. It was not included in the English translation of "My Concept of Poetry," but in the Urdu and Hindi versions Sant Darshan used it to illustrate the principles of nonsectarian "fellowship" and "brotherhood" that underlay his philosophy as an artist. Darshan Singh, "My Concept of Poetry," in *Love at Every Step*, 22.

The version of this verse in the Urdu "My Concept of Poetry" in *Matā'-e Nūr* and *Manzil-e Nūr* differs from the Hindi version of the essay. The Hindi transliteration of the Urdu verse substitutes the word *lā-makānī* (divine, godly) for the word *jāvidānī* (eternal, immortal). However, Sant Darshan himself in quoting this verse in a public talk used the word *lā-makānī*. Darshan Singh, "Priceless Gem," DVD 28, 1:02:50

46. "Where does the source of love exist? It is within us." Darshan Singh, *Wonders of Inner Space*, 157.

47. "God is love and the way back to Him is also through love. Being of the same essence as the Lord, our souls share in the nature of love, and it is through love alone that we can return to our Creator." Darshan Singh, *Streams of Nectar*, 70.

48. "It is said that the soul has been exiled from the inner kingdom and has been pushed into the outer world where it dissipates its energy." Darshan Singh, 51.

"The soul is a denizen of the heavens, and it must return to its true Home." Darshan Singh, 10–11.

49. When we look around, we find that religion, which purports to deal with the spiritual life, is taken up with elaborate rites and rituals. At best these rites and rituals are signs and symbols of the life within. But instead of directing our attention to that life, they tend to distract us from it. The result is that for most of us, what was meant as a help, turns ultimately into a hindrance. It is not surprising that whenever the great Saints and mystics have come, they have invariably sought to direct our attention away from such forms and ceremonies. . . . We have to turn within. Darshan Singh, 79.

50. Darshan Singh, 11.

51. "While God the Absolute is beyond comprehension, we may see Him in the person of someone who has become united with Him, in the saint. In such a being we behold the infinite in the finite and the invisible in the visible. To mortal eyes he may seem limited like the rest of us, yet he shares in God's omnipotence and omniscience, having become a conscious co-worker of the divine plan." Darshan Singh, 246.

52. "The Master teaches us the art of rising above body-consciousness, the art of dying while we are still living." Darshan Singh, 51.

"This practice of inversion[,] . . . [t]his process of leaving the body in meditation is similar to the experience we undergo at death. The only difference is that at death, the silver cord that connects the soul to the body is broken. In meditation, the silver cord remains intact and the soul can return to the body at will." Darshan Singh, 181.

53. "To understand what Naam is, we need to examine what the scriptures say about the beginning of creation. It is said that God in His formless state was all alone. He was an ocean of all-consciousness, all bliss, all love. He had no form and no name. Then He decided to become many from One. With this thought came a vibration which manifested in two principles: the Light of God and the Music of the Spheres or the Sound Current. This principle has been referred to in various scriptures by different names." Darshan Singh, 15.

"This Celestial Music has been called the *Word* in the Bible: 'In the beginning was the Word, and the Word was with God, and the Word was God.' The Hindu Vedas call it *Naad*, *Jyoti*, and *Sruti*. The Muslim Sufis call it *Kalam-i-Qadim*, or *Kalma*. The Zoroastrians call it *Sraosha*. The Buddhists call it *Sonorous Light*. The Sikhs call it *Naam*, *Shabd*, *Kirtan*, *Bani* and *Jyot*." Darshan Singh, *Spiritual Awakening*, 12.

> This God-into-expression Power . . . brought forth realm after realm of creation—the supracausal, the causal, the astral, and the physical planes. It also created humanity and all other species of life. This same current of the Light and Sound that flows out from God also returns to its source. Our soul is of the same essence as God, and is a drop of the ocean of all-consciousness. If we can come in contact with that current of Light and Sound within us, our soul can travel on it back to its source. . . . A realized soul connects us with Naam through his attention. At the time of initiation, he opens our inner eye and inner ear so that we can see the Light of God and hear the Sound Current reverberating ceaselessly within. He teaches us the art of meditation. Darshan Singh, *Streams of Nectar*, 16.

54. "Having received this [initial contact with the Light and Sound of God], we have to set to work. We have to labor hard in order to follow the teachings. The gift of Naam by itself does not ensure salvation. The Master teaches us the importance of truth, of the principle of nonviolence or ahimsa. He awakens us to the necessity of a strong ethical base for our lives." Darshan Singh, 412.

55. One who has set for himself one supreme goal, who has found a love which eclipses all earthly loves, cannot be enticed by the enchantments of the world. With each passing day one becomes increasingly anchored in the life within, in the life of the spirit. And the more one gets thus anchored, the less one is involved with the desires, ambitions, and attachments of worldly life. One may continue to live like one's fellow beings, meeting worldly obligations and raising a family. But one is like the exile who, though seemingly leading a normal life in the land of one's domicile, has one's thoughts forever anchored in the land of one's birth. Darshan Singh, 86.

56. The entire verse is as follows:

'eshq avval dar del-e ma'shūq peidā mī-shavad
tā nasūzad sham' kei parvāneh sheidā mī-shavad

Love first emanates from the beloved's heart;
Unless the candle burns, how will the moth be mad with love?

"This love is something which we imbibe from a spiritual Master. It is something to be caught, not taught. Master souls such as the saints are so imbued with divine love that they radiate it wherever they go." Darshan Singh, 44.

57. The love that the devotee has for the Master is a reflection of the love the Master radiates to him or her. Unless the Master, the Adept, chooses us and awakens us spiritually, we are unable to recognize him and to know that we are of the same color, of the same essence as he is. And so if a bond springs up between us and the Master, if we turn to the path of devotion and seek the Beloved, it is because the Beloved has walked tiptoe, and bestowed on us a secret kiss which has awakened us to life. Darshan Singh, 67.

58. The Master's spiritual power is passed mostly through the eyes, so unless we look at him lovingly how is he going to pass on his grace, his love, his charging? . . . Unless we look into the Master's eyes, unless our eyes meet, how will he transmit that charging, how will our souls become ignited, how will our hearts be changed? . . . The Master pours out his blessings through his eyes. These glances are termed lyrical glances. . . . One such glance can change the entire course of our lives. Darshan Singh, *Secret of Secrets*, 3–4.

"We bathe in his luminous eyes and become cleansed. . . . With one glance, one lyrical glance from a perfect Master, he can send our soul flying to its eternal Home, Sach Khand." Darshan Singh, 3.

59. "A devotee is in essence the true lover. One is caught up so completely in love that one knows no other reality, no other truth. In speaking of spirituality, the sages, the Mahatmas and the Sufis have dwelt on the supremacy of love. It is the secret whereby one loses oneself. One who loves, knows of nothing but the Beloved. One's mind dwells on the Beloved, remembers the Beloved, yearns for

the Beloved and has no room for anything else." Darshan Singh, *Streams of Nectar*, 70.

"By cutting us off from the desires of this world the Master frees us from the bondage of desire. The attachments and passions of centuries unnumbered are washed away by his gift of love. All desires come to an end, giving place to a single desire—union with the Beloved." Darshan Singh, 284.

"One who is maddened by the thought of the elusive Beloved cannot rest until one has sought her within." Darshan Singh, 86.

60. Love is an ordeal, and the path of love is one of anguish and tears. Once we have glimpsed the ineffable divine Beloved, nothing on this earth can satisfy us. Having enticed us and enraptured us, the Beloved then disappears. We pine and yearn for him, but he is nowhere to be found. Anyone who reads the writings of the mystics will notice how much they touch upon the torments which the seeker undergoes in his quest for the divine Spouse. Paradoxically, though the path is said to lead to the highest bliss, it is paved with the anguish of separation and tears. Darshan Singh, 171.

61. "And how different is this Light born of spiritual realization from the light of the intellect. Intellectual knowledge leads us into more and more specialization, into an ever greater awareness of what separates one object from another, rather than towards realization of the life impulse which unites them." Darshan Singh, 85.

"The true seeker has only a single preoccupation. He or she does not dissipate his or her energies in different directions. One proceeds unswervingly on one's quest. Having been drawn to the feet of a genuine Adept, one surrenders the ego completely." Darshan Singh, 55.

62. If we want to overcome all the problems of the world, there is only one remedy: to lose all awareness of oneself. And this becomes possible only through the grace of a perfect Master. By giving his own divine impulse he brings us the awareness of something beyond ourselves, and we are lost in that intoxication. Once we are in such a condition, all the troubles and all the problems of this world can pass over us without affecting us in any way. There is thus only one answer to the problem of suffering in this world: to be lost in the intoxication which makes us oblivious to suffering itself. Sufis speak of this state as Alam-e Bekhabri or Alam-e Bekhudi (Knowledge of Oblivion). But in reality it is not oblivion; it is knowledge of the highest Truth. Darshan Singh, 218.

"The wines of this world intoxicate us for an hour or two, or perhaps for a night, but then the effect wears off. The intoxication of the Word of God never passes away. Those who have been blessed with it are mad forever. In reality, they are not mad, but are the wisest of the wise. They know what ultimately matters. If they seem mad, it is because they are oblivious of themselves." Darshan Singh, 217–18.

63. "When we are in the presence of a saint we should focus our attention on his eyes. If we do this with full concentration, we become oblivious of ourselves. If we arrive at such a state of complete absorption, we become forgetful of the

physical world. In gazing on the Beloved we begin to identify with the Beloved, and the qualities of the Beloved begin to flow into us." Darshan Singh, 50.

64. "There is nothing quite as wondrous as gazing into the eyes of the Beloved. It is by far the quickest and easiest way to progress on the spiritual Path. It gives a boost to our spiritual practices. It cuts us free from time and space. It helps us surrender to his glorious lotus feet. And in that state, if we get one lyrical glance from him—just one—all our toils will cease; our soul will soar back Home." Darshan Singh, *Secret of Secrets*, 9.

65. "This world is false, consisting only of appearances, desire, and illusion. Its true nature remains concealed from our eyes. The perishable appears everlasting, and the physical body hides the true self." Darshan Singh, *Streams of Nectar*, 125.

66. "[The] tenth door, known as the third or single eye, [is] located between and behind the two eyebrows. This is the seat of the soul in the body. To regain the inner kingdom, we must invert our attention from the body and the world outside and focus it at the third eye. The attention, which has been directed outward into the world, must be reversed in order to enter the world within. Darshan Singh, 51.

    "[The] Power [of God], in the form of Light and Sound, can be contacted at the seat of the soul between and behind the two eyes. It acts like a magnet and draws the spirit to itself. If the soul were not covered by the rust of mind and matter it would go up in an instant." Darshan Singh, *Spiritual Awakening*, 13.

67. Darshan Singh, *Streams of Nectar*, 182.

68. Darshan Singh, 170.

69. Darshan Singh, 182.

70. "The radiant form of the Master . . . is so resplendent, so intoxicating, so enrapturing that the soul becomes lost in it. The Master, who we thought as our teacher and guide in the outer world, now is seen as the unfailing guide and friend who will stay with us on our journey Homewards. He becomes our alpha and omega." Darshan Singh, 182–83.

    "[The radiant form of the Master] is more beautiful, more resplendent than the form we know here in this physical world. He takes us under his wing and, stage by stage, he helps us to transcend not only the physical, but the astral and the causal planes. He brings us to the stage beyond these three worlds, where the soul stands fully purified, and all traces of mind and matter are left behind." Darshan Singh, 268.

71. Darshan Singh, 170.

72. Once we learn to drink the eyes of the Cupbearer, he gives us his own life impulse. With the imparting of this love glance, the seeker begins to partake of the bliss of Naam, of the intoxication of that inner Music of which all the scriptures, saints, and seers speak. We become a hearer of that unstruck and unsung Music which has been described in different ways and in different languages by those who have gone within. We become a partaker of the divine Symphony which, as Guru Nanak said, "Was, is, and shall ever be." . . . One who has once heard the magic of the divine Symphony within

is lost forever in its wonder. It is an intoxication which places the lover in perpetual communion with the Beloved. Darshan Singh, 355–56.

73. Darshan Singh, 355–56.

74. Once one has begun to taste of the joys of the spiritual world, of the bliss of Naam or the Word, the joys of this world become meaningless. . . . If we have tasted the joy and bliss of Naam, if we have found a true Beloved, it promises that we will be so lost to the pulls and attachments of this world and so detached from them, that we will pursue our spiritual goal undeterred. While living in this world and meeting all its commitments, we will, absorbed in our secret love, move steadily toward our ultimate goal. Darshan Singh, 74.

75. When the soul rises above physical consciousness and enters the astral plane, it sheds the physical body. As it proceeds further and enters the causal realm, it dispenses with the astral body. As it advances, it experiences its own increasing brilliance. When it crosses the causal plane and reaches the supracausal, it arrives at the fountain of life which the Sufis speak of as chashma-e kausar and which the Sikh scriptures refer to as Amritsar. On tasting its waters, it finally sheds its next covering, that of its causal body. It is purified of matter, mind and illusion. Mystics compare its brilliance to that of a dozen suns. On attaining this stage, the soul realizes its own innate divinity and cries out, "I am that." Darshan Singh, 168.

It has been said that the only veil between man and God is the individual's personal will or ego. The ego alone prevents the soul merging back into the Oversoul. This veil is the most subtle veil, it is the most delicate veil. Yet it is the hardest possible veil to penetrate. But still, with the Master's mercy and grace, this veil through which we cannot see Reality, in time becomes thinner and thinner, more and more sublime, until finally it becomes transparent. Through that veil God Himself is waiting, and through that veil we begin to get a glimpse of Him. But not until that veil vanishes altogether can we be reunited with Him. So it is the ego which is the cause of our separation and makes it difficult to transcend the physical body and soar into the Beyond, to wing our way back to the source of all life. We have to remove all traces of the ego, because the ego is the last curtain—the last barrier—between the lover and the Beloved. The lover is on one side of the curtain, and the Beloved on the other. This veil starts by appearing to be as opaque and impenetrable as the Himalayas. But eventually, with patience and perseverance, it becomes so clear that we can see through to the other side. It becomes totally transparent when we submit fully to the sweet will of the Master and carry out his behests with patience and perseverance. The demon ego having been vanquished, the hurdles on the path surmounted, there we find the glorious resplendent Master ready to draw us through the veil. When the veil vanishes, all illusion vanishes; we see the drop of the Ocean of All-consciousness merging back into the Ocean—the lover becomes one with the Beloved. There is no more separation, no difference between the two. Darshan Singh, *Secret of Secrets*, 71–72.

When speaking of the higher realms of spirituality, the great Sufis and the Masters of Sant Mat reveal an amazing similarity. If there is any difference, it is of terminology, not substance. In the literature of Sant Mat, the physical, astral, and causal planes are referred to as Pind, And, and Brahmand, and in Sufism as Kasif or Madi, Latif, and Latif-ul-Latif. The Sufis tell us that Baang-e Asmani (Word) brought the different regions into creation, and in like fashion Indian mystics declare that Naad brought the various realms into existence. For the Sufis, a spiritual Adept is never born, he only manifests; similarly, in the tradition of Sant Mat a Satguru is above birth and death. According to Kabir Sahib and Guru Nanak, the supreme challenge before the seeker is that of conquering his manas (mind), and according to the Sufis it is that of mastering nafs (mind). Both insist that the mind is not easy to subdue, and is fully mastered only when we go beyond the causal region, or beyond Brahmand or Alam-e-Jabrut. Just as the soul is the child of Satnaam (the Supreme Being), mind is the child of the lord of the causal region. On the physical plane we work through the *Pindi-Man* or *Nafs-e-Amara*, i.e., the physical mind. On the astral plane we work through the *Andi-Man* or *Nafs-e-Lavama* (the astral mind), and on the causal plane we work through the *Brahmandi-Man* or *Nafs-e-Mutmaena* (causal mind). The mind's power thus spreads from the physical to the causal region, and it is only when we reach the region beyond the causal that we are finally liberated from mind. In the literature of Sant Mat we speak of the need to move from Sahansdal Kanwal through Trikuti to Daswan Dwar. It is when the soul reaches Mansarovar or Amritsar, the pool or lake of Nectar, called Chashma-e-[Ab-e-H]ayat, the Fountain of the Elixir of Life, by the Sufis, that the soul is purified of all blemishes and washed clean of impurities. It at last becomes purified. It is at this point, after the soul recognizes that it is of the same essence as of God that it cries out "Sohang" or "I am that!" The Sufis use the term "Anahoo" or "I am Thou," to describe the same experience . . . of the pilgrim soul as it traverses Par Brahm, Bhanwar Gupha, or Alam-e-Hoot-ul-Hoot." Darshan Singh, *Streams of Nectar*, 214–15.

76. "This is the state which we arrive at when we have transcended the physical, the astral, and the causal. The Master now becomes Shabd Swaroop or Word-embodied. He first absorbs us in himself so that we become indivisible from him." Darshan Singh, 268.

77. "Turn within and concentrate on the Light and the Music which are within you. They are the outer vestment of the divine beloved. If you can forget everything else and dwell on these, you can begin to move inward and upward and arrive at the true Home of your Beloved." Darshan Singh, 43.

"Then [the Master] takes us up still higher until we are face to face with the Creator. At this stage there is neither one nor two nor three. The soul, the Master, and the Creator are all one and there is no awareness of separate identities. It is a state beyond description." Darshan Singh, 268.

"In this world which is bound by the limitations of time, he gives us the boon of eternal life." Darshan Singh, 57.

As [the soul] moves toward the ultimate stage, it comes face to face with the Creator in the realms referred to in the scriptures as the True Home or Sach Khand. This region is purely spiritual and is not subject to the limitations of time. The prodigal son returns Home. The soul becomes a conscious co-worker of the divine plan. The journey from our limited physical condition to our True Home may be described in linear terms, much as one describes a journey from a valley to the top of a mountain. But there are no terms for describing what follows: the progressive merging of the soul with its Creator. There are no earthly terms which may provide an analogy, a parallel. When complete union is achieved, there is no subject or object, no beholder or beholden, no lover or Beloved. They have become one. All that can be said is that the sunbeam has merged in the sun, the drop in the ocean. This is the ultimate goal of human life. Darshan Singh, *Wonders of Inner Space*, 12.

"When we have our first taste of divine love, it brings a joy that is beyond conception. Soul meets Oversoul; love meets its Source. What we experience is a bliss with which nothing from the world of time and space can compare. The soul at last finds its true Mate, its divine and eternal Beloved." Darshan Singh, *Streams of Nectar*, 171.

"This state of love is one of complete abandonment in the Beloved. We are no longer aware of our own self." Darshan Singh, 186.

The Roots of Urdu Poetry

78. Chatterji, *Indo-Aryan and Hindi*, 174–77; Masica, *Indo-Aryan Languages*, 27–28, 53–54; Beg, *Urdu Grammar*, 1–2.
79. Masica, *Indo-Aryan Languages*, 28.
80. Farooqi, *Language of Whose Camp?*; Ikram, *Muslim Civilization in India*, 35. The names Hindvi, Hindi, and Hindui have also been used over the centuries to refer to the language of India as a whole or to different North Indian dialects, such as Braj Bhasha and Awadhi—and even in earlier Urdu writing to Urdu itself. Masica, *Indo-Aryan Languages*, 29; Dalmia, *Nationalization of Hindu Traditions*, 152; Ahmed, *Intellectual History of Islam in India*, 91. What today is known as Modern Standard Hindi was cultivated as a separate language from Urdu during the first half of the nineteenth century by the British colonialists, missionaries, and Hindu schoolbook writers, and from the mid-nineteenth century until independence in 1947 by nationalistic Hindu elites concentrated in Benares and Allahabad. Dalmia, *Nationalization of Hindu Traditions*, 218.
81. Ikram, *Muslim Civilization in India*, 116, 117; Farooqi, *Language of Whose Camp?*; Faruqi, *Early Urdu Literary Culture*, 70.
82. Masica, *Indo-Aryan Languages*, 466nn8–9; Faruqi, "Urdu Literary Culture: The Syncretic Tradition," 2; Faruqi, *Early Urdu Literary Culture*, 23–24, 25; Faruqi, "Name and Nature of a Language," 7. Originally a Turkish word meaning "military encampment," *urdū* had by Mughal times come to refer to "the royal court." Faruqi, "Syncretic Tradition," 2.
83. Masica, *Indo-Aryan Languages*, 48, 50; Farooqi, *Language of Whose Camp?*; Ikram, *Muslim Civilization in India*, 37, 40, 42.
84. Farooqi, *Language of Whose Camp?*.
85. Masica, *Indo-Aryan Languages*, 28.

86. Faruqi, *Early Urdu Literary Culture*, 113; Masica, *Indo-Aryan Languages*, 57. Masica writes as follows: "The closest [language or dialect that] stands in direct *linguistic* antecedence to Modern Standard Hindi . . . is perhaps the mixed dialect of the Nirguṇa poets sometimes called *sādhū bhāṣā* which at least incorporates some elements of Khari Boli. . . . The Sant or Nirguṇa tradition of mystical poets . . . beginning with Kabir, has tended . . . to prefer a fluid mixed dialect with a strong Khari Boli element favoring widest possible intelligibility." Masica, 54, 57.

87. Farooqi, *Language of Whose Camp?*.

88. Farooqi; Faruqi, *Early Urdu Literary Culture*, 72.

89. Faruqi, *Early Urdu Literary Culture*, 111.

90. Ikram, *Muslim Civilization in India*, 80, 83; Ahmed, *Intellectual History of Islam in India*, 98–99; Faruqi, *Early Urdu Literary Culture*, 149.

91. Farooqui, *Comprehensive History of Medieval India*, 263–64; Ikram, *Muslim Civilization in India*, 204.

92. Faruqi, *Early Urdu Literary Culture*, 138–39.

93. Ikram, *Muslim Civilization in India*, 244; Farooqi, *Language of Whose Camp?*.

94. Farooqi.

95. Schimmel, *Classical Urdu Literature*, 167; Mir, *Zikr-i Mir*, 3.

96. Ikram, *Muslim Civilization in India*, 245; Ahmed, *Intellectual History of Islam in India*, 103, 104.

97. Darshan Singh, *Love at Every Step*, 5.

98. Darshan Singh, "My Concept of Poetry," in *Love at Every Step*, 41–2.

99. Lane, *Arabic-English Lexicon*, bk. I, pt. 6, s.v. "ġhazal," 2255; Platts, *Dictionary of Urdū, Classical Hindī, and English*, s.v. "ġhazal," 771.

100. Ġhālib, *Dīvān-e Ġhālib*, ed. Ḳhān, 19 (verses 1–2, 4 of ghazal); *Dīvān-e Ġhālib, Kāmil*, ed. Reẓā, 397–98.

101. Darshan Singh, *Matā'-e Nūr* (Urdu), 156 (first three verses of ghazal 48), *Matā'-e Nūr* (Hindi), 170.

102. Kiernan, *Poems by Faiz*, 32.

103. Kiernan, 22.

The Ghazal—Themes

104. Russell, "In Pursuit of the Urdu Ghazal," 121–22.

105. Kiernan, *Poems by Faiz*, 32.

106. Kiernan, 33.

107. Kiernan, 33.

108. Kiernan, 36.

109. Kiernan, 33.

110. Kiernan, 34.

111. Russell, "In Pursuit of the Urdu Ghazal," 113–14, 117.

112. Pritchett, "Convention in the Classical Urdu Ghazal: The Case of Mir," 60–77.

113. Kiernan, *Poems by Faiz*, 35.

114. Kiernan, 36.

115. The pain of love, of separation, is beyond all others and is unlike all others. In the case of other types of pain, time is said to be a healer. But if our love is true, the pain of separation knows no abatement; it only knows intensification. Yet, those who have this malady will not give it up for anything. Ask them if they would like to change it for any of the gifts or joys of this world. It is true, it is pain, but it is a pain which is a form of bliss, a kind of blessing. Compared to it, all other goods seem meaningless. One may seem to suffer, to be in agony on account of separation, but remembrance itself is a form of union, and one would not exchange it for anything else. This remembrance is like the termite which hollows out from within us, all the love and ephemeral attachments of this world. Those who have it are progressively purified of their spiritual weaknesses. Even when we seem to make no progress, continued remembrance is itself a form of progress, for slowly, steadily, and inexorably it is preparing the way for everlasting union. Darshan Singh, *Streams of Nectar*, 153.

The Lyric Voice of Darshan's Poetry

116. Pritchett, "Convention in the Classical Urdu Ghazal," 60–61.

117. Darshan Singh, *Love at Every Step*, 82.

118. Darshan Singh, *Love Has Only a Beginning*, 122.

119. Darshan Singh, "My Concept of Poetry," in *Love at Every Step*, 31.

Gender in the Ghazal

120. Darshan Singh, *Poetic Symposium*, side 1.

Mystical Symbols Frequently Encountered in Darshan's Poetry

121. Qureshi, "Female Agency and Patrilineal Constraints: Situating Courtesans in Twentieth-Century India," 312, 318.

122. Qureshi, 322.

123. Kirpal Singh, "What Is True Darshan?," 12–16; Kirpal Singh, *Spiritual Elixir* 1:42, 62–64, 93. See also endnotes 58, 63, and 64 for Sant Darshan Singh's discussion of *darshan*.

124. Schimmel, *My Soul Is a Woman: The Feminine in Islam*, 18.

Selected Poetry – *Matā'-e Nūr* – Treasure House of Light

125. Sant Darshan Singh used the following ironic verse of the Persian poet Moḥammad Ḥosein Nazīrī Nīshāpūrī (c. 1560–1612-1614), which contains the word *matā'* (wealth, treasure, treasure house), as the epigraph to *Matā'-e Nūr*:

matā'-e deir agar dārīm bar mā rad makon zāhed
beh 'azm-e ka'beh mī-raftīm rāh-e kārevān gom shod

Do not condemn me, devout one, for these treasures I've brought from the temple!
I left bent on reaching the Ka'ba but my caravan went astray.

The verse implies that, for seekers after truth, there is no real difference between the Ka'ba, the holiest shrine in Islam, and a Hindu temple—that is, the teachings of all religions are equally valuable and worthy of reverence because "all religions point to a single reality underlying existence" (Darshan Singh, *Love at Every Step*, 29), and the meditative practices of their founders "lead to the transcendent experience at the heart of every religion" (Rajinder Singh, "Meditation – Bringing Depth and Richness to Our Lives," *South Asian Times: Collector's Edition* (Spring 2009): 12).

"[Sant Kirpal Singh] was often asked how we can establish peace in the world. He said if kings rise above kingdoms, and priests rise above isms, there would be lasting peace. He did not teach any ism; he presented religion as a science. . . . All religions command us to love our neighbors – even our enemies. Only then can we fully understand the meaning of the Fatherhood of God and the brotherhood of man. We are all brothers and sisters in God, so we should love each other irrespective of our religion, color, caste or creed." Darshan Singh, *Sant Mat: The Teachings of the Masters*, 7–8.

> Each explorer of spirituality in his or her own time and clime discovered that there is a higher power that lies behind all creation and is also within us. . . . Within us is a divine spirit from which our intelligence and wisdom is derived. They also discovered that that part of us can exist without the physical body. They realized there is a controlling power in the universe that brought all physical matter into being. What is remarkable is that their findings cross all times of human history. . . . This group of scientists has been recognized as the saints, mystics, prophets, philosophers, and Masters of all religions and faiths. When they explored the science of spirituality they discovered the same truths. Rajinder Singh, *Silken Thread of the Divine*, 27.

Commentary on the Poems

126. Nurbakhsh, *Traditions of the Prophet*, 12; Derin, "From Rābi'a to Ibn al-Fāriḍ," 222.

127. Nurbakhsh, *Traditions of the Prophet*, 25.

128. Rūmī, *Maśnavī*, ed. Sobḥānī, bk. I, 114, lines 2654–56 (from "Dar nehādan-e 'arab bar eltemās-e delbar-e ḵhw̱īsh va sowgand ḵhordan keh darīn taslīm marā ḥīlatī o emteḥānī nīst" (How the Arab Set His Heart on Complying with His Beloved's Request and Swore That His Submission to Her Was Devoid of Trickery or Trial)).

129. Nicholson, *Selected Poems from the Dīvāni Shamsi Tabrīz*, 72 (eleventh verse in the ghazal beginning "man ān rūz būdam keh asmā nabūd"). Nicholson's book was originally published in 1898, and this ghazal does not appear in Forūzānfar's critical editions of the *Kulliyāt-e Dīvān-e Shams-e Tabrīzī*, published from 1957 to 1967.

130. Rūmī, *Kulliyāt-e Dīvān-e Shams*, ed. Forūzānfar, 950 (eighth verse in ghazal 2553, beginning "kojā shod 'ahd o peimānī keh mī-kardī namī-gū'ī").

131. Momin, *Dīvān-e Momin*, ed. Ḥasan, 141 (first verse of the ghazal beginning "shab tum jo bazm-e ġhair meṅ ānkheṅ churā ga'e").

132. Iqbāl, *Kulliyāt-e Iqbāl: Urdū*, ed. Faiṣal, *Bāl-e Jibrīl* (Gabriel's Wing), pt. 1, 249 (from penultimate verse of ghazal 14, beginning "apnī jaulāṅgāh zer-e āsmāṅ samjhā t'hā maiṅ").

133. Darshan Singh, *Wonders of Inner Space*, 175–76.

134. Darshan Singh, 179–80.

135 Darshan Singh, *Streams of Nectar*, 170.

136 Darshan Singh, *Streams of Nectar*, 207–8.

137. Darshan Singh, "True Freedom," 2.

138. Darshan Singh, "The Soul's True Home," 3.

139. Darshan Singh, *Streams of Nectar*, 214–15.

140. Darshan Singh, *Poetic Symposium*, side 1.

141. Darshan Singh, *Talāsh-e Nūr*, 87.

142. Darshan Singh, *Streams of Nectar*, 245.

143. Darshan Singh, *Wonders of Inner Space*, 12.

144. 'A<u>tt</u>ār, *Dīvān-e 'A<u>tt</u>ār-e Nīshābūrī*, 561 (first verse of ghazal 424); 'A<u>tt</u>ār, *Dīvān-e Qaṣā'ed va Tarjī'āt va Ġhazalīyāt*, 473 (first verse of ghazal 660).

145. Mīr, *Kulliyāt-e Mīr, Dīvān-e Avval*, 38.

146. Russell, *Three Mughal Poets*, 30–33, 35–36; Mir, *Zikr-i Mir*, 83–85.

147. Russell, *Three Mughal Poets*, 35; Mīr, *Zikr-i Mir*, 93–94.

148. Cahill, *Paradise Rediscovered*, vol. 2, 885; Elliot, *The History of India*, vol. 8, 430; *Vāzheh-nāmeh-ye Mo'īn* and *Loġhat-nāmeh-ye Dehḳhodā*, s.v. "Jām-e Jam," accessed October 22, 2017, http://vajje.com/search/index?query=جام+جم, archived at https://perma.cc/62AR-TKF3.

149. Ġhālib, *Dīvān-e Ġhālib*, ed. Ḳhān, 39 (first verse of the ghazal); *Dīvān-e Ghālib, Kāmil*, ed. Reẓā, 355.

150. Ġhālib, *Dīvān-e Ġhālib*, ed. Ḳhān, 90 (from the ghazal beginning "sab kahāṅ kuchh lālah o gul meṅ numāyāṅ ho ga'īṅ"); *Dīvān-e Ghālib, Kāmil*, ed. Reẓā, 426.

151. Iqbāl, *Kulliyāt-e Iqbāl: Urdū, Bāl-e Jibrīl*, pt.1, 246 (verse 4 of ghazal 10, beginning "matā'-e be-bahā hai dard o soz-e ārzūmandī!").

152. Iqbāl, *Bāl-e Jibrīl*, pt. 2, 279 (verse 2 of ghazal 33, beginning "ḳhirad-mandoṅ se kyā pūchhūṅ kĕh merī ibtidā kyā hai").

153. Kabir, *Kabīr Vachanāvalī*, 132. For variants of this verse, see Kabīr, *Mahābījak*, 981 (sākhī: sec. 8 – "Bhīkh ko Aṅg," verse 1); Kabīr, *Kabīr Grant'hāvalī*, ed. Pārasnāt'h Tiwārī, 241 (sākhī: sec. 32 – "Besās kau Aṅg," verse 16); Kabīr, *Kabīr-Vāṇī*, ed. Vaudeville, 38 (sākhī [KG1]: sec. 35 – "Besās kau Aṅg," verse 15).

154. Kabīr, *Mahābījak*, 982 (sākhī: sec. 8 – "Bhīkh ko Aṅg," verse 11).

155. Darshan Singh, *Spiritual Awakening*, 6.

156. Darshan Singh, 7.

157. Ġhālib, *Dīvān-e Ġhālib*, ed. Ḳhān, 9 (from the ghazal beginning "sitā'ish-gar hai zāhid is qadar jis bāġh-e riẓvāṅ kā"); *Dīvān-e Ghālib, Kāmil*, ed. Reẓā, 369.

158. *Shabdārt'h Srī Gurū Grant'h Sāhib Jī*, ed. Shromaṇī Gurduārā Prabaṅdhak Committee, vol. 2, Rāg Gūjrī kī Vār, M5, p. 518, salok 2, verse 1, line 4.

159. *Shabdārt'h Srī Gurū Grant'h Sāhib Jī*, vol. 3, Rāg Mārū, M5, p. 1007, shabad 31, verse 4, line 1.

160. All references to the Hindi version of *Matā'-e Nūr* are to the 2016 edition unless otherwise noted.

161. Kirpal Singh, *Morning Talks*, 182.

162. Rūmī, *Kulliyāt-e Dīvān-e Shams*, 304 (second verse from ghazal 730, beginning "īnak ān morġhān keh īshān beiẓeh'hā zarīn konand").

163. Rūmī, *Kulliyāt-e Dīvān-e Shams*, 665 (verses 1, 2, 6 of ghazal 1767, beginning "to cheh dānī keh mā cheh morġhānīm").

164. Darshan Singh, *Matā'-e Nūr* (Urdu), 137n1. This note was not included in the Hindi edition of *Matā'-e Nūr*.

165. Ġhālib, *Dīvān-e Ġhālib*, ed. Ḵhān, 19 (from the ghazal beginning "yĕh nah t'hī hamārī qismat kĕh viṣāl-e yār hotā"); *Dīvān-e Ghālib, Kāmil*, ed. Reẓā, 398.

166. Iqbāl, *Kulliyāt-e Iqbāl: Urdū, Bāng-e Darā* (Call of the Bell), pt. 3 ("from 1908 . . . ."), 131 (verse 44 of the *naẕm* (poem not in ghazal form) "Shikwah" (Complaint), beginning "kyoṅ ziyāṅkār banūṅ sūd farāmosh rahūṅ?").

167. Nurbakhsh, *Traditions of the Prophet*, 77.

168. *Shabdārt'h Srī Gurū Grant'h Sāhib Jī*, vol. 2, Rāg Gauṛī, Bhagat Ravidās, p. 345, shabad 2, verse 1, lines 1–2; rĕhā'u 1, lines 1–2; verse 2, line 1; verse 3, line 2.

169. Persian verse, sometimes attributed to Jalālu'ddīn Rūmī, but source unknown.

170. Darshan Singh, *Streams of Nectar*, 281–82.

171. *Shabdārt'h Srī Gurū Grant'h Sāhib Jī*, vol. 2, Rāg Sorat'hi, M3, p. 601, shabad 4, verse 1, line 2.

172. For the tippler's code of conduct, see Darshan Singh, *Spiritual Awakening*, 181.

173.
> Those who are familiar with mystic love . . . know that a lover must undergo many trials. Without a grumble they accept them as the normal lot of a lover. While many people are apprehensive of the trials and turmoils, the cruelties and tyrannies which the Beloved inflicts, real lovers revel in being caught in the coils of the Beloved's tresses. Those who have experienced being caught in love know that any attempt to shake off those coils ends in failure. A true lover relishes being a captive of the Beloved's curls and begins enjoying it. It becomes his way of life to experience ecstasy in his seeming captivity, and he surrenders to it. . . . A true lover is moved by one thought: how to reach the Beloved, how to woo the Beloved. The lover is prepared to pay any price for his Beloved. Darshan Singh, *Spiritual Awakening*, 229–30.

174. Rūmī, *Maśnavī*, bk. 3, 493, line 4393 (from Molāqāt-e ān 'āsheq bā Ṣadr-e Jahān (The Lover's Meeting with Ṣadr-e Jahān)).

175. This verse was the ninth verse in one of Darshan's earliest poems, a ghazal that he composed when he was seventeen at the prompting of his father, who gave him the first hemistich on which the rest of the poem was based. Darshan composed the poem for Hazur Baba Sawan Singh's birthday celebration in July 1938, and this verse was among those that elicited the greatest appreciation from Hazur. However, when the poem was published in *Talāsh-e Nūr* with the title "Tajalliyāt" (Resplendent Visions), this verse along with several others was omitted. This particular verse of Darshan's seems to be in direct response to a verse of Amir Khusro's:

nāḳhodā dar keshtī-ye mā gar nabāshad gū mabāsh
mā ḳhodā dārīm mārā nāḳhodā kār nīst

There is no captain on our ship? Silence! Why should it matter?
We have the Lord—what need have we for a captain?

Both Darshan's Urdu and Khusro's Persian verse contain a play on words between *ḳhudā* (Persian *ḳhodā*), *nā-ḳhudā*, and *nāḳhudā* (see 1:6 note).

Khusro's verse comes from another very famous ghazal that did not appear in any of the divans consulted (see endnote 250). The ghazal reads as follows:

kāfer-e 'eshqam mosalmānī marā dar kār nīst
har rag-e man tār gashteh ḥājat-e zonnār nīst

mā amīrān rā tamāshā-ye chaman dar kār nīst
dāġh'hā-ye sineh-ye mā kamtar az golzār nīst

'āsheqān rā rūz-e maḥshar bā qeyāmat kār nīst
kār-e 'āsheq joz tamāshā-ye jamāl-e yār nīst

az sar-e bālīn-e man bar ḳhīz ei nādān ṯabīb
dard-mand-e 'eshq rā dārū be-joz dīdār nīst

shād bāsh ei del keh fardā bar sar-e bāzār-e 'eshq
mozhdeh-ye qatl ast garcheh va'deh-ye dīdār nīst

nāḳhodā dar keshtī-ye mā gar nabāshad gū mabāsh
mā ḳhodā dārīm mārā nāḳhodā kār nīst

ḳhalq mī-gūyad keh Ḳhusrow bot parastī mī-konad
ārī ārī mī-konam bā ḳhalq o 'ālam kār nīst

Amīr Ḳhusrow, "Ġhazal-e Fārsī," *Paiġhām-e Ḥaq*, No. 6 (Jan.–Feb. 1999): 29.

I am an infidel for love, what have I to do with Islam?
Now with every vein a thread, what use have I for the sacred thread?

What need have noble souls like us for the garden's spectacle?
Are the wounds within my heart less splendorous than a garden!

No lover is concerned about the distress of Judgment Day;
A lover's only care is to behold the beloved's splendor.

Foolish physician, why are you here? Leave my bedside at once!
Nothing but the beloved's glance can cure those sick with love.

Rejoice at the happy news, my heart! She's ordered that tomorrow
You'll be slain in love's bazaar—with no promise you'll get her glance.

There is no captain on our ship? Silence! Why should it matter?
We have God—what business have we with a captain!

People say that Khusro has turned idolater;
Indeed, I have! But what have I to do with them or the world!

176. Darshan Singh, *Love Has Only a Beginning*, 119–21.

177. Kirpal Singh, *The Night Is a Jungle*, 283–86; Macauliffe, *The Sikh Religion*, vol. 2, 276–84.

178. Macauliffe, *The Sikh Religion*, vol. 1, 120.

179. Guru Nānak, verse from a janamsākhī, quoted in Waryām Singh, "Jau sukh kau chāhai sadā saran rām kī leh" (If You Yearn for Eternal Peace, Seek the Sanctuary of the Lord), *Ātam Mārg* (June 2009): 25.

180. Darshan Singh, *Spiritual Awakening*, 78–79.

181. Darshan Singh, 79.

182. Sant Darshan states that "the Master . . . happily accepts all that goes with the tasks [of making the disciple's soul fit for union with God] and takes upon himself the burden of vicarious suffering." Darshan Singh, *Streams of Nectar*, 297–98. Sant Kirpal Singh has written, "Out of their abundance of sympathy, love and kindness the Saints at times take upon their own shoulders some Karmic sufferings of their disciples through the law of sympathy." Kirpal Singh, *Man! Know Thyself*, 18.

183. Jigar, *Kulliyāt-e Jigar, Lama'āt-e Ṯūr* (Flashes from Sinai), 411 (from the nazm beginning "sāqī kī har nigāh pĕh bal khā ke pī gayā"), line 7.

184. Swāmi Shiv Dayāl Siṅgh, *Sār Bachan Poetry*, bachan 23, shabd 1 (quoted in Puri, *Radha Soami Teachings*, 207–8 (beginning "kāl jāl se ko'ī na bāchā / nij ghar apne ko'ī na āyā").

185. Kirpal Singh, *A Great Saint: Baba Jaimal Singh*, 135.

186. Rūmī, *Maśnavī*, bk. 1, 50 (from "Qeṣṣeh-ye makr-e ḵhargūsh" (The Story of the Hare's Strategem)), line 1066.

187. Rūmī, *Maśnavī*, bk. 4, 661 (from "Nemūdan-e Jebra'īl – 'alaihi's-salām – ḵhwod rā beh Muṣṯafá – ṣallá'llâhu 'alaihi wa sallama – beh ṣūrat-e ḵhwīsh va az haftṣad par-e ū chūn yek par ẕāher shod ofoq rā begereft va āftāb maḥjūb shod bā hameh-ye sho'ā'ash (How Gabriel – on Whom Be Peace – Showed Himself to Mustafa – May God Bless and Save Him – in His Own Form; and How, When One of His Seven Hundred Wings Became Visible, It Covered the Entire Horizon, and the Sun with All Its Radiance Was Veiled Over)), line 3804.

188. Sa'dī, *Būstān-e Sa'dī*, in *Kulliyāt-e Sa'dī*, ed. Forūġhī, 219 (from "Setāyesh-e Peiġhambar"), line 16.

189. Nicholson, *The Mathnawī of Jalálu'ddīn Rumī* 7:25, 27, 54, 182; 8:53–54.

190. Faiẓ, *Nusḵhah'hā-e Vafā*, 173 (from *Dast-e Ṣabā* (Hand of the Breeze)), first verse of the ghazal.

191. Darshan Singh, *Love Has Only a Beginning*, 119–21.

192. Darshan Singh, *Matā'-e Nūr* (Hindi), 140 (poem 29, verse 6).

193. Iqbāl, *Kulliyāt-e Iqbāl: Urdū, Bāng-e Darā*, pt. 3 ("from 1908 . . . ."), 213 (from the nazm "Ṯulū'-e Islām" (Rise of Islam)), stanza 5, verse 2.

194. Iqbal, *Secrets of the Self*, trans. Nicholson, 71.

195. Iqbāl, *Asrār-e Ḳhwodī* (*Secrets of the Self*), 44–46 (from "Marhaleh-ye sevvom nayābat-e elâhī" (Stage Three: Divine Vicegerency)), verses 4, 5, 10, 16, 17–18, 19, 23.

196. Iqbal, *Secrets of the Self*, trans. Nicholson, 71–74, lines 899, 902, 910–11, 924–929, 937–38.

197. While this widely quoted Persian verse is sometimes attributed to Hafez Shirazi, it did not appear in any of the Divans of Hafez (including recent critical editions) that were consulted. Akbar Allahabadi has used it as the final couplet of his nazm beginning "Ik Miss Sīmīṅ Badan se Kar Liyā London meṅ 'Aqab." Akbar, *Kulliyāt-e Akbar Allâhābādī*, 163–64.

198. Mīr, *Kulliyāt-e Mīr, Dīvān-e Avval*, 154 (from the ghazal beginning "dekh to dil kĕh jāṅ se uṭ'htā hai").

199. Jigar, *Kulliyāt-e Jigar*, from *Shu'lah-e Ṯūr* (Flames of Sinai), 210 (from the ghazal beginning "ab to yĕh bhī nahīṅ rahā iḥsās"), line 5.

200. "When you leave the body [in meditation] you will begin to understand how all this is going on under the Divine Will. The man who becomes a conscious co-worker of the Divine Plan never says I am doing this or that, he says it is His Will that is being done. 'Thy Will be done on earth, as it is in Heaven.' The man who learns to die, to leave the body at will, gets everlasting life, never to return." Kirpal Singh, *Morning Talks*, 81.

201. Mīr, *Kulliyāt-e Mīr, Dīvān-e Avval*, 34 (from the ghazal beginning "bār'hā gor-e dil jhankā lāyā").

202. Nasr, "Existence (*Wujud*) and Quiddity (*Mahiyyah*)," *Iqbal Review*: 30–31 (Oct. 1989–Apr. 1990): 150, 158–59, 163–65; Bāqir, *Bayān-e Ġhālib: Sharḥ-e Dīvān-e Ġhālib*, 246 (commenting on Ghalib's verse "ġharrah-e auj-e binā-e ʿālam-e imkāṅ nah ho / is bulandī ke naṣībon meṅ hai pastī ek din").

203. Gonḍvī, *Kulliyāt-e Aṣġhar*, from *Sarūd-e Zindagī*, 100 (sixth verse of ghazal entitled "har bun-e mū se mĕre us ne pukārā mujh ko" and beginning "yĕh jahān-e mah o anjum hai tamāshā mujh ko").

204. Akbar, *Kulliyāt-e Akbar Allâhābādī*, 76 (fourth verse of the nazm beginning "jo zāhidoṅ kī ṯaraf se terī nigāh-e futāṅ phirī nahīṅ hai").

205. Sāḥir, *Kulliyāt-e Sāḥir*, 84 (first verse of the nazm entitled "Fan-kār" (Artist)).

206. Darshan Singh, *Secret of Secrets*, 67.

207. Darshan Singh, *Love at Every Step*, 85.

208. *Shabdārt'h Srī Gurū Grant'h Sāhib Jī*, vol. 1, Sirī Rāg, M5, p. 79, chhant 2, verse 3, line 5.

209. Surindar Singh Kohli, *Dictionary of Guru Granth Sahib*, 81, 93, 149; Rabinder Singh Bhamra, *Sikhism and Spirituality*, sec. 9, "Mind," 52–53; Darshan Singh, *Secret of Secrets*, 210.

210. Ṣā'eb Tabrīzī, *Dīvān-e Ash'ār*, ghazal 6864 (sixth verse of the ghazal beginning "agarcheh hast beh ẕāher ḳharāb darvīshī").

211. Sa'dī, *Būstān-e Sa'dī*, in *Kulliyāt-e Sa'dī*, ed. Forūġhī, 473 (from *qaṣīdeh* "Dar Pand o Mow'eẕeh," beginning "ei keh panjā raft o dar ḳhwābī"), line 12.

212. Gopal Singh, *Guru Nanak*, 70.

213. This verse is sometimes attributed to Jalalu'ddin Rumi (see, e.g., Chaddha's commentary in *Matā'-e Nūr* (Hindi) at 181). However, the verse does not appear in the critical editions of Rumi's *Maśnavī* or *Kulliyāt-e Dīvān-e Shams* that we consulted.

214. Darshan Singh, *Talāsh-e Nūr*, 129.

215. Schimmel, *Mystical Dimensions of Islam*, 66, 68–69; Mojaddedi, "Ḥallāj, Abu'l-Mog̲īt̲ Ḥosayn," in *Encyclopaedia Iranica* (2003), 11:589–92.

216. Darshan Singh, *Talāsh-e Nūr*, 139.

217. Darshan Singh, *Spiritual Awakening*, 120–21.

218. Darshan Singh, *Wonders of Inner Space*, 97–98.

219. Darshan Singh, *Matā'-e Nūr* (Hindi), 150 (poem 35, verse 4). See also Darshan Singh, *Love Has Only a Beginning*, 76–77, 138–39.

220. Ġhālib, *Dīvān-e Ġhālib*, ed. Ḳhān, 130 (from the ghazal beginning "ko'ī ummīd bar nahīṅ ātī"); Ġhālib, *Dīvān-e Ghālib, Kāmil*, ed. Reẓā, 400–01.

221. Mata Harbhajan Kaur and Sant Rajinder Singh, private conversation with translator Barry Lerner, March 11, 1990, Chicago, IL.

222. Darshan Singh, photocopy of handwritten unpublished changes to ghazal beginning "tujhe kyā ḳhabar mere ham-safar," on file with translator Barry Lerner.

223. Darshan Singh, unpublished changes to ghazal.

224. Darshan Singh, unpublished changes to ghazal.

225. *Shabdārt'h Srī Gurū Grant'h Sāhib Jī*, vol. 3, Rāg Rāmkalī Anaṅd, M3, p. 921, verse 33, line 1; 922, verse 36, line 1.

226. Iqbāl, *Kulliyāt-e Iqbāl: Fārsī, Payām-e Mashreq* (Message of the East), 210 (from "Lāleh-ye T̲ūr (Tulip of Sinai)," verse 46).

227. *Shabdārt'h Srī Gurū Grant'h Sāhib Jī*, vol. 4, Salok, Bhagat Kabīr, p. 1367, verse 55, lines 1–2. For variations of this verse, see Kabīr, *Kabīr Grant'hāvalī*, 207 (sākhī: sec. 19 – "Jīvat Mrit kau Aṅg," verse 10); *Kabīr-Vāṇī*, ed. Vaudeville, 41 (sākhī [KG1]: sec. 41 – "Jīvan Mritak kau Aṅg," verse 2); *Kabīr-Vāṇī Saṅgrah*, ed. Tiwārī, 176 (verse 72).

228. Gopal Singh, *Guru Nanak*, 15–16.

229. Laliwala, *Islamic Philosophy of Religion*, 91–92; Sultan Bahoo, *Risala Roohi Sharif*, trans. Qadri, 221–22.

230. *Ferozu'l-luġhāt Urdū Jāmi'*, ed. Al-Hāj Maulvī Ferozu'ddīn, s.v. "ḥaqqu'l-yaqīn," 572.

231. Darshan Singh, *Secret of Secrets*, 135.

232. Faiẓ, *Nusḳhah'hā-e Vafā*, 265 (from *Zindāṅ-nāmah* (Prison Book), from the ghazal beginning "guloṅ meṅ rang bhare bād-e nau bahār chale").

233. Faiẓ, 280 (from *Zindaṅ-nāmah*, from the ghazal beginning "garmī-e shauq-e naẓārah kā aśar to dekho").

234. Rūmī, *Kulliyāt-e Dīvān-e Shams*, 99 (fourth verse of ghazal 132, beginning "dar mīyān-e pardeh-ye ḳhūn 'eshq rā golzār'hā").

235. Darshan Singh, *A Tear and a Star / Ek Ānsū Ek Sitārā*, 80–81.

236. Darshan Singh, *Wonders of Inner Space*, 6.

237. Annemarie Schimmel, "Sufism: Sufi Thought and Practice," in *Encyclopaedia Britannica Online*.

238. Iqbāl, *Kulliyāt -e Iqbāl: Urdū, Bāl-e Jibrīl*, 336 (from the nazm "Lālah-e ṣaḥrā" (Tulip in the Desert), beginning "yĕh gunbad-e mīnā'ī! yĕh 'ālam-e tanhā'ī").

239. Ġhālib, *Dīvān-e Ġhālib*, ed. Ḳhān, 21 (from the ghazal beginning "darḳhūr-e qahr o ġhaẓab jab ko'ī ham-sā nah hu'ā"); Ġhālib, *Dīvān-e Ghālib, Kāmil*, ed. Reẓā, 448.

240. Blake, "Auguries of Innocence," from *The Pickering Manuscript* (1803), in *William Blake: The Complete Poems*, ed. Ostriker, 506, lines 1–4.

241. Mīr, *Kulliyāt-e Mīr, Dīvān-e Avval*, 207 (first verse of the ghazal).

242. Darshan Singh, *Spiritual Awakening*, 177, 180.

243. Darshan Singh, *Secret of Secrets*, 130.

244. Kirpal Singh, *Jap Ji*, 134.

245. Darshan Singh, *Matā'-e Nūr* (Hindi), 209–10 (poem 72, verse 3).

246. Ḥāfeẓ, *Ġhazaliyāt-e Ḥāfeẓ*, ed. Borūmand, 379 (from the ghazal beginning "shāh-e shamshād-qadān, Ḳhusrow-e Shīrīn-dahnān"); *Dīvān-e Ḥāfeẓ: Nosḳheh-ye Shāhān-e Moġhalīyyeh*, 277; *Dīvān-e Kāmel-e Ḳhwājeh Shamso'ddīn Moḥammad Ḥāfeẓ-e Shīrāzī*, ed. Dorvash, 325; *Dīvān-e Ḥāfeẓ bar Asās-e Nosḳheh-ye Movarraḳh-e 818 Hijrī*, ed. Aḥmad, 157 (ghazal 282); Sharī'at, *Sharḥ-e Majmū'eh-ye Gol*, 786; *Dīvān-e Ḳhwājeh Ḥāfeẓ-e Shīrāzī*, ed. Shīrāzī, 214.

247. Translation adapted from Bicknell, *Hafiz of Shiraz*, 233.

248. Darshan Singh, *Matā'-e Nūr* (Urdu), 137. This note was not included in the Hindi edition of *Matā'-e Nūr*.

249. Kirpal Singh, *Jap Ji*, 82.

250. This verse comes from a ghazal attributed to Amir Khusro and is considered one of his most famous. It is widely quoted on the internet, but sources for the poem are never provided. This ghazal did not appear in any of the divans written by Khusro that were consulted for *Love's Last Madness*. It did appear in 'Sharmānī's book *Turkān-e Pārsī-gū'ī* (Persian-Speaking Turks) at 64–65, but two of the verses contain variations not found in the most-quoted forms of the ghazal. The source of the version of the ghazal presented in 66:7 note is *Paiġhām-e Ḥaq*, No. 6 (Jan.–Feb. 1999): 29.

251. Kirpal Singh, *The Night Is a Jungle*, 252.

252. This well-known verse traditionally comes from a ghazal of Amir Khusro's that begins "ei chehreh-ye zibā-ye to rashk-e botān-e āżarī." The verse is widely available on the internet (without source attributions) but was not included in the divans we consulted or in two books that quoted this ghazal (Raḥmān, *Amīr Ḳhusrow kī Jamāliyāt* 84, 132; Ṣalāḥu'ddīn, *Ḳhusrow-e Shīrīṅ-Zabāṅ*, 253–54). However, the verse was quoted in articles by two other scholars (Shahab Sarmadee, "Musical Genius of Amir Khusrau," in *Amir Khusrau: Memorial Volume* 47; Zoe Ansari, "Introduction," in *Life, Times & Works of Amīr Khusrau Dehlavi*, ed. Ansari, iii). Concerning Khusro's missing ghazals, Ansari writes that,

unlike his masnavis and eulogies Khusrau never tried to preserve any record of his ghazals until he had completed three diwans. He could comprehend that every poetaster, after he had composed ten to twelve ghazals, was regarded as the poet. But when he was compiling his fourth diwan 'Baqiya Naqiya', having become conscious of their artistic value, he was convinced by his friends also to include ghazals in his latest collection which in turn gave extra lustre to the beauty of his diwan.

The very ghazals for their immense popularity were scattered over the sky like . . . released birds and could never be recaptured. Daulat Shah Samarkandi relates that Sultan Sa'id Baisanghar Khan (the grandson of Amir Timur) in the 15th century appointed his favorite poet Saifi [to do] this hard task. Saifi after much endurance could collect only [one] hundred and twenty thousand couplets; later he also could find two thousand couplets that were not included in any diwan; ultimately he lost heart and discontinued his efforts.

Saifi's edited Kulliyat ([t]ranscribed in 924/1518) containing 894 pages, is still preserved in the Schedrin State Library of Leningrad, but there too the fifth diwan 'Nihayat-ul-Kamal' and many of the popular ghazals are missing, e.g.

[the ghazal with the radīf] shab jā'ī keh man būdam

[and]

[the ghazal containing the verse] man to shodam to man shodī . . .

. . . Different manuscripts were compiled under the title, "Kulliyat" [Complete Works] but none was complete. How silly it sounded when a few selections were prepared out of the different diwans of Khusrau and were titled as [Kulliyat], a tradition that continues till today. Ansari, "Introduction," in *Life, Times & Works of Amīr Khusrau Dehlavi*, iii–iv (the ghazal lines Ansari quotes are in Persian script).

253. Iqbāl, *Kulliyāt -e Iqbāl: Urdū, Bāng-e Darā*, pt. 3, 221 (from the ghazal beginning "kabhī ai ḥaqīqat-e muntaẓar, naẓar ā libās-e majāz meṅ").

254. Darshan Singh, *Streams of Nectar*, 208.

255. Darshan Singh, *Wonders of Inner Space*, 170.

256. Nurbakhsh, *Traditions of the Prophet*, 66.

257. Darshan Singh, "Divine Musician," DVD, 53:49.

258. While this verse is commonly attributed to Bulleh Shah (see, e.g., Chaddha's commentary in Darshan Singh, *Matā'-e Nūr* (Hindi), 219), we were unable to locate it in any of the more recent critical editions of Bulleh Shah's Punjabi verses that we consulted.

259. Darshan Singh, *Love Has Only a Beginning*, 119–20.

260. Platts, *Dictionary of Urdū, Classical Hindī, and English*, s.v. "manzil," 1076.

261. Ġhālib, *Dīvān-e Ġhālib*, ed. Ḳhān, 104 (from the ghazal beginning "kisī ko de ke dil ko'ī navā-sanj-e fuġhāṅ kyoṅ ho"); Ġhālib, *Dīvān-e Ghālib, Kāmil*, ed. Reẓā, 449–50.

262. Darshan Singh, *Spiritual Awakening*, 256.

263. Ġhālib, *Dīvān-e Ġhālib*, ed. Ḳhān, 119 (from the ghazal beginning "ishq mujh ko nahīṅ, vaḥshat hī sahī"); Ġhālib, *Dīvān-e Ghālib, Kāmil*, ed. Reẓā, 298.

264. See Harishchandra Chaddha's commentary in Darshan Singh, *Matā'-e Nūr* (Hindi), 225–26.

265. Rūmī, *Maśnavī*, bk. 1, 126 (from "Dar ṣefat-e pīr va moṯāve'at-e vei" (Concerning the Qualities of the Pir and Obedience to Him)), lines 2943–47.

266. Darshan Singh, *Matā'-e Nūr* (Hindi), 221 (poem 78, verse 7.)

267. Darshan Singh, *Streams of Nectar*, 182–83.

268. Iqbāl, *Kulliyāt -e Iqbāl: Urdū, Bāl-e Jibrīl*, pt. 2, 283, first verse of ghazal 40.

269. Mir, *Kulliyāt-e Mīr, Dīvān-e Avval*, 6 (from the ghazal beginning "jis sar ko ġhurūr āj hai yāṅ tāj-varī kā").

270. Rūmī, *Maśnavī*, bk. 1, "Prologue," 5, lines 9–10.

271. Darshan Singh, "Two Ways Before Us," *Sat Sandesh* 27, Nos. 11–12 (Nov./Dec. 1994): 13.

272. Darshan Singh, *Matā'-e Nūr* (Hindi, 1991 ed.), 190 (poem 68, verse 4); *Matā'-e Nūr* (Urdu), 196.

273. Darshan Singh, *Matā'-e Nūr* (Hindi, 2016 ed.), 202.

274. Ġhālib, *Dīvān-e Ġhālib*, ed. Ḳhān, 184 (from the ghazal beginning "shabnam bah gul-e lālah nah ḳhālī zĕ-adā hai"); Ġhālib, *Dīvān-e Ghālib, Kāmil*, ed. Reẓā, 268–69.

275. Mīr, *Kulliyāt-e Mīr, Dīvān-e Avval*, 141 (from the ghazal beginning "hai ġhazal Mīr yĕh shifā'ī kī").

276. Ġhālib, *Dīvān-e Ġhālib*, ed. Ḳhān, 19 (first two couplets of the ghazal); Ġhālib, *Dīvān-e Ghālib, Kāmil*, ed. Rezā, 397.

277. Moayyad, "Farhād (1)," in *Encyclopaedia Iranica* (December 15, 1999); Renard, *Islam and the Heroic Image*, 69.

278. Moayyad.

279. Moayyad; Renard, 69.

280. Darshan Singh, *Love Has Only a Beginning*, 129–30.

281. Darshan Singh, *Manzil-e Nūr* (Hindi), 119.

282. Kirpal Singh, *Crown of Life*, 26, 148.

283. Kirpal Singh, 153–54.

284. Darshan Singh, *Manzil-e Nūr* (Hindi), 137 (stanza 28).

Bibliography

Ahmad, Aziz. *An Intellectual History of Islam in India*. Edinburgh: Edinburgh University Press, 1969.

Akhtar, Jāṅ Nisār. *Hindostāṅ Hamārā*. Bombay: Hindustani Book Trust. Vol. 1, 1965. Vol. 2, 1973.

Ali, Abdullah Yusuf. *The Holy Qur'an*. Elmhurst: Tahrike Tarsile Qur'an, 1987.

Ansari, Zoe, ed. *Life, Times & Works of Amīr Khusrau Dehlavi*. New Delhi: National Amīr Khusrau Society, 1975.

Arberry, A.J. *The Qur'an Interpreted*. New York: Macmillan, 1976.

'Attār-e Nīshābūrī, Farīdu'ddīn. *Dīvān-e 'Attār-e Nīshābūrī: Matn-e Enteqādī bar Asās-e Nuskheh'hā-ye Khattī-ye Kohan*. Edited by Mahdī Madāyenī and Mehrān Afshārī. Tehran: Nashr-e Charkh, 2014.

'Attār-e Nīshābūrī, Farīdu'ddīn. *Dīvān-e Qaṣā'ed va Tarjī'āt va Ġhazalīyāt*. Edited by Sa'īd Nafīsī. Tehran: Kitābkhāneh-ye Sanā'i, [1960?].

Bahoo, Sultan, *Risalah Roohi Sharif*. Translated by Ambreen Moghees Sarwari Qadri. Lahore: Sultan-ul-Faqr Publications, 2015.

Bāqir, Muḥammad, *Bayān-e Ġhālib: Sharḥ-e Dīvān-e Ġhālib*. Amritsar: Āzād Book Depot, [1980?].

Beg, M. K. A. *Urdu Grammar: History and Structure*. New Delhi: Bahri Publications, 1988.

Bhamra, Rabinder Singh. *Sikhism and Spirituality*. Bloomington: Xlibris, 2015.

Bicknell, Herman. *Hafiz of Shiraz*. Tehran: Imperial Organization for Social Services, 1976.

Blake, William. *William Blake: The Complete Poems*. Edited by Alicia Ostriker. London: Penguin Books, 1977.

Cahill, Michael. *Paradise Rediscovered: The Roots of Civilisation*. Vol. 2. Brisbane: Glass House Books, 2012.

Chatterji, Suniti Kumar Chatterji. *Indo-Aryan & Hindi*. Calcutta: Firma K. L. Mukhopadhyay, 1969.

Cohn, Bernard S. "The Command of Language and the Language of Command." In *Colonialism and Its Forms of Knowledge: The British in India*, 16–56. Princeton: Princeton University Press, 1997.

Dalmia, Vasudha. *The Nationalization of Hindu Traditions*. Delhi: Oxford University Press, 1997.

Derin, Suleyman. "From Rābi'a to Ibn al-Fāriḍ: Toward Some Paradigms of the Sufi Conception of Love." PhD diss. University of Leeds, September 1999.

Eliot, Sir Henry Miers. *The History of India, as Told by Its Own Historians: The Muhammadan Period*. Vol. 8. London: Trübner, 1877.

Faiz̤, Faiz̤ Aḥmed. *Nusḳhah'hā-e Vafā*. Delhi: Educational Publishing House, 1993.

Farooqi, Mehr Afshan. "Language of Whose Camp?" *Outlook India*, February 21, 2008. https://www.outlookindia.com/website/story/language-of-whose-camp/236758, archived at https://perma.cc/7M8Z -WK7X.

Farooqui, Salma Ahmed. *A Comprehensive History of Medieval India from the Twelfth to the Mid-Eighteenth Century*. Delhi: Pearson India Education Services, 2011.

Faruqi, Shamsur Rahman. "A Modest Plea: Please, Could We Have a Proper History of Urdu Literature?" Keynote Address: Urdu-Fest 2008, University of Virginia, Charlottesville, VA, September 12, 2008. http://www.columbia.edu/itc/mealac/pritchett/00fwp/srf/srf_lithistneeds_2008.pdf, archived at https://perma.cc/8P4P-RYS5.

Faruqi, Shamsur Rahman. *Early Urdu Literary Culture and History*. New Delhi: Oxford University Press, 2001.

Faruqi, Shamsur Rahman. "The Name and Nature of a Language: Would Urdu by Any Other Name Smell as Sweet?" Keynote Address: Conference on a Historical Appraisal of India's Composite Cultural Ethos: Perspectives from Urdu Literature, Allahabad, India, March 2014. http://www.columbia.edu/itc/mealac/pritchett/00fwp/srf/srf_nameofurdu_2014.pdf, archived at https://perma.cc/Y7HJ-3B6H.

Faruqi, Shamsur Rahman. "Urdu Literary Culture: The Syncretic Tradition." Keynote Address: Shibli Academy, Azamgarh, India, December 17, 2008. http://www.columbia.edu/itc/mealac/pritchett/00fwp/srf/txt_syncretic2007.html, archived at https://perma.cc/AQ6E-X7SU.

Ferozu'l-luġhāt Urdū Jāmi', edited by Al-Hāj Maulvī Ferozu'ddīn. Lahore: Ferozsons Ltd., 1989.

Ġhālib, Mirzā Asadu'llâh Ḳhān. *Dīvān-e Ġhālib*. Edited by Ḥāmid 'Alī Ḳhān. Lahore: al-Faiṣal Publishers, 1995.

Ġhālib, Mirzā Asadu'llâh Ḳhān. *Dīvān-e Ghālib, Kāmil: Nusḳhah-e Rez̤ā, Tārīḳhī Tartīb se*. Edited by Kālīdas Guptā Rez̤ā. Bombay: Sākār Publishers, 1995.

Gibb, H.A.R. *Arabic Literature*. London: Oxford University Press, 1974.

Gonḍvī, Aṣġhar. *Kulliyāt-e Aṣġhar*. Edited by Krishan Kānt. Amritsar: Āzād Book Depot, 1976.

Government of India. *Amir Khusrau: Memorial Volume*. New Delhi: Publications Division, Ministry of Information and Broadcasting, 1975.

Ḥāfez̤-e Shīrāzī, Ḳhv̱ājeh Shamso'ddīn Moḥammad. *Dīvān-e Ḥāfez̤ bar Asās-e Nosḳheh-ye Movarraḳh-e 818 Hijrī*. Edited by Naẓīr Aḥmad. New Delhi:

Markaz-e Taḥqīqāt-e Fārsī, Rāyizanī-ye Farhangī, Sefārat-e Jomhūrī-ye Eslāmī-ye Īrān, 1988.

Ḥāfeẕ-e Shīrāzī, Ḵhwājeh Shamso'ddīn Moḥammad. *Dīvān-e Ḥāfeẕ: Nosḵheh-ye Shāhān-e Moġhalīyyeh*. Patna: Ḵhudā Baḵhsh Oriental Library, 1992.

Ḥāfeẕ-e Shīrāzī, Ḵhwājeh Shamso'ddīn Moḥammad. *Dīvān-e Kāmel-e Ḵhwājeh Shamso'ddīn Moḥammad Ḥāfeẕ-e Shīrāzī*. Edited by Faẕlo'llâh Dorvash. Tehran: Enteshārāt-e Dāyerat-ul-Ma'ārif-e Īrān-Shenāsī, 2002.

Ḥāfeẕ-e Shīrāzī, Ḵhwājeh Shamso'ddīn Moḥammad. *Dīvān-e Ḵhwājeh Ḥāfeẕ-e Shīrāzī*. Edited by Sayyed Abū'l-Qāsem Anjavī-ye Shīrāzī. Tehran: Sāzmān-e Enteshārāt-e Jāvīdān, 1982.

Ḥāfeẕ-e Shīrāzī, Ḵhwājeh Shamso'ddīn Moḥammad. *Dīvān-e Kohneh-ye Ḥāfeẕ*. Edited by Īraj Afshār. Tehran: Mo'asseseh-ye Enteshārāt-e Amīr Kabīr, 1987.

Ḥāfeẕ-e Shīrāzī, Ḵhwājeh Shamso'ddīn Moḥammad. *Ġhazaliyāt-e Ḥāfeẕ*. Edited by Adīb Borūmand. Tehran: Sherkat-e Enteshārātī-ye Pāzhang, 1988.

Haleem, M.A.S. Abdel. *The Qur'an*. Oxford: Oxford University Press, 2015.

Ḥussain, Sayyid Akbar. *Kulliyāt-e Akbar Allâhābādī*. Lahore: Sang-e Mīl Publications, 2008.

Ikram, S. M. *Muslim Civilization in India*. New York: Columbia University Press, 1964.

Iqbāl, Muḥammad. *Kulliyāt-e Iqbāl: Fārsī*. Lahore: Shaiḵh Ġhulām 'Alī and Sons, 1973.

Iqbāl, Muḥammad. *Kulliyāt-e Iqbāl: Urdū*. Edited by Muḥammad Faiṣal. Lahore: al-Faiṣal Nāshirān wa Tājirān-e Kutub, 1995.

Iqbal, Mohammad. *Secrets of the Self: A Philosophical Poem*. Translated by R.A. Nicholson. New Delhi: Arnold-Heinemann, 1978.

Kabīr. *Kabīr Bānī*. Edited by Bhagīrat'h Miśhra. Indore: Kamal Prakāśhan, 1972.

Kabīr. *Kabīr Grant'hāvalī*. Edited by Pārasnāt'h Tiwārī. Allahabad: Hindī Parishad, Prayāg Viśhvavidyālay (Allahadbad University), 1961.

Kabīr. *Kabir Granthavali (Doha)*. Edited by Charlotte Vaudeville. Pondichéry: Institut Français D'Indologie, 1957.

Kabīr. *Kabīr Vachanāvalī*. Edited by Ayodhyāsiṅh Upādhyāy 'Hariaudh.' Kashi: Nāgarīprachāriṇī Sabhā, 1964.

Kabīr. *Kabīr-Vāṇī*. Edited by Charlotte Vaudeville. Pondichéry: Institut Français D'Indologie, 1982.

Kabīr. *Kabīr-Vāṇī Saṅgrah*. Edited by Pārasnāt'h Tiwārī. Allahabad: Lokbhāratī Prakāśhan, 1970.

Kabīr. *Mahābījak: Kabīr Sāhab kī Sampūrṇ Vāṇiyoṅ kā Saṅgrah*. Edited by Āchārya Mahant Gaṅgāśharaṇ Śhāstrī. Varanasi: Kabīr Vāṇī Prakāśhan Kendra, 2000.

Karhānī, Shamīm. *Intikhāb-e Kalām-e Shamīm Karhānī.* Aligarh: Anjuman Taraqqī Urdū Hind, 1962.

Karhānī, Shamīm. *Intikhāb-e Kalām-e Shamīm Karhānī.* Edited by Ḥanīf Kaifī. New Delhi: Urdu Academy Delhi, 1999.

Ḳhusrow, Abū'l-Ḥasan Yamīnu'ddīn. *Dīvān-e Amīr Ḳhusrow Dehlavī.* Edited by Anwāru'l-Ḥasan. Lucknow: Rājah Rām Kumār Book Depot, 1967.

Ḳhusrow, Abū'l-Ḥasan Yamīnu'ddīn. *Dīvān-e Amīr Ḳhusrow Dehlavī Moṯābeq-e Nosḳheh-ye Yamīnu'ddīn Abū'l-Ḥasan Ḳhusrow.* Edited by Iqbāl Ṣalāḥu'ddīn. Tehran: Mo'asseseh-ye Enteshārāt-e Negāh, 2001.

Ḳhusrow, Abū'l-Ḥasan Yamīnu'ddīn. *Dīvān-e Ḳhusrow.* Islamabad: National Committee barā-ye Sāt Sau Sālah Taqrībāt-e Amīr Ḳhusrow, 1975.

Ḳhusrow, Abū'l-Ḥasan Yamīnu'ddīn. "Ġhazal-e Fārsī." *Paiġhām-e Ḥaq* No. 6 (January–February 1999): 29.

Ḳhusrow, Abū'l-Ḥasan Yamīnu'ddīn. *Kulliyāt-e Ġhazaliyāt-e Ḳhusrow, Jeld-e Avval.* Edited by Iqbāl Ṣalāḥu'ddīn. Lahore: Packages Limited, 1972.

Kiernan, Victor G. *Poems by Faiz.* London: George Allen & Unwin, 1971.

Kohli, Surindar Singh. *Dictionary of Guru Granth Sahib.* Amritsar: Singh Brothers, 2005.

Kulke, Hermann and Dietmar Rothermund. *A History of India.* Abingdon: Taylor & Francis e-Library, 2004.

Lāl, Inderjīt. *Naġhmah-e Rūḥ: Ṣūfiānah Ġhazaloṅ kā Intiḳhāb.* New Delhi: Salūjah Prakāshan, 1982.

Laliwala, Jaferhusein I. *Islamic Philosophy of Religion: Synthesis of Science, Religion and Philosophy.* New Delhi: Sarup & Sons, 2005.

Lane, Edward William. *An Arabic-English Lexicon.* Bk. 1, pt. 6, edited by Stanley Lane-Poole. Beirut: Librairie du Liban, 1968.

Lelyveld, David. "*Zuban-e Urdu-e Mu'alla* and the Idol of Linguistic Origins." *Annual of Urdu Studies* 9 (1994): 57–67. http://www.urdustudies.com/pdf/09/14LelyveldZuban.pdf, archived at https://perma. cc/7M6T-TJVT.

Ludhiyānvī, Sāhir. *Kulliyāt-e Sāhir.* Delhi: Nāz Publishing House, 1995.

Macauliffe, Max Arthur. *The Sikh Religion – Its Gurus, Sacred Writings and Authors.* Vols. 1 and 2. Oxford: Clarendon Press, 1909.

Masica, Colin P. *The Indo-Aryan Languages.* Cambridge: Cambridge University Press, 1991.

Matthews, D. J. and C. Shackle. *An Anthology of Classical Urdu Love Lyrics.* London: Oxford University Press, 1972.

Mir, Mir Muhammad Taqi. *Zikr-i Mir: The Autobiography of the Eighteenth Century Mughal Poet: Mir Muhammad Taqi 'Mir.'* Edited and translated by C. M. Naim. New Delhi: Oxford University Press, 1999.

Mīr, Muḥammad Mīr Taqī. *Kulliyāt-e Mīr*. Lahore: Sang-e Mīl Publications, 1987.

Moayyad, Heshmat. "Farhād (1)." In *Encyclopaedia Iranica*, December 15, 1999, accessed April 24, 2018. http://www.iranicaonline.org/articles/farhad%20(1), archived at https://perma.cc/8X6M-KWCJ.

Mojaddedi, Jawid. "Ḥallāj, Abu'l-Mogīṯ Ḥosayn." In *Encyclopaedia Iranica*, edited by Ehsan Yar-Shater, 11:589–92. New York: Encyclopaedia Iranica Foundation, 2003, accessed September 30, 2017. http://www.iranicaonline.org/articles/hallaj-1, archived at https://perma.cc/JWC2-ZE84.

Momin, Ḥakīm Momin Ḳhān. *Dīvān-e Momin*. Edited by Anwāru'l-Ḥasan. Delhi: Idārah Ṣubh-e Adab, 1971.

Morādābādī, Jigar. *Kulliyāt-e Jigar*. Delhi: Educational Publishing House, 2003.

Nanavati, G.T. *Justice Nanavati Commission of Inquiry (1984 Anti-Sikh Riots) – Report*. Vol. 1. New Delhi: Government of India, February 9, 2005. https://mha.gov.in/sites/upload_files/mha/files/pdf/Nanavati-I_eng.pdf, archived at https://perma.cc/35RV-JFD2.

Nasr, Seyyed Hossein. "Existence (*Wujud*) and Quiddity (*Mahiyyah*) in Islamic Philosophy," *Iqbal Review* 30–31 (October 1989–April 1990): 150, 158–59, 163–65. http://www.allamaiqbal.com/publications/journals/review/oct89/10.htm, archived at https://perma.cc/U9XM-JJLP.

Nicholson, Reynold A. *The Mathnawī of Jalálu'ddīn Rumī*. Vols. VII–VIII. London: Luzac, 1937.

Nurbakhsh, Javad. *Traditions of the Prophet: Ahadith*, New York: Khaniqahi-Nimatullahi Publications, 1981.

Platts, John T. *A Dictionary of Urdū, Classical Hindī, and English*. London: Oxford University Press, 1974.

Pritchett, Frances W. "Convention in the Classical Urdu Ghazal: The Case of Mir." *Journal of South Asian and Middle Eastern Studies* (Fall 1979): 60–77. http://www.columbia.edu/itc/mealac/pritchett/00fwp/published/txt_convention.html, archived at https://perma.cc/6UCU-8QAS.

Puri, Lekh Raj. *Radha Soami Teachings (As Given in Swami Ji's Book 'Sar Bachan' Poetry)*. Beas: Radha Soami Satsang Beas, 1982.

Qureshi, Regula Burckhardt. "Female Agency and Patrilineal Constraints: Situating Courtesans in Twentieth-Century India." In *The Courtesan's Arts: Cross-Cultural Perspectives*, edited by Martha Feldman and Bonnie Gordon, 312–31. Oxford: Oxford University Press, 2006.

Raḥmān, Shakīlu'r. *Amīr Ḳhusrow kī Jamāliyāt*. New Delhi: Modern Publishing House, 1996.

Rahman, Tariq. *From Hindi to Urdu: A Social and Political History*. Karachi: Oxford University Press, 2011.

Renard, John. *Islam and the Heroic Image: Themes in Literature and the Visual Arts*. Columbia, SC: University of South Carolina Press, 1993.

Rūmī, Maulānā Jalālu'ddīn Muḥammad Balkhī. *Kulliyāt-e Dīvān-e Shams-e Tabrīzī*. Edited by Badī'a'zzamān Forūzānfar. Tehran: Mo'asseseh-ye Chāp-e Enteshārāt-e Amīr Kabīr, 1966.

Rūmī, Maulānā Jalālu'ddīn Muḥammad Balkhī. *Maśnavī-ye Ma'navī*. Edited by Towfiq H. Sobḥānī. Tehran: Enteshārāt-e Rowzaneh, 2003.

Rūmī, Maulānā Jalālu'ddīn Muḥammad Balkhī. *Masnavi-ye Ma'navi*. Edited by Reynold Alleyne Nicholson. Tehran: Mo'asseseh-ye Enteshārāt-e Amīr Kabīr, 1977.

Russell, Ralph. "In Pursuit of the Urdu Ghazal." *Journal of Asian Studies* (Nov. 1969): 107–24.

Russell, Ralph and Khurshidul Islam. *Three Mughal Poets*. Cambridge: Harvard University Press, 1968.

Rypka, Jan. *History of Iranian Literature*. Dordrecht: D. Reidel, 1968.

Sa'dī-ye Shīrāzī, Sheikh Moṣleḥo'ddīn. *Kulliyāt-e Sheikh Sa'dī*. Edited by Moḥammad 'Ali Forūghī. Tehran: Ketāb-forūshī-ye Mūsá 'Elmī, 1957.

Ṣalāḥu'ddīn, Iqbāl. *Ḵhusrow-e Shīrīṅ-Zabāṅ*. Lahore: Maktabah-e Merī Library, 1970.

Ṣā'eb Tabrīzī, Mirzā Moḥammad 'Alī. *Dīvān-e Ash'ār*. http://ganjoor.net/saeb/divan-saeb/ghazalkasa/sh6864, archived at https://perma.cc/4QZ8-948M.

Schimmel, Annemarie. *Classical Urdu Literature from the Beginning to Iqbāl*. Wiesbaden: Otto Harrassowitz Verlag, 1975.

Schimmel, Annemarie. *My Soul Is a Woman: The Feminine in Islam*. New York: Continuum, 2003.

Schimmel, Annemarie. *Mystical Dimensions of Islam*. Chapel Hill: The University of North Carolina Press, 1978.

Schimmel, Annemarie. "Sufism: Sufi Thought and Practice." In *Encyclopaedia Britannica Online*, accessed December 31, 2017. https://www.britannica.com/topic/Sufism/Sufi-thought-and-practice, archived at https://perma.cc/2ZDP-EGL5.

Shāh, Bullhe. *Bullhe Shāh kā Kalām / Tarjumah*. Edited by 'Alī Akbar 'Abbās. Lahore: Punjab Council of the Arts, 1989.

Shāh, Bullhe. *Kalām-e Bullhe Shāh*. Edited by Sayyid Nażīr Aḥmad. Lahore: Packages, 1976.

Shāh, Bullhe. *Mukammal Kāfiyāṅ*. Edited by Muḥammad Sharīf Ṣābir. Lahore: Sayyid Ajmal Ḥusain Memorial Society, 1991.

Shahrānī, 'Enāyatu'llâh. *Turkān-e Pārsī-Gū'ī*. Kabul: Kānūn-e Farhangī-ye Qeizīl Chowpān, 2015.

Shromaṇī Gurduārā Prabaṅdhak Committee, ed. *Shabdārt'h Srī Gurū Graṅt'h Sāhib Jī*. Amritsar: Vol. 1, January 1959. Vol. 2, October 1959. Vols. 3–4, January 1964.

Sharī'at, Muḥammad Ṣadeq. *Sharḥ-e Majmū'eh-ye Gol: Sharḥ va Tafsīr-e Dīvān-e Ġhazaliyāt-e Ḥāfeẓ-e Shīrāzī*. Tehran: Qāṣedak-e Ṣabā, 2011.

Singh, Darshan. "The Divine Musician." Public talk given in New York, NY, on September 2, 1988. DVD 48, 53:49, Naperville, IL: SK Publications, 2010.

Siṅgh, Darshan. *Jādah-e Nūr* (Urdu). Delhi: Sawan Kirpal Publications, 1992.

Siṅgh, Darśhan. *Jādaye Nūr* (Hindi edition with translation by Hariśhchandra Chaḍḍhā). Delhi: Sawan Kirpal Publications Spiritual Society, 1996.

Singh, Darshan. *Love at Every Step*. Bowling Green, VA: Sawan Kirpal Publications, 1989.

Singh, Darshan. *Love Has Only a Beginning. Volume I: Autobiography of Darshan Singh*. Naperville, IL: SK Publications, 1996.

Siṅgh, Darśhan. *Manzil-e Nūr* (Hindi edition with commentary by Hariśhchandra Chaḍḍhā). Delhi: Sawan Kirpal Publications Spiritual Society, 2016.

Siṅgh, Darshan. *Manzil-e Nūr* (Urdu). Delhi: Sawan Kirpal Publications, 1989.

Siṅgh, Darśhan. *Matā'-e Nūr* (Hindi edition with commentary by Hariśhchandra Chaḍḍhā). Delhi: Sawan Kirpal Publications Spiritual Society, 1991.

Siṅgh, Darśhan. *Matā'-e Nūr* (Hindi edition with commentary by Hariśhchandra Chaḍḍhā). Delhi: Sawan Kirpal Publications Spiritual Society, 2016.

Siṅgh, Darshan. *Matā'-e Nūr* (Urdu). Delhi: Sawan Kirpal Publications, 1988.

Siṅgh, Darśhan. *Mauj-e Nūr*. (Hindi edition with commentary by Hariśhchandra Chaḍḍhā). Delhi: Sawan Kirpal Publications Spiritual Society, 1999.

Siṅgh, Darshan. *Mauj-e Nūr* (Urdu). Delhi: Sawan Kirpal Publications Spiritual Society, 1996.

Siṅgh, Darshan. Photocopy of handwritten unpublished changes in Urdu to ghazal no. 65 in *Matā'-e Nūr* (beginning "tujhe kyā ḳhabar mere ham-safar"), n.d. On file with translator Barry Lerner.

Singh, Darshan. *Poetry Symposium: Master Recites His Own Poetry – July 18, 1978, Chicago*. Audiotape #52. Bowling Green, VA: Sawan Kirpal Publications, n.d.

Singh, Darshan. *Portrait of Perfection*. Bowling Green, VA: Sawan Kirpal Publications, 1981.

Singh, Darshan. "The Priceless Gem." Public talk given in Baltimore, MD, on August 12, 1983. DVD 28, 1:02:50, Naperville, IL: SK Publications, 2008.

Singh, Darshan. *Sant Mat: The Teachings of the Masters*. Pamphlet: Bowling Green, VA: Sawan Kirpal Publications, n.d.

Singh, Darshan. *Secret of Secrets*. Bowling Green, VA: Sawan Kirpal Publications, 1982.

Singh, Darshan. "The Soul's True Home." Satsang talk given at Kirpal Ashram, Delhi, India, November 21, 1981. http://santdarshansingh.org/TK0282.PDF, archived at https://perma.cc/Z5FE-2HNZ.

Singh, Darshan. *Spiritual Awakening*. Bowling Green, VA: Sawan Kirpal Publications, 1982.

Singh, Darshan. *Streams of Nectar*. Naperville, IL: SK Publications, 1993.

Siṅgh, Darshan. *Talāsh-e Nūr*. Delhi: Sawan Kirpal Ruhani Mission, 1980.

Singh, Darshan, *A Tear and a Star / Ek Ānsū Ek Sitārā*. Delhi: Sawan Kirpal Publications, 1992.

Singh, Darshan. "True Freedom." Talk given at Hayden Hall, Boston University, Boston, MA, July 4, 1983. http://santdarshansingh.org/tk0983.pdf, archived at https://perma.cc/F6FR-GKP5.

Singh, Darshan. "Two Ways Before Us." *Sat Sandesh* 27, Nos. 11–12 (Nov./Dec. 1994): 12–19.

Singh, Darshan. *The Wonders of Inner Space*. Bowling Green, VA: Sawan Kirpal Publications, 1988.

Singh, Gopal. *Guru Nanak*. New Delhi: National Book Trust, India, 1967.

Singh, Kirpal. ". . . and the Darkness Comprehended It Not." Public talk at the First Unitarian Church in San Francisco, CA, November 13, 1972. http://www.kirpalsingh-teachings.org/it/talks/third-world-tour/601-q-and-the-darkness-comprehended-it-notq75.html, archived at https://perma.cc/XFB6-QP8R.

Singh, Kirpal. *The Crown of Life*. Bowling Green, VA: Sawan Kirpal Publications, 1980.

Singh, Kirpal. "Delusion of Doership." *Sat Sandesh* 2, No. 4 (April 1969): 2–9, 32.

Singh, Kirpal. *Godman*. Bowling Green, VA: Sawan Kirpal Publications, 1979.

Singh, Kirpal. "A Grand Delusion," *Sat Sandesh* 2, No. 7 (August 1969), 2–16.

Singh, Kirpal. *A Great Saint: Baba Jaimal Singh – His Life and Teachings*. Delhi: Ruhani Satsang, 1973.

Singh, Kirpal. *Heart to Heart Talks*. Vol. 2. Delhi: Ruhani Satsang, India, 1976.

Singh, Kirpal. *The Jap Ji: The Message of Guru Nanak*. Bowling Green, VA: Sawan Kirpal Publications, 1981.

Singh, Kirpal. "The Law of Karma." Public talk given in Chicago, October 1972. http://www.kirpalsingh-teachings.org/index.php/en/talks/third-world-tour/496-the-law-of-karma.html, archived at https://perma.cc/KSW2-29BD.

Singh, Kirpal. *Man! Know Thyself*. Bowling Green, VA: Sawan Kirpal Publications, 1983.

Singh, Kirpal. *Morning Talks*. Bowling Green, VA: Sawan Kirpal Publications, 1981.

Singh, Kirpal. *The Night Is a Jungle*. Tilton, NH: The Sant Bani Press, 1975.

Singh, Kirpal. *Spiritual Elixir*, 2 vols. Delhi: Ruhani Satsang, India, 1972.

Singh, Kirpal. "What Is True Darshan?" *Sat Sandesh* 6, No. 7 (July 1973): 12–16.

Singh, Rajinder. *Inner and Outer Peace through Meditation*. Rockport, MA: Element Books, 1996.

Singh, Rajinder. "Meditation – Bringing Depth and Richness to Our Lives." *South Asian Times* (Spring 2009): 12. http://lovetomeditate.net/pdf/Collector-Edition-Sant-Rajinder-Singh.pdf, archived at https://perma.cc/436D-HZB3.

Singh, Rajinder. "Relationship between Science and Spirituality." In *Silken Thread of the Divine*, 23–37. Naperville, IL: SK Publications, 2005.

Singh, Waryām. "Jau sukh kau chāhai sadā saran rām kī leh."*Ātam Mārg* (June 2009): 25.

Thapar, Romila. *The Penguin History of Early India: From the Origins to AD 1300*.

About the Translators

Barry Lerner received an MA in South Asian Languages and Civilizations in 1984 from the University of Chicago, where he studied Hindi, Urdu, and Persian Literature, with a concentration in literary criticism. Lerner was awarded a Hindi Language Fellowship by the American Institute of Indian Studies in New Delhi in 1980, and studied Arabic on his return from India. His translation of some Persian verses of Sa'di was published in Ehsan Yarshater's book *Persian Literature* (1988). He lives in Arlington, Virginia, and works as an editor and research writer at the Law Library of Congress. Lerner received spiritual initiation from Sant Kirpal Singh in 1973 and, in 1988, was personally asked by Sant Darshan Singh to translate Sant Darshan's poetry.

Harbans Singh Bedi, the younger brother of Urdu short story laureate Rajinder Singh Bedi, received his MA in English Literature, with minors in Persian and Urdu literature, from India's Government College, Lahore, in 1945. He taught English at Government College, Rupar, until he entered government service, retiring in 1980 as Assistant Director General, Defense Lands and Cantonments. He now lives in Arlington, Virginia. Bedi received spiritual initiation from Hazur Baba Sawan Singh in 1942. From 1978–89, he translated Hazur's and Sant Kirpal Singh's Punjabi and Hindi-Urdu spiritual discourses into English for *Sat Sandesh* magazine in Delhi under the direction of Sant Darshan Singh, who also requested his assistance in editing the Urdu manuscript of *Matā'-e Nūr*.

www.ingramcontent.com/pod-product-compliance
Lightning Source LLC
Chambersburg PA
CBHW030821090426
42737CB00009B/815
* 9 7 8 1 9 4 8 7 9 6 3 8 5 *